HISTORY
OF
ENGLAND

Volume Two: *The Tudors and the Stuart Era*
by G. M. TREVELYAN, O.M.
Master of Trinity College, 1940–1951. Formerly Regius Professor of Modern History in the University of Cambridge

Doubleday Anchor Books

DOUBLEDAY & COMPANY, INC., GARDEN CITY, NY.

First Edition, June 1926
Second Edition, July 1937
Second Edition revised, April 1942
Third Edition, October 1945
Reissue (with minor corrections), 1952
PRINTED IN THE UNITED STATES OF AMERICA

DESIGNED BY DIANA KLEMIN

A History of England was originally published by Longmans, Green & Co., Ltd. in 1926. The Anchor Books edition is published by arrangement with Longmans, Green & Co., Inc.

Anchor Books edition: 1953

CONTENTS

BOOK THREE

The Tudors. Renaissance, Reformation and Sea-Power

INTRODUCTION *11*

CHAPTER ONE Character of Henry VII. The machinery of Tudor government. Powers of the Council and decline of the aristocracy. Economic and social change. Cloth Trade, Poor Law and Agriculture *18*

CHAPTER TWO The revival of Lollardry. The Renaissance Scholars. Colet and the young Henry VIII. Wolsey and the Balance of Power. The era of discovery. The Cabots. Henry VIII founds the Royal Navy *37*

CHAPTER THREE The Royal and Parliamentary Reformation under Henry VIII. London and the Reformation. Lutheranism. The Divorce. The Breach with Rome. The dissolution of the Monasteries. The Six Articles *49*

CHAPTER FOUR Interludes, Protestant and Catholic. Edward VI. Latimer and Cranmer. Somerset and Dudley. Agrarian and religious strife. Mary. Submission to Spain and Rome. The Protestant Martyrs *67*

CHAPTER FIVE The policy and character of Elizabeth. The Elizabethan Church Settlement. Spain and France. The Scottish Reformation and the future Great Britain. Cecil and Knox. The Rising of the Earls and the end of English feudalism *81*

CHAPTER SIX The Origin of English Sea-Power. France, England, and Spain in the new age. Drake and the new naval tactics. Cecil and Walsingham. Philip and Elizabeth. Drake's voyage. The Armada. The Regular War *99*

CHAPTER SEVEN The great Elizabethan era. Wales. Ireland. Religion. The boundaries of Elizabethan freedom. The Bible, poetry and music. Apprenticeship and some conditions of industry. The gentry and Parliament *123*

BOOK FOUR

The Stuart Era. Parliamentary Liberty and Overseas Expansion

INTRODUCTION *146*

CHAPTER ONE James I. Parliaments, Puritans and Recusants. Decline of English Sea-Power. The Spanish match. Buckingham and the Thirty Years' War. Charles I. The King, Parliament and the Common Law. Coke and Eliot. Laud and Strafford *152*

CHAPTER TWO England and Scotland. The Scottish Revolt. The Long Parliament. First Session: fall of the Prerogative system and execution of Strafford. Second Session: the Church Question and the division of parties *173*

CHAPTER THREE The Great Civil War, 1642–46. Resources of the two sides. Arms and tactics. Course of the War. Politics, religion and military reorganization. The Scottish Alliance. Cromwell and the New Model. Causes of the victory of Parliament *185*

CHAPTER FOUR The Failure to reach a Settlement. Regicide. The Revolutionary Governments. Ireland and Scotland. Blake and the Revival of the Navy. Domestic, Ecclesiastical and Foreign Policy of the Protectorate. The Death of Oliver and the Restoration *198*

CHAPTER FIVE English village and town life and its expansion overseas. Character of colonization and Colonial policy in the Seventeenth Century. New England, Virginia, and the absorption of the Dutch middle Colonies. England, France, and Holland *219*

CHAPTER SIX The Restoration in State and in Church. Clarendon and the Cabal. The 'just balance of the constitution.' The Dutch wars. Danby's policy. The formation of the Whig and Tory Parties. Faction and fury. The Court left supreme *236*

CHAPTER SEVEN James II. Monmouth's Rising. Illegal proceedings of James. The Tories and the Church alienated. Union of parties against the Court. The Revolution. The Revolution Settlement *261*

CHAPTER EIGHT Scotland and Ireland from the Restoration to Queen Anne. The character of the Two Settlements *275*

CHAPTER NINE The Wars of William and Marlborough. The downfall of Louis XIV and the Rise of Great Britain to Maritime and Commercial Supremacy. Whig and Tory interaction. The Death of Anne and the Dynastic Crisis *287*

INDEX *311*

MAPS

1 England and Wales in Counties, Tudor period (Inset— Tudor London) *29*
2 Europe in the time of Henry VIII. Rise of the Great Continental Monarchies *45*
3 Europe in the time of Elizabeth *105*
4 Spanish and Dutch Netherlands *114*
5 An Army in Battle Array: Great Civil War *189*
6 England and Wales in the winter of 1643–44 *190*
7 Ireland in the Seventeenth Century *206*
8 English American settlements, latter part of Seventeenth Century *223*
9 Europe after the Treaty of Utrecht, 1713 *296*

GENEALOGICAL TREES

Henry VII's descendants: the Stuart claim   94
James I's descendants: the Hanoverian claim   163
Charles I's descendants: Orange and Jacobite claims   252

HISTORY OF ENGLAND
VOLUME TWO

BOOK THREE

The Tudors
Renaissance, Reformation
and Sea-Power

INTRODUCTION

The Europe of to-day is divided perpendicularly into a
number of separate States, each absolute sovereign in its
own territories, and each purporting to represent a racial
or national idea. But in the Middle Ages, Europe was divided horizontally into Estates and corporations of clergy,
nobles, villeins and burghers,—governed locally by their
own domestic laws, in convents, castles, manors and walled
cities. In the shelter of that framework the arts of civilization, torn up by the barbarian inroads, took root again
and flourished in new forms. But the individual had little
freedom in the feudal village and less in the monastery;
while, even in the chartered town and guild, initiative was
checked and the unprivileged stranger excluded. Expansion, progress and individuality were hampered, until these
rigid corporations had lost some of their power, and until
the close control of the mediæval Church over the lives
and thoughts of all men had been loosened.

The only power strong enough to effect a social revolution of such extent and gravity was the power of the national State. The despotism of the State laid indeed
restraints of its own upon liberty, but it cleared more el-
bow room for the individual than he had enjoyed in the
mediæval world. The era of private enterprise and expanding genius associated with Drake and Raleigh, Shakespeare and Bacon, was the outcome of two hundred years
of social disruption and rebirth, of the appeal of Renaissance
and Reformation to the individual mind and conscience,

and the subjection of corporate power to the national will embodied in Crown and Parliament.

The mediæval system passed away, not by chance or by the whim of a King impatient to be divorced, but on account of profound changes in the habits of the English people, most of which we have seen already at work in the Fourteenth and Fifteenth Centuries. The emancipation of the villeins; the growth of London; the rise of educated and active-minded middle classes; the spread of cloth manufacture and other trading activities outside the chartered towns; the unifying effect of the Common Law, the royal administration and the national Parliament; the national pride engendered by the Hundred Years' War and the democratic triumphs of the English archer over the mounted aristocrat; the adoption of the English language by the educated classes; the invention of cannon to shatter the noble's stronghold, and of the printing-press to undermine the churchman's monopoly of learning; the studies of the Renaissance, which on the one hand set religion in the light of a scholarly examination of the Scriptures, and on the other revealed in ancient Greece and Rome ideals unknown to mediæval Christendom; the discovery of the ocean trade routes and of the New World, which had held no place in the intellectual outlook or commercial habits of any former age—all these changes, spiritual and material, combined to dissolve the fabric of mediæval society in England.

At the same time all Western Europe was tending to group itself into national States—France, Spain, Portugal. Inside each modern State, power was increasingly concentrated in the King's hands. But whereas in France and Spain the new monarchy was allied with the old Church, in England it was allied with the old Parliament. In France and Spain mediæval religion was preserved, while mediæval Parliaments decayed and the Roman Imperial law was received as the basis of the Prince's absolute power. In England mediæval religion was changed, while we preserved mediæval Parliaments, native Common Law, and the constitutional character of the Kingship. The distinction between England and continental Europe, particularly

Latin Europe, which the Norman Conquest had obscured, was emphasized once more by these opposite developments on the two sides of the Channel. English and French civilization, at one time not very easily distinguishable, became not only separate but mutually repellent.

Tudor England, while effecting a great revolution in the social system, characteristically preserved the form and even the spirit of much that was old. Most of the orders, corporations and institutions which had been the principal channels of mediæval life, remained intact on condition of submitting to the sovereign authority of the State. Universities, nobles, lawyers, Bishops, secular clergy and town corporations survived ostensibly in the old forms. Some institutions, like the cosmopolitan orders of monks and friars, could not be fitted into the new national scheme of things, and were ruthlessly destroyed by the State. Rights like those of Sanctuary and Benefit of Clergy were reduced or abolished, because they set limits to the execution of the national law. Noble and commoner, clergy and laity were made equal before the law of the land. The class of villeins excluded from these benefits disappeared, and the nobleman's coercion of the royal courts through his retainers became a thing of the past. The ecclesiastical courts exercised diminished powers over the laity, by the authority no longer of the Pope but of the Crown. Cosmopolitan feudalism and the cosmopolitan Church went down before the new idea of a national State with a national Church attached. The 'liberties' of the mediæval clergy and aristocracy, slices of sovereignty held in private or corporate hands, were resumed in favour of the liberty of the ordinary English subject, sheltered behind the power of the State.

So, too, the regulation of trade, instead of being as formerly an affair of each chartered town or guild, became the business of the national authorities. We have already seen Plantagenet Parliaments trying to regulate wages and prices by their Statutes of Labourers, to be enforced by the King's Justices of the Peace. In Tudor times this national control of economy was carried still further. The law of apprenticeship was regulated no longer by each

local guild, but by the Statute of Artificers passed by
Queen Elizabeth's Parliament. The provision for the poor,
formerly left to the monasteries and guilds and to private
charity, was provided for as a duty incumbent on society
at large, and enforced by the State. The chief agents of
this statutory control of the nation's economic life,—as also
of its political and judicial life,—were the unpaid Justices
of the Peace appointed by the Crown, who formed the
link between the views of the central authority and the
facts of local administration. They performed as servants
of the State many functions which the feudal baron had
performed in his own personal right.

When the Crown in Parliament effected a series of revolutions in ecclesiastical and religious affairs, it was demonstrated beyond all question that the State had acquired
unlimited sovereign authority. In the Middle Ages such
radical legislation would have been regarded as altogether
beyond the legal and moral competence of any power in
England. But in the Tudor epoch the nation asserted its
new strength, and, expelling all foreign authorities and
suppressing all local immunities, claimed the right to do
whatever it liked within its own frontiers. These novel
claims of complete independence for the nation and omni-
competence for the State, were embodied in the person
of the Prince. This is the general cause of the Kingworship
of the Sixteenth Century.

The plenary powers of the new State could, in that age,
have been exercised only by the King. Parliament, half
debating society and half court of law, had neither the
strength nor the ambition for such a part. Indeed it was a
main function of the Tudor Kings and their Privy Council
to teach to the Parliament men at Westminster and to the
Justices of the Peace in the countryside the work of real
government, which had been so sadly neglected in the previous century. Parliament was ready to be the scholar and
servant of royalty, like a prentice serving his time and fit-
ting himself to become partner and heir.

So, too, the peculiar religious circumstances of that age
of transition favoured the power of the Crown in England.
By putting himself at the head of the Anti-clerical revolu-

tion that destroyed the mediæval power and privilege of
the Church, Henry VIII not only became the heir of much
of that power, but set the new Monarchy in alliance with
the strongest forces of the coming age,—London, the middle classes, the seagoing population, the Protestant preachers, the squirearchy bribed and reinforced by the abbey
lands; together they proved more than a match for the
forces of the old world,—the monks and friars, the remnant
of the feudal nobility and gentry in the North, and popular
Catholic piety which was strongest in districts farthest removed from London. The secular clergy acquiesced, at
first as neuters; but in the course of the long reign of Elizabeth, the parish clergy and the schoolmasters became the
chief instruments of Protestant propaganda and instruc-
tion.

Roman Catholic zeal in England was at its lowest ebb
when Henry struck at the mediæval Church, and it failed
to revive when his daughter Mary gave the old religion
another chance. It only recovered vigour with the Jesuit
reaction well on in the reign of Elizabeth. That revival
came a generation too late for success, and it came from
continental sources that infuriated the rising nationalism of
the English. Catholic was identified in the vulgar mind
with Jesuit, and Jesuit with Spaniard. The issue became
involved in the struggle of our seamen for the free use of
the ocean and the world beyond, which the Pope had
divided with a stroke of the pen between Portugal and
Spain. The new commercial and naval aspirations of England, embodied in the Tudor Royal Navy, in Drake and
his captains, and in the trading companies of London,—
and Raleigh's prophetic visions of colonial Empire, were
all arrayed against the old religion and sailed under the
banner of the new monarchy.

In the Tudor epoch as a whole, Catholic zeal had the
feebleness of age and Protestant zeal the feebleness of
immaturity. Neither dared to defy the Crown, as Catholics and Protestants then defied it in France and in Scotland, and as the Puritans afterwards defied it in England.
Hence the bewildering changes of religion with every fresh
Tudor monarch were accepted by laity and clergy alike

much as a change of Cabinet is accepted to-day. The only successful defiance of the Tudors' claim to settle the faith of their subjects was the passive resistance of the three hundred Protestant martyrs burned in Mary's reign, and that was successful only on condition of being passive. Wyatt's Protestant rebellion failed as hopelessly as the Catholic Pilgrimage of Grace and the rising of the Earls. It was not an age of religious zeal in England, like the age of Becket or the age of Cromwell, yet the greatest of all religious questions then came up for decision. It was, therefore, the supreme moment for the Erastian Prince, who stepped into the place whence the Pope had been deposed, fully prepared, with the help of Parliament, to define the faith of all his subjects, as the great mass of them heartily desired that he should do. So long as men persisted in the mediæval error that there should be only one religion tolerated, so long the only alternative to priestly rule of society was the Erastian State. Liberty of conscience slowly grew up out of the struggles between the Erastian State and the various phases and sects of religious enthusiasm.

Only towards the end of Elizabeth's reign are there indications that the House of Commons might some day acquire enough political strength and enough religious conviction to dispute the control of ecclesiastical affairs with the Crown. In that case the ensuing confusion might enable the individual conscience to come by its own. The assumption by the State of the persecuting powers of the old Church was, as we can now see, provisional in its nature; however little questioned for the moment, it was bound to break down in the end if persistently challenged by the private conscience.

The Tudors gave a new direction to the external and expansive energies of the English people. The attempt to conquer France was not seriously resumed; little England, with its four to five million inhabitants, was thrown upon the defensive in Europe by the strength of the new French and Spanish monarchies. Her rising school of diplomacy, from Wolsey to Cecil, pursued the 'Balance of Power' as England's only chance of security in face of the great continental States now being formed. Partly owing to these apprehensions, Henry VIII made, for the first time in our history, a really fine Royal Navy. Celtic Wales and the anarchic Welsh March were reduced to order and annexed on terms of equality to England,—the first successful act of English Imperialism of the modern type, due to Henry VIII and his inherited understanding of things Welsh. Scotland he misunderstood, but under Elizabeth the future union of the two Kingdoms was prepared, when Scotland was detached from her old French connections and bound in friendship to England on the basis of common Protestant interests. The future Great Britain, the heretical sea-power on the flank of the great continental despotisms, was already clearly visible in outline. At the same time the conquest of Ireland, after being neglected by England for four hundred years, was at length undertaken in earnest, in an age too late for the happiness of either party.

Last, but not least, just when social and economic change at home was setting free individuals of all classes to wander and seek fortune afar, the new paths of the ocean were opened to the adventurous, the avaricious and the valiant, where the restless spirit of the race could find better work to do than vexing France with fresh Agincourts and England with fresh Towtons and Barnets. The descendants of the archers and retainers thronged the decks of the privateers bound for the Spanish Main, and manned the merchantmen trading to Muscovy, the Levant and the further East. England had ceased to be at the world's extremity and was found, as the new *mappa mundi* yearly unfolded itself, to be each year nearer to the strategic centre. While the Armada was going to pieces on the rocks, England was at last entering on the wider spaces of her destiny; and the sense of adventure in untrodden regions of mind and matter inspired the rising generation, who went out in the spirit of free individual initiative to explore new worlds of land and water, knowledge and imagination. At that propitious moment the English language reached its perfection of force and beauty in the

mouths of men, and at that moment Shakespeare lived to
use it.

CHAPTER ONE

Henry VII. The Machinery of Tudor Government.
Economic and Social Change. Cloth Trade, Poor
Law, and Farming

KINGS: Henry VII, 1485–1509; Henry VIII, 1509–
47

Shakespeare was well advised to leave the reign of Henry
VII as a blank in the sequence of his historical plays. For,
having once drawn Richmond, the open-hearted young
champion of Bosworth Field, gambling gaily with his life
and addressing his little band of brothers with the ingen-
uous fervour of the Prince in the fairy tale, how would
he have reconciled that portrait with the character in
which Henry as King impressed himself upon posterity, as
the English counterpart of Louis XI, cautious and thrifty
to a fault, moving silently about with keen, inscrutable
glance, opening his heart to no man and to no woman?
There may have been a certain truth in both pictures, each
in its turn, for life is long and 'one man, in his time, plays
many parts,' especially if he is an able man with an eye for
the change of circumstances. After Bosworth, England
wanted, not more adventures in shining armour, but peace,
retrenchment and, above all, the enforcement of order. It
was by putting these prosaic ideals on to a new institu-
tional basis that Henry VII left England in a position to
seize her great opportunities in the coming era.

The Tudor monarchy had a pedestrian beginning, and
became a very far-shining affair under Queen Elizabeth,
but she would have been the last to deny that her glory
was founded on the spade-work of her shrewd, patient
grandfather, to whose character her own bore a family
likeness for double-dealing, caution and thrift as to means,
and clear, tenacious purpose as to ends. Had they not both
been cruelly schooled to self-suppression by long experi-

ence of the world's treachery and danger before ever they came to the throne? And if Elizabeth's other name and nature was that of 'Gloriana' or 'the good Queen Bess,' Richmond too had known how to win the people's love in showing the high courage of his race on that gallant Bosworth campaign.

Henry VII, like his grand-daughter, ascended a throne surrounded by snares and challenges, domestic and foreign; but whereas Elizabeth's dangers could largely be traced to the religious differences of her subjects, Henry's arose from the social state of the country. Habits of disorder were general among high and low. 'There is no country in the world,' wrote the Venetian envoy to his masters, 'where there are so many thieves and robbers as in England; insomuch that few venture to go alone in the country excepting in the middle of the day, and fewer still in the towns at night, and least of all in London,'—although the English appeared, to this representative of the Venice of Carpaccio, to be richer than any other people in Europe, especially the merchants and the clergy, and to wear the finest clothes in the world.[1] Robin Hood bands, with masked or blackened faces, were destroying the deer in royal forests and private parks, with none to say them nay. In most houses and castles, the retainers down the long hall tables pricked up their ears as they heard their lord discussing with guests on the dais the likelihood of fresh dynastic disturbance, and meanwhile contented themselves with occasionally beating the men and robbing the granges of a neighbouring squire, or carrying off the cattle and burning the gate of an abbey with whose servants they had some quarrel. Benefit of Clergy and the Right of Sanctuary greatly impeded the execution of justice in every shire, and juries were still intimidated or bought.

Closely involved in these habits of disorder was the dynastic question, not yet at rest. Some fifteen years passed before it was certain that Bosworth Field had

[1] Another Italian visitor, Polydore Vergil, had a similar impression of the wealth of early Tudor England, and the thriving condition of a meat-fed peasantry, as compared to those of the continent.

ended the Wars of the Roses. By marrying the heiress of the House of York, Henry somewhat strengthened his own title to the throne, more by offering to the nation a prospect of reconcilement and peace, through the blending of the Roses, than by securing an indisputable hereditary claim. For in fact several persons still alive could show a better title by lineal descent. It was on the popular will and *de facto* occupation that the Tudor claim to the throne rested, not on the hereditary right divine, invented later by the Stuarts and their partisans.

The lords and gentlemen who were gambling on a Yorkist restoration were not to be appeased by Henry's marriage. They remained bold and confident in the North, much like the Jacobite party in days to come. In Ireland they were for a while supreme.[2] It was perhaps fortunate for Henry that they twice over chose to pin their fortunes to impersonators like Lambert Simnel and Perkin Warbeck, but the trouble which these sorry knaves caused for years on end, reminds us how weak was the habit of loyalty and how feeble the arm of the State when the Tudor rule began.

There was no standing army, beyond a bodyguard of 'beefeaters.' Only the rallying of gentlemen, yeomen and burghers to the King, enabled him to defeat at Stoke [1487.] the army of Irish adventurers and German mercenaries who were parading Lambert Simnel about in the North as Edward VI, and to round up at Blackheath [1497.] the Cornishmen who had marched unimpeded to within sight of London by way of protest against taxation.[3] Small bodies of foreign mercenaries were occasionally hired by the Crown for a campaign in Scotland or else-

[2] See Vol. I., p. 274.

[3] Latimer long afterwards told the real Edward VI from the pulpit, 'My father was a yeoman. . . . He had a walk for an hundred sheep, and my mother milked 30 kine. He was able and did find the King a harness, with himself and his horse, while he came to the place that he should receive the King's wages. I can remember that I buckled his harness when he went unto Blackheath field.'

where, but there was no money to keep them in pay as a regular force.

Neither Henry VII nor any Tudor after him made a standing army, or paid a centralized bureaucracy to govern the countryside. Tudor policy differed from that of contemporary despots on the continent. Henry and his descendants preserved the old mediæval institutions—King's Council, Parliament, Common Law, Justices of the Peace and jurymen—but breathed into them all a new vigour and compelled them all to become no longer checks on governmental efficiency, but instruments of royal power. In this way the English were trained in the habits of obedience to law necessary to modern civilization, without forfeiting their ancient liberties or breaking the continuity of their national life. The Venetian envoy had observed—'If the King should propose to change any old established rule, it would seem to every Englishman as if his life were taken from him,' and wondered how then Henry VII would be able to enforce order, which to the Latin mind could only be done through the setting up of despotism. Nevertheless another way was found, for the Tudors understood the people they ruled.

The pivot of this new constitution working through the old forms was the King's Council. Under the House of Lancaster, the Council had become, even more markedly than Parliament, a battle-ground of aristocratic factions.[4] The presence of great nobles at the Council-board had in itself secured that the arm of the State should not be exercised against them. But Henry VII and VIII, following up the beginning made by Yorkist Kings, excluded from the Privy Council all nobles save those of the King's own choice and obedience.

This exclusion of the aristocracy remained a first principle of Tudor statecraft: the list of sixteen regents named in Henry VIII's will to govern on his son's behalf, contained not a single peer of twelve years' standing. Very different had been the complexion of the Council during

[4] In the reign of Henry VII the term 'Privy Council' becomes usual for the more confidential and political body inside the larger Council.

the minority of Henry VI. The change was partly the fault
of the nobility themselves, for in the first Parliament of
Elizabeth it was stated that 'the wanton bringing up and ignorance of the nobility forces the Prince to advance new
men that can serve,' and Latimer declared in the reign of
Edward VI that 'the only reason why noblemen be not
made Lord Presidents is that they have not been brought
up in learning.'

Under the first Tudor the chief Privy Councillors were
middle-class clergy of the civil-servant type, such as Morton and Fox, or lawyers like Empson and Dudley; these
men owed all to Henry VII, and were valued by him for
their skill in filling his exchequer by means however ex-
tortionate.[5] After the Reformation the lawyer element remained, but the clergy became less prominent in the
Council and the civil service. There arose a new type of
Privy Councillor, men like the Cecils, Walsinghams and
Bacons, aspiring to be numbered among the country gentlemen, but connected with the trading community; these
men pushed their fortunes at Court, after training themselves at the Universities and by foreign travel and legal
study for all diplomatic and political business. The great
successes of government under Elizabeth were largely due
to such men, who were more enlightened and independent in spirit than the councillors of Henry VII, but not less
loyal servants of the Crown.

In working out the policy dictated by the Tudor monarchs the Council displayed great legislative activity,
partly by ordinances and proclamations which had an au-

[5] Bacon's *Henry VII* tells us: 'There is a tradition of a di-
lemma that Bishop Morton used to raise up the Benevo-
lence to higher rates, and some called it his "fork" and some
his "crotch." For he had couched an article in the instruc-
tions to the Commissioners who were to levy the Benevo-
lence, that if they met with any that were sparing, they
should tell them that they must needs have because they
laid up; and if they were spenders, they must needs have
because it was seen in their port and manner of living.'
Empson and Dudley 'being lawyers in science and privy
councillors in authority turned law and justice into worm-
wood rapine.'

thority and a scope not yet seriously challenged by Parliament, and partly by Bills which the Councillors promoted in Parliament itself. For Parliament was an essential part of the Tudor system, especially after Henry VIII broke with Wolsey and embarked on his Reformation policy. The reign of Henry VII and the early years of his son were not a great Parliamentary period; the Houses were occasionally summoned, but there was little popular interest in Parliament, no resentment at its abeyance for half-a-dozen years on end, no competition for seats even when it met, and no constitutional resistance to Henry VII's exaction of unauthorized 'benevolences' from the wealthy. This indifference disappeared as Parliament became more important under the later Tudors, and was made the instrument in constant changes of religion. Privy Councillors took seats in the Lower House and guided its proceedings, somewhat as the Ministerial Bench does to-day, save that their power depended not on the Commons, but on the Crown, whose wishes they interpreted to their fellow-members. This leadership was the chief process of education by which the House of Commons was trained to face the real problems of government and to deal with high affairs of State. It is partly for lack of such an intervening period of tutelage that some Parliaments in other countries than our own, when suddenly entrusted with power, have failed in the practical qualities necessary for the conduct of affairs.

Besides greatly increased legislative activity in its own right by Ordinances, and indirectly through Parliamentary Statutes, the Council under the Tudors organized its ancient judicial authority anew so as to bring it to bear with more weight and frequency. It delegated a sub-committee of its own members to exercise its judicial power, which was as old as the Curia Regis of the Norman Kings. This new 'Star Chamber,' as it was called, in which some of the greatest men in the Privy Council had seats, was a court which no subject in the land could hope to overawe. It was popular because it protected the weak against the strong. It was the chief instrument by which Henry VII at length put down the illegal habits of riot, retainers and maintenance. Nor, as readers of the *Merry Wives* will remember, was this use of the Star Chamber yet exhausted in Shakespeare's day:

> *Shallow:* 'I will make a Star-Chamber matter of it: if he were twenty Sir John Falstaffs he shall not abuse Robert Shallow, esquire. . . . The Council shall hear it: it is a riot. . . . Knight, you have beaten my men, killed my deer, and broke open my lodge.'
> *Falstaff:* 'But not kissed your keeper's daughter?'
> *Shallow:* 'Tut, a pin! This shall be answered. . . . The Council shall know it.'

Largely through the wholesome fear that the Star Chamber instilled into the minds of men, the ordinary law-courts recovered their real independence, and were no longer intimidated by sinister local influences. Juries became less afraid of giving verdicts against powerful neighbours, and more afraid of being called to answer before the Star Chamber for verdicts not in accordance with the facts of the case or with the wishes of the Crown. Another expression of the judicial power of the Council, analogous to that of the Star Chamber, was found in the prerogative courts of the Councils of Wales and of the North, districts where the feudal and military traditions of borderland would have made a mock of the unsupported courts of Common Law.[6]

Under Henry VII the jurisdiction of the prerogative courts and of the King's ordinary courts grew together in harmony under the shadow of the throne. But by the end of Tudor times, a sharp antagonism was felt between the courts where the Common Law was administered and the prerogative courts emanating from the Council, because the latter strove to introduce the Roman Civil Law as studied by the jurists of the Renaissance. By the end of Tudor times the prerogative courts were many and active: Star Chamber, Requests, Admiralty, Councils of Wales and the North, and the ecclesiastical Court of High Commission, an outgrowth of the royal Reformation. All these courts were giving a favoured position to the King's servants as against the common subject of the land, according

[6] For the settlement of Wales by the Tudors, see pp. 124–25, below.

to the principles of continental law, known in France as the 'droit administratif'; some of the prerogative courts used the procedure of the *ex officio* oath by which the prisoner was constrained to bear sworn witness against himself; and the Privy Council on occasion used the Tower rack, though torture was illegal in the English Common Law. The battle of the Common Law against its rivals, first clearly ranged by Coke in the reign of James I, was one of the chief issues of the struggle between the Stuart Kings and their Parliaments. The victory of Common Law was decided in 1641 and confirmed in 1688. It was well for the liberties of the subject that the future of English law did not lie with the prerogative courts, but the great part they played in Tudor times was neither unpopular nor unnecessary.

In the Sixteenth Century the English resented high taxation as quickly as in the next century they resented taxation not voted by Parliament, and the result was scarcely less effectual in limiting the power of the Crown. Since the people were armed and the government was not, the Tudor monarchs had to be thrifty. When Cornwall alone rose against the taxes in 1497, the State was seriously shaken. Partly, then, to keep down expenses, Henry VII and his successors, instead of setting up a paid bureaucracy in the countryside, laid more and more duties upon the unpaid and therefore independent country gentlemen, who held the royal commission as Justices of the Peace. Tudor England was governed by the Privy Council through the Justices of the Peace, and this involved a measure of agreement between the King and the gentry which the Crown had to consider in framing its plans for Church and State.

Every new reign added to the duties of the Justices of the Peace, until, when Elizabeth died, hardly anything in the countryside was alien to their province. They tried small offences in petty sessions. They kept up roads, bridges and prisons so far as they were kept up at all, they licensed ale-houses, they arrested criminals. They became the agents of the vast and intricate economic control taken over by the State from the old corporations—regulation of wages and prices, relations of master and apprentice. They enforced the new Poor Law. Even Elizabeth's religious policy, involving hunts after Jesuits, recusants and nonconformists, depended largely on their activity and good will.

The Privy Council saw that all these multifarious duties were well and truly performed by the local magistrates. In Elizabeth's reign they were probably performed with more efficiency than at any time before, or for many generations after. The function of the Tudor Privy Council was to teach not only Parliament to legislate but Justices of the Peace to govern, and judges and juries to execute justice. The habits of self-government in England gained far more than they lost by the Tudor rule. This great process was set going by Henry VII, and was carried on with ever-increasing momentum by his son and grandchildren.

We may well ask why did the nobles submit to be thus supplanted alike in the Privy Council and in the countryside. It is not enough to point out that the Wars of the Roses had temporarily reduced the numbers of the aristocracy.[7] It was of more permanent importance that the expense of those campaigns and the confiscations that followed each of them had impoverished the noble houses, while the same confiscations had so enriched the Crown that Henry VII, by careful 'husbanding,' found the means to carry out his system of good but cheap government through unpaid Justices of the Peace. Furthermore the middle classes of town and country were heartily with the King against the nobles; the squires, merchants and yeomen, who often intermarried with one another, were acquiring greater wealth and more trained intelligence, and could no longer be relegated to a subordinate part in the national life. It is time to examine the industrial and ag-

[7] The number of Earls and Barons summoned to the Parliament of 1454, the last before the outbreak of the Wars of the Roses, was 53; in the last Parliament of Edward IV, 45; in the first of Henry VII, 29, partly because there were so many attainted or under age. As the minors grew up and a few new peerages were created, the average number of lay peers in the Tudor epoch rose again to about 50.

ricultural changes which were giving these classes a new
importance.

The history of the change from mediæval to modern England might well be written in the form of a social history
of the English cloth trade.

From prehistoric times coarse cloth had been manufactured in our island, and under the manorial system the
mediæval villagers not only span but wove much of their
own poor clothing. But in those days little was woven fit
for export, or even for the home market, so that our well-
to-do classes must needs bring English wool home again
in the form of Flemish cloth. The export of raw wool to
the looms of Flanders and Italy gave a modest trading
wealth to Plantagenet England, besides helping her to pay
the Pope's agents the sums which their master extorted.
But when at last the English themselves learnt to weave
fine cloth for the foreign market, unexpected consequences
followed in every department of life and thought.

The great change began when, under the patronage of
Edward III, a large number of Flemish weavers brought
their skill to this island. Many of them were refugees and
allies of the English cause in the Hundred Years' War, for
the French feudal nobility was constantly at war with the
liberties of the burgher democracy of Ghent and the neighbouring cities led by the Van Arteveldes. The Flemish immigrants were, indeed, so little popular over here that some
hundreds were massacred by the London mob in the rising
of 1381, but the survivors were protected by the wise
policy of the King, until their descendants became by in-
termarriage indistinguishable from the other English. The
gift of their skill became a national treasure, destined to
multiply a thousand-fold. The French and Flemish Huguenots who flocked over in Elizabethan and Stuart times
found more popular favour, as being sufferers in the Protestant cause, and they were no less helpful than their
mediæval forerunners in developing ever new branches of
the English weaving industry.

In the Fifteenth and Sixteenth Centuries, East Anglia,
with Norwich for its capital, was greatly enriched by the

cloth trade, as its many fine churches bear witness. Its example was followed by Taunton and the western Cotswolds, Kendal and the Yorkshire dales, and favoured spots in Hants, Berkshire and Sussex. East and West, North and South saw weaving colonies spring up, not only inside old walled towns, but even more in rural villages like Painswick and Chipping Campden. Thence new wealth and new ideas spread among the yeomen and squires, drawing the whole countryside into a conspiracy to produce cloth. In such districts 'speed-the-shuttle' became as popular as 'speed-the-plough,' and sheep had a new value in the farmer's eyes. Stone villages of the noblest Tudor architecture, encircled for miles round by Tudor farms built in the same lavish style, tell the tourist on Cotswold the tale of the ancient prosperity of the loom. And the history of the Kendal cloth trade can still be read in the stout stone walls and oak furniture of Westmoreland and Cumbrian sheepfarms.

The weaving industry was conducted on 'domestic' lines, that is, the weavers and their families worked their looms in their own cottages and were supplied with material by middlemen who disposed also of the finished goods. The long trains of pack-horses, each animal with a wool-sack or a bale of cloth slung across its back, were shuttles for ever moving across the warp and woof of English life, drawing distant regions and classes together in a solid national texture. The farmer in Lincolnshire was growing fine wool for looms in Yorkshire, while the merchants and seamen of Hull and London were busy finding new markets for it in the Levant and Baltic, in the East and West Indies, and finally in Virginia and Massachusetts. The Cotswold shepherds and weavers had Gloucester and Bristol at hand in the plain below to push their wares across the sea.

All this widespread energy was taken into account by the statesmen of the Privy Council, who framed the nation's policy, foreign and economic. For all these various individual interests looked one way, when wisely guided by Cecil and Elizabeth. The town corporation and local guild could not command so wide a field of national vision as the State. Indeed the municipalities did little to control

EMERY WALKER LTD. SC.

Map 1 England and Wales in Counties, Tudor Period,
Inset—Tudor London

the new movement, for even when the cloth manufacture was not conducted, as it usually was, in rural surroundings, it was often set up in the 'liberties' just outside the borough jurisdiction, in order to avoid the pettifogging rules that hampered commerce within the walls. The great days of mediæval corporate life in guild and borough were on the downgrade throughout Tudor times, so far as economic regulation was concerned. On the other hand, there was a great increase in the wealth and political power of London and other towns, particularly the sea ports, for the cloth trade and the discovery of the ocean routes combined to make a new era in English maritime commerce.

The influence of the cloth trade was national and individualist, not cosmopolitan or corporate. All through the Wars of the Roses, through the changes and violences of Henry's Reformation and Mary's Counter-Reformation, in the golden days of Elizabeth, on through the civil wars of King and Parliament, enterprising cloth merchants, weavers and sheep-farmers were making and spreading wealth among many classes high and low, by their own individual initiative, subject only to State protection and control. They were at once more individualist and more nationalist than the mediæval churchmen and nobles whose place they were slowly taking as leaders of the English, for they had no corporate sense of belonging to a cosmopolitan order, like the mediæval Bishop, monk, noble and burgher. They had therefore no jealousy of the Tudor national monarchy, until the House of Commons engendered in them a new sentiment of democratic co-operation on a purely national basis.

The Protestant religion, setting up the domestic and individual forum for conscience and Bible-study, suited these men and their character well. In the Fifteenth Century great founders of chantries to save their own souls and perpetuate their own fame, with a strong tendency to anti-clericalism in early Tudor times, they became Bible-readers and Reformation men for the most part as the Sixteenth Century drew on. The richer of them, buying land and intermarrying with needy squires, founded new 'county families.' Not a few shared in the Abbey lands, having ready cash with which to join in the fierce land speculation that followed the dissolution of the monasteries. At the Universities and Inns of Courts their sons trained themselves to public service. The men of the new wealth were an indispensable mainstay first of Elizabeth and then of the Parliamentary cause in the era that followed. Through them the Tudor and Stuart navy came to rule the seas. For one chief advantage that England had over Spain in the exploitation of the New World, was that we had cloth to sell there in exchange for its goods, while the Spaniards had nothing to send out except soldiers, priests and colonists.

The effect of the cloth trade on rural development was not wholly for the good. The employment and wealth that it created for high and low greatly surpassed what it destroyed. But, like every other process of economic change, it had its army of victims and its tale of agony. Since it overthrew status and custom in favour of cash nexus and the fluidity of labour, it brought to the newly emancipated villein great opportunities and great risks, and to the capitalist farmer and landlord temptations to grow rich quickly at the expense of others. In certain districts there was 'enclosure' of the open fields of the village for pasture, implying the eviction of many ploughmen to make room for a few shepherds. The Tudor Privy Council frequently interfered to prevent enclosure leading to depopulation, though its efforts were neither continuous nor always successful. The centre of the evil was Leicestershire and Northamptonshire, and to a less degree the counties bordering on them to the south and east.[8] Thence many of the evicted ploughmen wandered off to swell the ranks of the 'sturdy beggars,' 'staff-strikers,' and 'rogues forlorn,'

[8] On the other hand, Somerset, Devon, Cornwall, Suffolk, Essex and Kent were counties largely enclosed in pre-Tudor times by the peasants themselves, because of woodlands, physical conditions, fruit-farming, or local circumstances now forgotten, and in the West partly because of old Celtic custom.

who figure so largely in the literature and the Statute Book of Tudor times.

The 'beggars' were the characteristic evil of the Sixteenth Century as the 'retainers' had been of the century before; and enclosing landlords who set them adrift on society were denounced by moralists like More and Latimer, just as the noblemen who kept the retainers had been denounced by Fortescue and his contemporaries. Many of the sturdy 'beggars' were *quondam* retainers, robbers and outlaws, who had not thrown off the lawless habits of Fifteenth Century society. Under a stronger government they began to figure less often as bullies and more often as victims; the stocks, the whip and the bed of 'short and musty straw' became their lot, instead of the fellowship of the merry green wood or the licence to rob in their lord's livery. With them were joined the innocent sufferers from seasonal unemployment in the cloth trade and other industries of a modern character, and, last but not least, the evicted ploughmen of the Midlands. But unless tramps were very different in the Sixteenth Century from those of later date, many ne'er-do-wells must have claimed commiseration by posing as evicted ploughmen, in an era when everyone was talking of the wrongs of that much injured class.

The promiscuous charity distributed at the monastery door bred beggars as well as relieved them. And the sudden suppression of the monasteries, before the Poor Law had been fully developed to take their place as an agency of relief, naturally increased distress, as much perhaps by turning adrift the large companies of monastic servants, as by stopping the monastic alms; these had latterly been a much smaller proportion of the conventual income than is often assumed.[9] The 'beggars' became the objects both of fear and of pity. Their entry into a village (usually called a 'town' by our Tudor ancestors) has been immortalized in nursery rhyme:—

Hark! hark! the dogs do bark; the beggars are coming to town.

[9] See pp. 112–18 of R. H. Snape's *English Monastic Finances in the Later Middle Ages* (Cam. Press, 1926).

and then we know how—

Some gave them white bread, and some gave them brown,
And some gave them a good horsewhip, and sent them
out of the town.

Both bread and whip, at first the expression of individual charity and self-protection, were organized as compulsory social duties by the series of Tudor poor laws culminating in the Poor Law and parish Poor Rate of Elizabeth. Gradually the distinction between the able-bodied who would not work, the aged and feeble who could not work, and the unfortunate who could not find work, became clear to Tudor society and took its place in the Poor Law. The abolition of the monastic dole had helped to make England consider the problem in a national light and to make scientific provision for the poor a civic duty enforceable by law. With all its imperfections the Elizabethan Poor Law marked a step forward in social organization, and by the end of her reign foreigners marked with surprise an absence of beggars to which they were unaccustomed in other lands.[10]

To regard 'enclosure' of open land by permanent walls and hedges as a thing invariably or even usually bad in itself, would be to misinterpret the whole history of British agriculture. In the first place, by no means all enclosure, even in the Sixteenth Century, converted arable into pasture. Much of it was directed to convert unused land into pasture, or to improve the method of arable farming, processes essential to increase the wealth, trade and population of the island. In the second place, many of the Tudor enclosures were made, not by 'engrossing landlords' or 'capitalist farmers,' but by small yeomen. By enclosing modest portions of the domain or of the open village field into compact farms and hedged fields, they increased the employment and wealth of the humble. The

[10] See p. 124 and note, below. Actually several Poor Laws had been put on the Statute Book before the dissolution of the Monasteries. 'The Dissolution no doubt made a Poor Law more necessary, but they do not stand to each other in the simple relation of cause and effect.' Tanner, *Documents*, 470.

good farmer was freed from the drag of his slovenly, dishonest or less skilled neighbours in the common field. The
constant quarrels and litigation due to the removal of balks
and boundaries of the scattered strips came to an end. The
free individual initiative given by enclosure to the yeoman
farmer was an advantage to himself and to everyone else.
The pity is that so much of the best land in the Midlands
was still left 'open field,' till in the Eighteenth and Nineteenth Centuries it was enclosed under economic and social conditions more generally unfavourable to the small
farmer than those of the Tudor age.[11]

Hugh Latimer's pulpit eloquence was fearlessly directed
against enclosure accompanied by eviction on behalf of engrossing capitalist landlords; but it is probable that his own
father, whom he held up as the type of yeoman of the true
breed, had an 'enclosed' farm of the right sort. We know
at least that his leasehold farm, containing 200 acres arable,
fed also 100 sheep and 30 milch cows besides the oxen
for the plough, enabled him to employ six men besides
women servants, to give his daughters portions of £50
apiece and to send Hugh to school, college and ultimately
to bishop's bench and martyr's stake. It was such yeomen
who bred the new England, a better England on the whole
than that of mediæval lord and villein. These yeomen
with small copyholds or moderate-sized leasehold or freehold farms, were as important a feature in the new rural
economy as were the engrossing landlords with their large
estates. The great importance of the yeomen, particularly
the freeholders, in the wars and politics of Stuart times,

[11] The Elizabethan agricultural poet, Tusser, thus describes the advantages of enclosure 'in severall,' as against
the open field ('champion') :—
'More profit is quieter found / (Where pastures in severall
bee) / Of one seelie aker of ground, / Than champion
maketh of three, / Againe, what a joie is it knowne / When
men may be bold of their owne!'

The extent of the Tudor enclosures is often exaggerated.
The shires where there was most of it, Leicester and North-
ampton, were still very largely open and 'champion' at the
time of the enclosing movement of the Eighteenth Century.

was an outcome of the economic changes of the Fifteenth and Sixteenth Centuries.[12]

Nor must we judge the enclosure movement entirely by its immediate social consequences. There is also its agricultural and economic justification. The historian of British farming has pointed out that the exhaustion of the corn-land, especially in open-field farms, by centuries of use, in many cases necessitated the restoration of its fertility by a long period of rest under grass; and moreover that the enclosures as a whole so benefited corn-production, that whereas in Tudor times men feared that bread would grow scarce if the open-field farms were broken up, the Hanoverians had learnt from experience that only by further enclosure could their over-populous island be saved from starvation.[13]

Tudor times saw not only the segregation of compact yeoman farms for the occupier, but the formation by proprietors of great landed estates, to which the superb country houses of Elizabeth's richest subjects bore monumental evidence. This movement, that made a few men 'spacious in the possession of dirt,' was destined to culminate in the Eighteenth and Nineteenth Centuries at the expense of the smaller freeholds; but in Tudor and Stuart England large and small properties flourished side by side. The concentration of landownership was furthered by the English custom of primogeniture, which remained a social habit long after it had ceased to be a legal obligation. The country gentlemen in their wills provided only the eldest son with land, having previously sent his brothers out from the manor-house door to seek their fortunes as apprentices in trade or manufacture, in the liberal professions or in overseas adventure. This custom, so different from that of the continental nobility, destroyed class barriers and greatly helped to build up English commerce and Empire. It built up also the great landed estates.

[12] The word 'yeoman,' prior to the late Eighteenth Century, was normally used for a free peasant farmer, irrespective of whether his land were freehold or held on lease. A villein was not a yeoman, nor was a landless labourer.

[13] Lord Ernle, *The Land and the People*, Chaps. I. and II.

Sheep-farming and enclosure were not the only signs of a new spirit in the English countryside. Formerly, the object of 'subsistence agriculture' was to enable each village to grow its own food; but many men, small and great, were now investing capital in land with their eyes on the national market and its ever-growing demand for corn, wool, cattle, horses, poultry, dairy produce, and a hundred other requirements. Throughout Tudor and Stuart times the old subsistence agriculture and the new capitalist agriculture were flourishing side by side, but the latter was always gaining ground. One of its earlier triumphs was the introduction of hops from Flanders, which in Tudor times went far to change the drink of the Englishman and the appearance of Kent. The feeding of cattle and sheep during the winter began to be seriously studied; turnips were known over here in time for Shakespeare to mention them, and under the Stuarts artificial grasses and other methods were slowly introduced in imitation of the scientific farmers of Holland. Horses were slowly taking the place of oxen at the plough.[14]

BOOKS FOR FURTHER READING, *Tudor Period generally:* I. POLITICAL AND GENERAL: H. A. L. Fisher, *Political History of England,* 1485–1547; A. F. Pollard, *ditto,* 1547–1603; Innes, *England under the Tudors;* Tanner, *Tudor Const. Documents;* Holdsworth, *History of English Law,* Vol. IV. (admirable on this period); Pollard, *Factors in Modern History;* McIlwain, *The High Court of Parliament; Tudor Studies,* by twelve colleagues of Professor Pollard, 1924.

It does not seem necessary to refer readers to the well-known controversial histories of the period by Froude and

[14] 'Hops, Reformation, bays and beer / Came into England all in one year'

is as truthful as such traditional rhymes can be expected to be. Put 'era' for 'year,' and it is correct. 'Bays' were a new kind of cloth introduced by Flemings into Norwich. There are various versions of the rhyme, some of them mentioning 'turkeys,' which came from America.

It is Anne Page in the *Merry Wives,* who declares that sooner than marry Dr. Caius, she

'had rather be set quick i' the earth, / And bowl'd to death with turnips.'

his opponents, who between them have elicited so much information. The present generation of historians seems to be in a calmer and more judicial mind.

II. ECONOMIC AND AGRICULTRAL CHANGES: Ashley, *Economic Organization in England,* and *Economic History,* Pt. II.; Ernle, *British Farming,* and *The Land and the People,* Chap. II.; Tawney, *Agrarian Problem in 16th Century;* A. H. Johnson, *Disappearance of the Small Freeholder;* Gonner, *Common Land and Enclosure;* Leonard, *English Poor Relief;* Tawney and Power, *Tudor Economic Documents.*

III. EDUCATION, ETC.: Leach, *English Schools at the Reformation;* Foster Watson, *English Grammar Schools to 1660;* Einstein, *Tudor Ideals;* Seebohm, *The Oxford Reformers.*

CHAPTER TWO

> The Revival of Lollardry. The Renaissance Scholars. Wolsey and the Balance of Power. The Era of Discovery. The Cabots. Henry VIII Founds the Royal Navy

> KINGS: Henry VII, 1485–1509; Henry VIII, 1509–47

The Fifteenth Century, if we exclude its last twenty years, was intellectually barren beyond any other epoch in our history since the Norman Conquest. The violent suppression of freedom of thought at Oxford and subsequently throughout the country by the persecution of Wycliffism [1382.], was not made good by any moral or intellectual revival of a more orthodox character. There was nothing analogous to the 'coming of the friars' of two hundred years before. The triumph of mere obscurantism reached its height in the trial and imprisonment of poor Bishop Pecock, because in arguing against the Lollards he had appealed partly to human reason instead of wholly to the authority of the Church. [1457.] Among the laity, the same period was unproductive of great literature, if we except some of the popular ballads. Chaucer had readers, reproducers and imitators, but not successors. There was, however, the

new printing-press, and an adequate supply of new
schools for the middle classes; though the education given
was of poor quality, the number of educated people in the
island offered a wonderful field for the sower of wheat or
tares. And Henry VII's reign was a season of seed.

The restoration of peace and order was a condition favourable to intellectual revival. We observe two portents in
the early Tudor world, before the Lutheran controversy
arose,—first a revival of Lollardry and Bible-reading among
the poor, and secondly the coming of the Renaissance
learning from oversea. To these two movements we should
perhaps add another tendency, that favoured them both,
the sheer anti-clericalism of large sections of the population: it was said that, if Abel had been a priest, Cain would
have been acquitted by a jury of London citizens. The
squires and nobles, though none of them were any longer
Lollards, cared so little for the Church that they were prepared to support a policy of spoliation provided the spoils
came their way. Ecclesiastical privilege, left intact for centuries while all else had been changing in England, had
aroused an anti-clerical temper in the ordinary Englishman which rendered him ready to listen to the new doctrines. The Church had lost her moral and intellectual
leadership, while retaining to the full her privileges, her
wealth and her persecuting power. Her decision to defend herself against Wycliffism by repression unaccompa-
nied by reform, though successful for a while, was fraught
with danger.

A generation before Luther sprang to sudden fame,
Lollardry, long suppressed, had come into the open once
more. It was native to the soil of England, and had been
faithfully preserved in cottage and workshop as a poor
man's tradition, by the spiritual ancestors of John Bunyan.
Peasants in the Chilterns and other parts of the Home
Counties, humble persons in London, Bristol and other
towns, with here and there a priest and here and there
a man of means, met secretly to read 'the epistles and gos-
pels in English and Wycliffe's damnable works,' and to
strengthen one another's faith in what we should now call
'Protestant' doctrine. Between 1490 and 1521 many of the

Lollards actually went to the stake, while more recanted to save their lives. The persecution was hotter than ever before, but this time failed of its purpose.

In the same years a different movement was stirring the Universities to fresh life. Italy was the land of the Renaissance, and thence the new studies came to Oxford in the last two decades of the Fifteenth Century.[1] From Italy, Grocyn, Lily and Linacre brought home a new interest in Greek literature, Latin grammar and scientific medicine. Slowly the long-lost world of Hellas began to take shape, as in a glass darkly, revealing to a few ardent minds a world of thought not bounded by the mediæval heaven and hell, just as the material world was expanding beyond all the limits of mediæval cosmography, with every new voyage of Columbus and Cabot. At the same time, studies conducted in Ciceronian Latin, replacing the useful but inelegant Latin of the Middle Ages, suggested ideals of conduct on the 'antique Roman' pattern. If these influences should once spread from Court and college into common grammar schools at Stratford and elsewhere, life even here, upon this bank and shoal of time, would become a gracious and noble adventure.

Another element formative of modern England was introduced by young Colet, a London merchant's son. [1497.] On his return from Italian groves of Academe, he astonished Oxford by the announcement that he would lecture on St. Paul's epistles. By sheer force of genius he compelled not only the enthusiastic undergraduates but the disapproving Abbots and doctors of divinity to listen to a young man scarcely yet ordained priest, while he set aside every landmark erected by the scholiasts, and gave straight from the text a realistic and humanist exposition of the life and teaching of St. Paul. He was seeking to

[1] Early in the reign of Henry VI, Humphrey Duke of Gloucester, an English statesman allied to the Royal House, had patronized Italian scholars of the new classical renaissance. His gift of 'Duke Humphrey's Library' to Oxford proved the beginning of the Bodleian collection, but some time passed before the classical writers were studied there in the unmediæval spirit of Duke Humphrey and his Italians.

discover what the Epistles had meant to him who wrote
and to those who received them, not at all what they had
meant to the dialecticians of the last three hundred years.
The studies and learning of the Middle Ages crumbled
like a corpse exposed to the air. Duns Scotus had once
been in the van of intellectual advance, but those who
were still faithful to the Subtle Doctor were now held in
derision as 'dunces' by the rising generation at Oxford and
Cambridge, and presently on every school bench in the
land.

Dutch Erasmus was rapidly rising by the help of the
printing-press to a European reputation without previous
parallel. He was much in England, and both he and Sir
Thomas More were Colet's friends and allies. Between
them they gave a new character to the Renaissance
studies, making them moral and religious in Northern Europe, instead of artistic and pagan as in Italy. To the Italian scholars and their patron Princes and Cardinals, the
Renaissance meant the ancient poets and philosophers,
marble nymphs and 'brown Greek manuscripts.' To Colet
and Erasmus, and through them to the English generally,
the Renaissance meant these things indeed, but it meant
also the New Testament in Greek and ultimately the Old
Testament in Hebrew. The difference was profound, and
produced yet another rift between England and the
Franco-Italian civilization which had nurtured her child-
hood. For the men of the Italian Renaissance lived, and
their spiritual successors in France and Italy have lived
ever since, in a world of art, letters and science seldom
touched by religion, in effect abandoning ecclesiastical affairs to the unaided efforts of the monks and clergy. But
in England the men of the Renaissance, following the lead
of Colet, used the study of Greek and Latin to reform
not only the schools but the Church herself, and called on
clergy and laity to act together in the task.

This movement, at once moral and intellectual, classical
and Christian, did not, as is sometimes said, perish in the
storms of the English Reformation. On the contrary, its
spirit found expression in the educational and religious policy of the reformed schools and of the reformed Church of

England that emerged under the later Tudors from the confused violence of the earlier struggle. If Colet had seen a typical Elizabethan grammar school, he would have been well pleased. If the old endowments that were confiscated under Henry and Edward are set against the new endowments that were made under Elizabeth, the quantity of educational provision was little if at all increased under the Tudors; but the quality was immensely improved.

These Oxford Reformers, as Colet and Erasmus were called, began, in the names of scholarship, religion and morality, a series of bitter attacks on the monks as obscurantists, on the worship of images and relics, on the extortion of the ecclesiastical courts and the worldliness of the clergy. On these matters no Lollard could use stronger language, although they were no Lollards. Their influence was spreading from Oxford to London, to the Court, and ere long to Cambridge. Colet became Dean of St. Paul's [1505.], and delighted the citizens and perturbed the clergy of the capital by sermons denouncing Church abuses and practices in a manner not heard from the official pulpit since the silencing of Wycliffe's priests a hundred years before. Colet also founded, in the shadow of the Cathedral, St. Paul's School with Lily as its first headmaster, to teach Greek and Ciceronian Latin, and to become the prototype of the reformed grammar school.

What would be the attitude of the new monarchy towards the New Learning? Much indeed turned upon that, for in the situation then reached by England, the nation could do nothing against the will of the Crown, and the Crown nothing against the will of the nation, but the two together could do anything they chose, even to the altering or preserving of religious doctrine and ecclesiastical privilege.

Henry VII was too busy in his great task as England's policeman to concern himself with the New Learning. The clergy to him were useful civil servants, the Pope a figure on the diplomatic chessboard. For the rest he was orthodox; he once took part in converting a Lollard at the stake, and leaving him to be burned in spite of his recantation, such being the standard of Christian charity of those times.

But what of the younger Henry? In 1509 he succeeded to the throne and to the marriage with Catherine of Aragon, since his elder brother Arthur who was to have enjoyed the lady and the realm had prematurely died. The young King of eighteen exceeded the ordinary run of his subjects in body and in brain. He was a paragon of Princes, the patron alike of all true English sportsmen and of the men of the New Learning. Succeeding with a clear title to the peace, wealth and power that his father had painfully accumulated, and cutting off the heads of Empson and Dudley as an earnest of the great love he bare his people, he won their hearts from the first. He was as true an Englishman as 'Farmer George,' but on a more brilliant pattern. He could bend a bow with the best forester in the realm, and when complimented on his archery by the French Ambassador could reply 'it was good for a Frenchman.' His colossal suit of tilting armour in the Tower reminds us that once he flashed through the lists like Launcelot, laying low his adversaries and calling for more. He was a champion at tennis and a mighty hunter. Orthodox like his father, he continued to encourage the burning of Lollards, wrote his book against Luther, and was dubbed by the Pope *Fidei Defensor*. [1521]. But he was also a friend to Colet and More, forcing the latter to take up the dangerous profession of courtier, and defending Dean Colet against the obscurantist clergy, with the declaration 'Let every man have his doctor, this is mine,' even when the fearless Dean denounced his war against France as unchristian. [1513.] For 'Henry loved a man.' And 'pastime with good company he loved,' as we read in the song which he is said to have composed and set. Among other accomplishments this Admirable Crichton was no mean musician, and played well on all known instruments. Poetry and music flourished in his Court, when the English lyrical and the English musical genius were moving forward again towards the moment of their fine flowering under Elizabeth.

It was said that Henry's Court had better store of learned men than any University. These early friends of his implanted in his mind a dislike of monks, of image worship, of relic worship, and a respect for the study of the Bible—all perfectly compatible with doctrinal orthodoxy on the Eucharist, as his subjects were to find out in days to come when this handsome young athlete and lover of all things noble had been turned by thirty years of power and worship into a monstrous egoism moving remorselessly over the bodies of old friends and new foes towards a clearly conceived middle policy in religion, with the Royal substituted for the Papal power. All the various aspects of that later policy can be traced to opinions imbibed during his early life, and to the movement of the age in a nation which, even in his days of bloated and ferocious tyranny, Henry understood with an instinct that even Elizabeth never surpassed.

For the present those days were far ahead. As yet the Cardinal ruled—the last Cardinal and almost the last churchman ever to rule over England. While 'Harry our King was gone hunting' morning after morning, or was holding high festival at night 'with masque and antique pageantry,' Wolsey was labouring over the details of home and foreign policy which in later years Henry took into his own industrious hands. But youth must be served, at least such a youth as Henry's, and that was the Cardinal's day.

Wolsey, like all the greatest servants of the Tudor monarchy, was of comparatively humble birth—his father was probably an East Anglian grazier or wool merchant—but he was haughty and ostentatious to a degree that would hardly have been tolerated in a Prince of the Blood. He 'is the proudest prelate that ever breathed' reported a foreign observer, and such was the general opinion. The one blot on his splendid equipment as a diplomatist was the fury of his temper; one day he laid violent hands on the Papal Nuncio and threatened him with the Tower rack over some dealings with France. The state which Wolsey kept, in the high hall at Hampton Court or when he travelled, for a while pleased his master and dazzled his countrymen, but in the end helped to turn them all against him, and pointed for poets the moral of his fall.

In his hands the Balance of Power in Europe first became clearly defined as the object of England's foreign policy. It was dictated by the rise of the great monarchies of France and Spain, for if either of these overcame the other, it would be lord paramount of Europe, and little England's position would be ignominious and unsafe. For several years Wolsey kept the balance with consummate skill and with a minimum of expense to English blood and treasure. In 1513 the double victory over the invading Scots at Flodden and over the French at the Battle of Spurs near Guinegatte on the Netherland border, raised England to a strong position as holder of the balance. But after 1521 Wolsey's skill and foresight failed him. He backed Charles V, monarch of Spain and the Netherlands and Emperor in Germany, at a time when he should rather have supported the weakening cause of France. At the battle of Pavia [1525.] the capture of Francis I and the destruction of his army laid Italy at the feet of Spain for the next 180 years, reduced France and England temporarily to impotence, and began that Hapsburg supremacy in Europe which in the days of Philip II and Elizabeth almost proved the destruction of England, and would have destroyed her but for the growth of popular, maritime and religious forces in the island which Wolsey overlooked or opposed.

The power of Spain was not confined to the Old World. The era of ocean discovery and commerce had begun, replacing the ancient trade routes across Asia and Egypt, of which the European end had been in the hands of Genoa and Venice. From the Italian cities and the land-locked Mediterranean with its oared galleys, power and wealth were passing to the lands of Western Europe, which could send out a new type of seaman and new type of ship to sail the far ocean, to reach the markets of Asia by sea, and to discover Africa and America on the way.

It did not seem at first that England would be the chief gainer by this change. In the Fifteenth Century, Portuguese seamen, under Prince Henry the Navigator, had been beforehand along the coast of Africa and round the Cape route to India, founding a Portuguese Empire on the

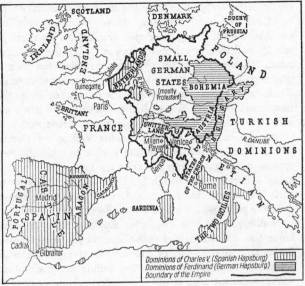

EMERY WALKER LTD. SC.

Map 2 Europe in the Time of Henry VIII. Rise of the Great Continental Monarchies

African littoral, destined to survive till the present day. Spain was long disunited and struggling with the Moors, but when joined into one State by the marriage of Ferdinand of Aragon with Isabella of Castile, she soon made an end of the Moors on her own side of the Straits of Gibraltar, employed Columbus [1492.] and sent out the Conquistadores, who made her a present of the mines of Mexico and Peru and the wealth of the Spanish Main. [1519–35.]

The Pope had risen to the occasion. He had drawn a line down the globe from pole to pole, a hundred leagues west of the Azores, giving all lands discoverable to the west of it to Spain, and on the east to Portugal. [1493.] The competition thus set on foot had incited the great voyagers in the pay of the two Iberian monarchies, had sent Magellan round by the Horn and across the Pacific, and set Amerigo Vespucci to trace the southern coastline of the continent that bears his name. As yet no one openly impeached the validity of the Pope's division. As yet Portugal and Spain had no rivals on the ocean and in the lands beyond. The Italian maritime States supplied the master mariners—Columbus, Vespucci and Cabot—but neither Venice nor Genoa ventured upon their own account on the new ocean traffic. It was as if the heart of Italy had been broken by the decline of the old Asiatic trade-routes of which she had been mistress; neither Venice nor Genoa, as communities, had the requisite vitality to build the new type of ocean-going ship and train the new type of ocean-going sailor: it was enough for their declining powers to carry on the wrecks of the old Levant trade, and engage galley to galley with the Turkish war fleets.

Neither as yet was France or England ready to challenge the commercial and colonial monopoly of Spain and Portugal in Africa, Asia or America. In Henry VII's reign John Cabot and his boy Sebastian, sailing in a cockle-boat with 18 gallant men of Bristol, visited certain regions in Labrador, Newfoundland or Nova Scotia. [1497.] They had sailed west to find the fabled Cathay and the Seven Cities of the East, with their spices and their gold, and found the way blocked by the foggy cod banks and dripping pine forests of North America—a better heritage for the English had they known it. But England dared not yet arouse the wrath of Spain by laying hands on this heritage; her time was not yet. Henry VII had encouraged maritime adventure, but Wolsey discouraged it. The voyages of the Cabots and the men of Bristol to North America merely staked out a claim that lay dormant for several generations as regards inland discovery or plantation, though before the middle of the new century the Newfoundland fisheries had become an important nursery of our seamen.

Such was the situation with which Henry VIII had to deal. His policy was both wise and strong. While not encouraging transoceanic adventure in the face of predominant Spanish power, he made possible the future liberation of his country's energies by the only means—the foundation of a Royal Navy. The 'narrow seas' had been held during the Hundred Years' War—so far as they had been held at all—by the pugnacious seamen of the merchant navy, fighting sometimes as individual pirates, sometimes, as at Sluys, united under the royal command. Henry V had begun to build a royal fleet, but his work had not gone far and had subsequently been neglected. Henry VII had encouraged the mercantile marine, but had not built a fleet for fighting purposes only. It was Henry VIII who built an effective fleet of royal fighting ships, with royal dockyards at Woolwich and Deptford; he also founded the corporation of Trinity House.

Henry's maritime policy had a double importance. Not only did he create ships specially manned and commissioned to fight, and to fight in the public service alone, but his architects designed many of these royal ships on an improved model. They were sailing vessels better adapted to the ocean than the rowed galleys of the Mediterranean powers, and better adapted to manœuvring in battle than the more clumsy 'round' ships of the mediæval type in which the English merchants sailed the sea, and in which the Spaniards crossed the Atlantic. The new type of English warship was three times the length of its beam or more, while the normal 'round' ship was only twice the length of its beam. Hitherto sea-battles had consisted of ramming, archery and boarding, very much like the battles of the old Greek and Roman navies. But a new age was at hand. From the port-holes of Henry VIII's fleet protruded the iron mouths of great cannon in a row, ready to give the shattering 'broadside,' the operation of war to which, more than to any other, British maritime and colonial power owe their existence. It was Henry VIII himself who had insisted that his naval architects should mount heavy cannon in the body of the ship; they had devised the expedient of piercing apertures in the very hold itself through which the great shot could be discharged.[2]

[2] On the technical question of the build of the ships in Henry VIII's navy see Callender, *Naval Side of British History*, Chap. IV., and the Introduction to Corbett's *Drake and the Tudor Navy*. The word, as well as the deed, 'broadside' often occurs in Hakluyt's accounts of our ships

In 1545, at the end of Henry's reign, a French armada attempted to invade England, but was foiled by the Royal Navy. England was saved from invasion, and the same year a baby called Francis Drake was born on a farm near Tavistock.

The Royal Navy was Henry's creation, and it saved both himself and his daughter after him when they adopted an island policy and defied the Catholic powers of Europe. Wolsey had no notion of the importance of sea power to England. He was a great mediæval churchman, a civil servant of the old school, and a diplomatist of the Renaissance type. But of the future development of England at home and on the sea Wolsey had no vision at all. His master, with that curious instinct of oneness with the English people which was the secret of Tudor greatness, saw deeper. He could use Wolsey's consummate administrative powers during the years of his own apprenticeship in statecraft, and then pass over him along a path of his own which no Cardinal could be expected to tread.

Wolsey was a great man, but it was not he who made modern England. He had no interest in the navy and no trust in Parliament. He had indeed an active distrust of it, because the growing anti-clericalism of the country had been demonstrated in the Parliament of 1515 by an attack on Benefit of Clergy, mortuary fees, and the currency of Papal decrees in England. There had been strange talk on the judicial bench of the penalties of *præmunire* incurred by Convocation. Judges and Parliament had stood up for the royal power, as representing popular rights against clerical privilege. Neither Wolsey nor his master had been unobservant of these things. For the present indeed the Cardinal ruled and Henry watched. So Parliament was not summoned again for eight years. But if ever Henry should tire of the Cardinal and desire to rob or to reform the Church and to defy the Pope, he would know to what institution he could look for support.

fighting in Queen Elizabeth's reign. 'I commanded to give the broadside, as we terme it,' says Captain Downton, describing his destruction of 'the Portugalls' mightie carack of the East Indies' in 1593.

CHAPTER THREE

The Royal and Parliamentary Reformation under
Henry VIII

Those who conceive of opinion in Tudor England as
sharply divided between two mutually exclusive and
clearly defined parties of Catholic and Protestant, can
never understand the actual course taken by the Reformation before the latter years of Elizabeth. Opinion was in
the making, not yet made. Honest men, as well as time-
servers, were perpetually altering their views. Few held a
consistent body of doctrine which would have satisfied the
Catholic or Protestant partisans of a later day. Sir Thomas
More, a scathing critic of the religious orders and the popular superstitions they fostered, became the martyr of Papal
Supremacy, whereas Bishops Gardiner and Bonner, though
famous as Papalists under Mary, had defended Henry's
original breach with Rome. Queen Elizabeth herself would
have preferred a celibate priesthood. Opinion among the
mass of men was more interested in preserving the King's
Peace than in raising difficulties over his religious policy.

In the North and extreme South-West, considerable
zeal was shown for the defence, not indeed of the Papal
jurisdiction, but of the monasteries and the old forms of religion. In London and the neighbourhood the party of
change prevailed. The contrast between the citizens of
Tudor London and those of Valois Paris, in their attitude
towards the clergy and the doctrines of the mediæval
Church, goes a long way to explain the different fortunes
of the Reformation in England and in France.[1]

[1] Professor Pollard has written:—'Tudor despotism consisted largely in London's dominance over the rest of England,' and Miss Davis has added, 'The history of the English
Reformation might well be rewritten from that point of
view. Almost all its changes were anticipated there (in
London), and Henry VIII, Elizabeth and Burghley succeeded, where Wolsey, Cromwell, Somerset and Mary
failed, because they seldom flouted the City and never lost
its allegiance.' For a monarch without a standing army,

But the party of change, in London and elsewhere, was not wholly inspired by Protestantism or by the New Learning of Dean Colet and his friends. It was also under the influence of a passion which can best be described as anti-clerical. Anti-clericalism was in some persons a greedy desire to plunder the Church for the benefit of their own families. In others it was a rational and honourable dislike of the powers and privileges enjoyed by the priesthood. For the clergy still had the legal right to extort money in innumerable ways, and to adjudicate in their spiritual courts on points of doctrine and morals for all men, in an age when the laity had become well able to think and act for themselves. The change from mediæval to modern society in the sphere of religion, consisted mainly in a reduction of the power of the priesthood, and the raising up of the laymen, first collectively through the action of the State, then individually through the freedom of private conscience. It was the first of these movements that took place under the Tudors, in the subjection of the Church to the State, and it was a movement quite as much anti-clerical as it was Protestant.

Henry VIII burnt Protestants, while hanging and beheading the Catholic opponents of an anti-clerical revolution. And this policy, which appears so strange to-day, then met with much popular approval in England. In the babel of voices heard during his reign, the strongest note is a Catholic, Nationalist anti-clericalism. It was only after Henry's death that the logic of the new situation at home and abroad drove the English Anti-clericals and Nationalists to defend themselves against Catholic reaction by alliance with the Protestants, to whose doctrines they became, in Elizabeth's reign, very fair converts.

Anti-clericalism, in fact, was not destined to become the

the presence of such a storehouse of wealth, arms, and men, two miles from his Palace gate, was a chief consideration in policy. *Tudor Studies,* pp. 287–88. Moreover, in the Sixteenth and early Seventeenth Centuries, London had a practical monopoly of the printing-press, except for Oxford and Cambridge; Elizabeth actually forbade printing outside London and the two Universities.

shibboleth of a permanent party in England, as it became in France and Italy from the time of Voltaire onwards. Dislike of clerical domination and respect for religion are both more general in England than in most parts of Europe, and both found satisfaction in our post-Reformation churches and sects. The spirit of opposition to clerical predominance sometimes supported Anglicanism against Roman or Puritan claims to govern men's lives, and sometimes joined Nonconformity against the pretensions of the State clergy. But while the power of the Pope and the mediæval Church was being broken by Henry VIII, anti-clericalism appears as an independent force on the flank of both Catholicism and Protestantism, and for a few decisive years it was the strongest of the three.

[1519.] The prelude to Henry's breach with the Pope was the German Reformation under Luther, which for some years almost annihilated the prestige of Rome as a centre of religious authority. In 1527 the Holy City was sacked by the armies of Charles V, Emperor in Germany and King of Spain. German heretics and Spanish Catholics rivalled each other in looting churches, raping nuns and besieging Pope and Cardinals in the Castle of St. Angelo, while a Roman Catholic wrote thus to Charles V:—

Everyone considers that this has taken place by the just judgment of God, because the Court of Rome was so ill-ruled. Some are of opinion that the Holy See should not continue in Rome, lest the French King should make a patriarch in his Kingdom, and deny obedience to the said See, and the King of England and all other Princes do the same.

If ever there was a moment when European opinion made it easy for England to break with the Papacy, it was the generation that followed the revolt of Luther and the sack of Rome.

The Lutheran doctrines had no sooner been proclaimed at Wittenberg than they became a power in England, though still under the ban of Church and State. They at once absorbed the Lollard into the Protestant movement. Their effect on the men of the New Learning was twofold:

some, particularly the younger men, eagerly joined the more thorough-going movement; others, particularly the older men who had brought the Renaissance to England, shrank back and reacted towards orthodoxy. Erasmus feared Protestantism; More opposed it and wrote against it. Oxford, where so much had been done for progress in the past, held back in doubt, but Cambridge stepped for the first time into the van of the national movement. From 1521 onwards, students met at the White Horse tavern in that town, to discuss Luther's propositions.[2] The tavern was nicknamed 'Germany' and the scholars who haunted it 'Germans,' but they were the makers of the new England—Tyndale and Coverdale who first gave her the Bible in Tudor English, Cranmer who gave her the Prayer Book, Latimer the soul of the popular movement, and many other future apostles and martyrs.

Latimer and Cranmer represented, each very nobly, the two aspects of the reformed English Church of the future—the moral and the reflective. Latimer was as fearless as Luther on points of religion, and was far less timorous than the German Reformer on social questions and in face of secular power. Cranmer, mild and cautious, a student scrupulously slow to choose between two sides in intellectual controversy, was a man of perpetual moral hesitations and mental revisions, but with occasional bursts of courage on behalf of his hard-won opinions, like the courage of a timid woman turning to bay in defence of her children. Both men won Henry's regard, and though Latimer's views were too uncompromising to suit the King's purposes for long, Cranmer's favour lasted through all the violent changes of royal affection and policy, to which Wolsey, More, Cromwell and so many others of both sexes fell victims. Cranmer, indeed, remained the last personal friend that Henry cared to keep: the brutal and self-willed King

[2] There was, of course, nothing disreputable about a 'tavern' in those days; it had not the associations of a modern 'public house.' Gentlemen often took their wives to spend the evening at the ale house, as a natural place to meet friends. 'Mine host' held an important social position, for instance in *The Merry Wives of Windsor*.

was to die murmuring of his faith in God, his hand lying trustfully in that of the gentle and perplexed founder of Anglicanism. If one could rightly interpret the inner meaning of that scene one would know much of the curiosities of human nature.

But Henry had a good deal to do before he came to die. At the time of the sack of Rome [1527.] he was thirty-six years old, and had reached in his slow development the prime of his intellectual power. Hunting and tournaments could no longer be a substitute for politics and government as an outlet to his immoderate energies. He was, at last, prepared to take over from Wolsey the heavy burden of administration. Moreover, like all his subjects, he was getting tired of the Cardinal, who had failed abroad and given personal offence at home, and whose fall could scarcely have been delayed much longer, even without the question of the Royal Divorce.

That question, the immediate cause of the breach with Rome that had been preparing for centuries in England, was not, strictly speaking, a question of 'divorce' at all. Technically, it was a question whether or not Henry had ever been properly married to Catherine of Aragon, since his brother Arthur had been her first husband. A former Pope had granted a dispensation for her marriage to Henry, but Clement VII was now asked to declare that the marriage had never been valid, and that Henry was yet a lusty bachelor. For he desired to marry Anne Boleyn. Like the generality of monarchs of that era and of many eras before and after, he would have been perfectly content with her as his mistress, which she soon was, had he not desired a legitimate male heir to secure for England an undisputed succession and strong rule after his death. He could expect no more children from Catherine, and the Princess Mary was their only child. There had never been a Queen Regnant in England, and the unfamiliar idea of a female succession seemed to threaten the country with civil war or the rule of a foreign Prince as Consort.

The refusal of the Pope to liberate Henry was not due to scruples: he had only recently divorced Henry's sister Margaret, Queen of Scotland, on a far less reasonable ex-

cuse, and his predecessors had released monarchs like
Louis XII of France, when they desired divorce on no
grounds save reasons of state. But he could not oblige
Henry, because after the sack of Rome he was in the power
of Charles V, who was Catherine's nephew and zealous
protector. The Temporal Power of a Pope, so far from
giving him freedom, made him a slave to mundane considerations, then as in other ages. Because he was an Italian Prince, Clement could not afford to displease the *de
facto* lord of Italy.

To Henry it seemed intolerable that the interests of
England should be subjected, through the Pope, to the
will of the Emperor. In his anger at this personal grievance,
he came to see what many Englishmen had seen long before, that England, if she would be a nation indeed, must
repudiate a spiritual jurisdiction manipulated by her foreign rivals and enemies. The full-grown spirit of English
nationalism, maturing ever since Plantagenet times, asked
why we should look abroad for any part of our laws, either
matrimonial or religious. Why not consult our own churchmen? Why not act through our own Parliament?

[1530.] Wolsey's failure to obtain the 'divorce' from Rome
sealed his doom. His death in disgrace saved him from
preceding to the scaffold many high-placed victims of the
Terror that now began to walk by noonday. Cranmer,
learnedly arguing in favour of the 'divorce' and of England's competence to decide the question for herself, rose
thereby to royal favour and became Archbishop of Canterbury. [1532.] But Henry needed also a rougher and less
scrupulous servant and found one in Thomas Cromwell.
The revolution—anti-Papal, anti-clerical, Anglican and
Erastian all in one—was launched on the flood-tide, and
was carried through with the accompaniment of violence
and injustice that usually attends all great social revolutions, whether the driving force be a man or a mob.

What was the attitude of the English people towards the
question? The average Englishman retained the feeling of
his ancestors against the Pope's interference in England,
but held it more strongly than ever in the light of the new
times, and supported Henry in his decision to settle the

question once for all. The nationalism of England was fully grown; she would no longer submit to be governed by a religious authority that was seated a thousand miles beyond seas and mountains, and that judged English questions by Italian, Spanish, Imperial and occasionally by French standards and interests, but never by English. On the other hand, even in London, the sympathies of the common people went out to the blameless and injured Catherine and her daughter Mary. Anne Boleyn was unpopular. A mistress raised to be a wife at another's expense can scarcely win respect, and Anne was a light woman with no claims of her own for a reversal of so natural a verdict.

But the political and ecclesiastical sides of the question soon swallowed up the personal, and as this change took place, Henry's position with his subjects grew stronger. In the great revolution, by which he freed the English Church and State from the bonds of Rome, suppressed the monks and friars who represented the old cosmopolitan order, and reduced the power and privilege of the clergy, he had the support of London and the South. The unpopular divorce policy involved the popular breach with Rome, and the breach with Rome involved the anti-clerical revolution at home, which enlisted in its defence the most powerful forces in the country. But neither Henry nor his subjects yet understood that these changes must lead in turn to the toleration of the Protestant religion. It was the hour of a persecuting Catholic anti-clericalism as peculiar, some would say as monstrous, as Henry himself. [1533–47.] But for the moment it won more support than any other more logical or more merciful policy. Henry, sending the noble Sir Thomas More to the scaffold for his refusal to repudiate the Papal authority, and poor Protestants to the stake for their denial of transubstantiation, moves the angry disgust of readers accustomed to religious toleration as the basis of modern society. But these tragic scenes affected the minds of contemporaries in a different manner, —with pity indeed for the victims, but with respect for a Government that was keeping order in Church and State according to the persecuting standards inherited from the past of Christian practice and never yet called in question.

King-worship under the Tudors reached its culmination in these years, in the acceptance of one man's will as the *salus publici*. It was disastrous to the character of Henry, whose egoism became a disease. But the disease affected the heart and not the brain. One result of King-worship under a strong King was that England secured the great change in her institutions without civil war, though Henry had no army with which to keep order. Brave blood was shed, but it was not shed in rivers, as in France, Holland and Germany during the wars of religion.

The instrument chosen by Henry to effect his Royal Reformation was Parliament. It could scarcely be Convocation: the ecclesiastical assemblies of Canterbury and York wherein there was no representation of the laity, could not be made active instruments in an anti-clerical revolution. The mediæval Church was organized as a purely clerical body and therefore the laity could only assert themselves from outside, through Parliament and not through Convocation.

In both Provinces Convocation acquiesced only under threat of the penalties of Præmunire. Yet we must not suppose that the whole body of secular clergy were averse to all the changes which they were compelled to accept. They had little love for the monks and friars. They bitterly grudged the Annates and other heavy tolls levied from them by the Pope. Many in Convocation recognized that Benefit of Clergy, sanctuary and the abuses of the spiritual courts must be reformed. There was also a small but growing party of more advanced reformers like Cranmer and Latimer, whence Henry chose several of his bishops.

The attitude of the English clergy, though not heroic, was more patriotic, more useful and more morally sound than fanatical intransigence and the preaching of civil war in defence of outworn privileges. Because the clergy accepted much which they could not be expected to like, they saved England from a war of religion, and they soon recovered what they had long lost, a great place in the affection of the country, under a new regime s. modern times.

To be freed from the Pope was well perhaps; to subjected to the King was perhaps less well. But the clerg, had no third choice. Convocation acknowledged with a sigh that Henry was Supreme Head of the Church of England [1531.], with the scrupulous addition 'so far as the law of Christ allows,'—an elastic phrase that was stretched far in the next few years.[3] The clergy had thus forsworn the authority of the Pope and accepted that of the English State in its place. But Henry must seek elsewhere than in Convocation the active instrument of the layman's revolution that followed. He found it in Parliament.

The Reformation had the effect of doubling the importance of Parliament. Hitherto it had been almost as much a court of law as a legislative assembly, and under Henry VII and Wolsey its importance was on the decline. If English history had remained a branch of European history instead of going off on a course of its own, that decline would have continued until the English Parliament had followed into oblivion the mediæval Estates of France and Spain. But Henry VIII chose otherwise.

[1529–36.] The Reformation Parliament was not packed. It was not necessary to pack it. The legislation that completed the breach with Rome, destroyed the monasteries and established the supremacy of the State over the Church in England, was prepared by Privy Councillors and passed after discussion by both Houses. The Reformation Parliament, unlike its predecessors, sat for seven years, and in the course of its eight sessions acquired a continuity of personal experience among its members which helped to build up the traditions of the modern House of Commons as a great instrument of government. In Henry's Parliaments debate was fairly free, at least on subjects with which the King wished the Houses to deal; he knew the value of genuine advice and criticism,—provided al-

---

[3] In the Act of Supremacy, passed by Parliament in 1534, this qualification was omitted, and Henry was styled 'only Supreme Head in earth of the Church of England called *Anglicana Ecclesia.*'

ways that he had his way in the main, and that was ensured
by the nature of the times and by the character of the
royal programme. Yet, in Henry's reign, several measures
desired by government were rejected, and others amended
by the Commons.

Louis XIV is commonly believed to have said *'L'état,
c'est moi,'* and he certainly acted as if he thought so.
Henry's authority was of a different kind, as he was the
first to acknowledge. In 1543 he told the Commons, while
confirming them in the valuable privilege of freedom from
arrest:—

We be informed by our Judges that we at no time stand so
high in our estate royal as in the time of Parliament, when
we as head and you as members are conjoined and knit
together in one body politic.

And indeed, when a series of Royal Parliamentary
Statutes had revolutionized the fundamental law of Church
and State, which had from time immemorial been set high
above the competence of Crown or Parliament to alter,
then indeed the 'Crown in Parliament' had more than
doubled its power. It had become, what it had never been
before, 'omnicompetent' to make any law it would within
the Realm of England.

But while Parliament, and particularly the House of
Commons, was gaining a new position in the State, it remained in royal leading strings. The Reformation Parliament and the 'Tractable Parliament' that followed it, seem
to have been unduly dazzled by the right divine of the
new Pope-King of England. The Statute of Treasons of
1534 spread the net far too wide for the safety of the
loyal subject, and in the hands of Henry VIII and Thomas
Cromwell such a weapon was not left in the sheath. Fortunately it was repealed under the liberal Protector,
Somerset, at the beginning of Edward VI's reign, and the
relation of Crown to Parliament found its normal Tudor
level once more.

The suppression of the orders of monks and friars, and the
secularization of their property did much to secure the
Royal Parliamentary Reformation on a basis of vested in-

terest. [1536–39.] Henry VIII sold great parts of the confiscated Abbey lands to Peers, courtiers, public servants
and merchants, who at once resold much of it to smaller
men.[4] Syndicates of middlemen of the commercial class
bought the lands to speculate in real estate. It was largely
owing to these transactions that, when the Papal reaction
began under Mary, it was suspect to this new element in
the squirearchy. Many an Abbey had become a manor-
house, or the quarry out of which a manor-house was being built, and the squire had no wish to see it an Abbey
again. Such persons, though they themselves were never
found at the martyr's stake, learnt the wisdom of encouraging the Protestant preachers who were more willing to
serve God for nought.

In those days land meant power of a direct kind over
those who lived upon it. The Reformation would never
have been permitted to flourish among the tenants on
monastic estates. But when land in every shire changed
from the hands of corporations devoted to the Papal
authority and the old religion, into the hands of laymen
bound to the new order of things by the very fact of their
possessing land confiscated by sacrilege, the influence exerted over a very great body of tenantry was reversed.[5]
In London, as in every other town, valuable and conspicuous sites of religious houses and much house property
belonging to them passed into lay hands, removing the
last check on the ever-increasing Protestantism, anti-clericalism and commercialism of the capital. At Oxford and

[4] Except a few who resisted Henry and were executed
in terrorem, the old inhabitants of the monasteries were
well treated at the Dissolution. Many of the heads of the
dissolved houses became Bishops or Deans, and the monks
were handsomely pensioned; very many of them took livings as well as their pensions. Baskerville, *English Monks
and the Suppression of the Monasteries*, 1937.

[5] The strongly Protestant family of which Francis Drake
was born in 1545 held a farm on the Russell estates in
Devonshire confiscated from Tavistock Abbey. Francis
Russell stood godfather to the baby, and gave him the
Christian name which he was to make famous in two
hemispheres.

Cambridge the monks and friars had been very numerous
and had formed the backbone of resistance to the New
Learning. The first result of their disappearance was a fall
in the numbers of those attending the Universities, which
alarmed Latimer; but ere long the ranks of the students
were swelled by an increased proportion of gentlemen's
sons. This new class of lay undergraduate made the Universities a path to court favour and public service. The
Cecils and Bacons fitted themselves by their academic
studies to govern the country under Elizabeth, and to
foster a new order of intellectual ideas which would never
have taken root if Oxford and Cambridge had been left
to the guidance of the monks and friars, checked only by
the secular clergy.

Nevertheless, the way in which the monastic lands were
distributed was a crime against education. The wealth of
the monasteries, and after them of the chantries which
suffered like spoliation in the last years of Henry and the
first of Edward VI [1545–49.], should have gone to multiply
and enlarge the schools formerly attached to a few of the
monasteries and many of the Chantries. The example
had already been set, for Wolsey had used the wealth of
religious houses which he suppressed for the benefit of his
Cardinal College, afterwards Christ Church. At Cambridge,
a nunnery put down on account of scandals had been converted into Jesus College as early as 1496. Henry VIII
made, indeed, the splendid foundation of Trinity College,
Cambridge, largely out of monastic lands, a deed that
should never be forgotten if only to remind us what might
have been done with the rest of the monastic spoil. England might have become an educated democracy before
the Industrial Revolution, and she might in that case have
been able to direct that great change into nobler and more
humane channels. But in the corrupted currents of the
world such a scheme for the bestowal of these Abbey and
chantry lands wholesale on the public seemed a 'devout
imagination,' in England and in Scotland both. The Exchequer was empty and the courtiers greedy, and a hasty
sale of the lands to private persons was the course adopted.

The monks had not been good managers of their property, for they were terribly in debt. In relation to their tenants they were on the average neither much better nor much worse than laymen. As is the way with corporate bodies, they were often conservative in their policy as land-lords—that is less efficient, but less severe. But even this rule had many exceptions. Enclosure with depopulation had taken place on many monastic estates, and Bishop Langland in 1526 said of some monasteries that 'more than the seculars or the laity, they flay their tenants' (*'excoriant firmarios suos'*). It is true that when the monasteries were dissolved, many of the tenants suffered by a rise in rents, due to land speculation and frequent sales of the con-fiscated estates among the class of laity who were scram-bling for them. But this, too, was far from being always the case; very often the monks had wholly dissociated themselves from the management of their lands, letting them on long leases which necessarily remained untouched when the estates changed hands.[6]

Both the monks and the nuns, and those of the laity who lived upon pensions and 'corrodies' charged on the monastic endowments, were to a large extent aristocratic and well-to-do in their origin and connections.[7] The monasteries were no longer either a democratic or an intellectual force. The proportion of their income that actually went in alms to the poor had become scanty. The chronicle-writing which had distinguished the English cloister in the past had practically ceased, and no other form of intellectual activity had taken its place. To Colet, More and Erasmus the monk was an obscurantist, and the friar an exploiter of the worst popular superstition. The revived classical and biblical scholarship of the Renaissance found scarcely an echo in the monastery. Manual labour had died out among the monks, and the ascetic life which had

[6] See note at end of chapter, p. 66.

[7] On this point see Professor Savine's *English Monasteries at the Dissolution* (Clar. Press, 1909), pp. 240–45 and 263–67. On English Nunneries see Miss Power's *Medi-æval English Nunneries* (1922). There were never more than about 2000 nuns in mediæval England. On poor re-lief see pp. 32–33, above.

formerly given them so much influence over an admiring world was now neither admired nor practised. Occasionally there were bad scandals, both in monasteries and in nunneries, but for the most part the 'religious' on the eve of the Dissolution lived a life of easy sauntering comfort, without grave offence but without marked benefit to the world around them. For several generations pious endowments had been going no longer to monasteries, but to chantries and elsewhere. The numbers of the monks had fallen by some twenty-five per cent. in three hundred years, and stood at about 7000 at the time of the Dissolution. Years before the breach with Rome the movement for suppressing monasteries was being carried on by orthodox Bishops and Cardinals.

There was, in fact, a strong case for applying their endowments to other public purposes more suited to the new age, and if the breach with the Pope was to be permanent his militia must be disbanded. But there was nothing to be said for collecting vile charges on insufficient evidence,[8] judicially murdering the Abbot of Glastonbury and several other 'religious' in order to hasten the surrender of their property, and letting it nearly all pass into private hands in return for a merely temporary relief to the exchequer.

[1536.] The monks and the old religion were still beloved in Lincolnshire, Yorkshire and the counties of the Northern border where feudal and mediæval society still throve. The rising known as the Pilgrimage of Grace was the result. Henry had no troops save a few Yeomen of the Guard. If the rest of the country had risen, or had refused to support him, he must either have fallen or reversed his policy. But London, the South and the Midlands stood by him and the storm was weathered. Nor is this popular attitude surprising: long before the King and the gentry

---

[8] No historian goes to the reports of Henry VIII's Commissioners for evidence about the state of the monasteries. But there is plenty of good evidence in the Episcopal Visitations of those monasteries which were subject to them. See Tanner, *Constitutional Documents*, pp. 50–57, for an excellent summary.

rose against the monasteries, the peasants and townsfolk had so risen in 1381, at St. Albans, Bury St. Edmunds and elsewhere.

Neither did the rest of the Church feel called on to espouse the quarrel of the 'religious.' The secular clergy had for centuries regarded the monks and friars as their rivals, who took from them tithes and fees, competed against their ministrations, and rejected the jurisdiction of their Bishops. These feelings of rivalry between the two parts of the Catholic Church in England were just as strong on the eve of the Reformation as at any former time, and this fact largely accounts for what followed. The cosmopolitan orders which stood isolated alike from the clergy and the more progressive of the laity, and looked to Rome for protection, could not possibly survive when the spirit of nationalism undertook in earnest the formation of an English Church.

In that Church the Bishops retained their place, little altered in form or in law. It was easy for them to take King instead of Pope for master, for they had long been accustomed to act as Royal rather than as Papal servants. The typical English Bishop of the Middle Ages was not Becket but William of Wykeham. Their experience as civil servants, their active part in Parliament and Privy Council, the habit of compromise between the rival claims of Church and Crown, helped the Bishops to accommodate themselves and their office to the great change. But the Abbots had, most of them, stood outside the national life, few of them attending Parliament, and hardly any of them mixing with business outside their own conventual affairs. It was natural then, that in modern England there was a great place found for the Bishop but none for the Abbot. The disappearance of those Abbots who had sat beside the Bishops in the House of Lords left the spirituality in that Chamber in a minority instead of a majority, a change of great significance.

Henry, as Supreme Head of the Church, proceeded to reform the religion of his subjects and so complete the breach with Rome. The study of the Canon Law, that

intellectual link with Papal Europe, was suppressed.[9]
There were also changes of a more purely devotional character. In his morose and terrible old age, Henry put into
effect the ideals which he had imbibed from the Oxford
reformers in his fresh and generous youth, the more readily
as he could thereby counteract the influence of monks,
friars and Papalists over the multitude. Relic-worship,
image-worship and pardon-mongering, the grosser forms
of popular superstition and pious fraud which Colet and
Erasmus had attacked, were put down by the heavy hand
of the royal authority. All over the country relics were
being destroyed, miracle-working images taken down, and
their crude machinery exhibited to the people on whose
credulity it had imposed. 'Dagon is everywhere falling,'
said the reformers; 'Bel of Babylon is broken in pieces.'
The shrine and cult of Thomas Becket, so long the chief
centre of English pilgrimage, was utterly and easily suppressed, in a new age which spoke of 'the holy blissful
martyr' as 'a rebel who fled the realm to France and to the
Bishop of Rome to procure the abrogation of wholesome
laws.'

Meanwhile, under the influence of Cranmer, an approach
was being made towards a new type of appeal to the
religious instincts of the masses. The Archbishop himself
was drawing up forms of prayer in English which found
their places in the Prayer Book of the next reign. But,
meanwhile, Henry ordered priests to recite to their congregations, and fathers to teach their children the Lord's
Prayer, the Commandments and the Articles of Faith in
English. Above all, at Cranmer's instigation, the Bible in
English was not only permitted to circulate freely, but was
ordered to be set up in every parish church. A version
based on that of Tyndale, the noble scholar and martyr,
and on another by his less learned successor, Miles Cover-

[9] An indirect effect of the Reformation was to reduce not
only the independence of the Church Courts, but the scope
of their jurisdiction over the ordinary affairs of life. For
instance, actions for defamation or libel gradually passed
to the lay courts during the Tudor and Stuart epochs. See
Holdsworth, III. 410–11, V. 205–6.

dale, became known, as Tyndale had desired, to craftsmen and to 'the boy that driveth the plough.' The English Reformation, which had begun as a Parliamentary attack on Church fees, and proceeded as a royal raid on Abbey lands, was at last to find its religious basis in the popular knowledge of the Scriptures which had been the dream of Wycliffe. In this way it acquired the strength that resisted the Marian persecution, when cobblers, clothiers and poor women willingly offered themselves for a cause they at last understood.

Henry, having thus let in the sea, proceeded to ordain the limits of the flood. The disagreeable appearance of one of his later brides, Anne of Cleves, whom Cromwell brought over from anti-Papal Germany, helped, together with graver considerations of European policy, to remind the King that things were going too far, or at least too fast. Cromwell was beheaded. [1540.] The Act of Six Articles had already been passed decreeing death against any one who denied Transubstantiation, or the necessity of auricular confession and clerical celibacy. [1539.] A man was hanged in London for eating flesh on Friday. The burning of Protestants proceeded quietly, but with no indecent haste. Latimer was permitted to retire to private life, but Cranmer remained Archbishop. It was an oscillation, not a reversal of policy. Catherine Howard, the fifth wife, was a Catholic Anne Boleyn, who had much the same faults and suffered the same fate as her Protestant prototype. [1542.] Catherine Parr, the famous survivor, was a moderating influence on religious policy, inclining cautiously to the Reformers.

Henry in fact was trying to prevent further change and to frighten people who were too prone to discuss religion, a subject on which the King's Grace had finally pronounced —at least for the present. Meanwhile men could read the Bible and think what they liked in silence. The Act of Six Articles was not unpopular, for at the moment the great majority were neither Papalists nor Protestants, and no one believed in toleration. The Act was not rigorously or regularly enforced. Henry was still in touch with the desires of the generality of his subjects, and he had their loyal support against hostile foreign powers in the last years of his reign. But times were bound to alter, and there are signs that he was meditating yet another move forward when he was called before the only spiritual authority that was any longer competent to summon a King of England. [1547.]

BOOKS FOR FURTHER READING: Pollard, *Henry VIII,* and *Cranmer,* and *Wolsey;* R. W. Chambers, *Thomas More,* and books in list, pp. 36–37, above.

NOTE (to p. 61, above), MONKS AS LANDLORDS: Mr. Leadam, in his close analysis of Wolsey's *Domesday of Enclosures* of 1517 (I. pp. 48–49, 263), comes to the conclusion, based on statistics, that 'leaving out of account the question whether the evictions were the work of landlord or tenant, there was no superior security, as fancied by later generations, for the cultivators of ecclesiastical soil.' It is not surprising therefore that, while the monasteries still existed, they had no such reputation for good landlords as they acquired in the sentimental retrospect. In Sir T. More's *Utopia* we read: 'noble men and gentlemen, yea, and certain Abbots, holy men God wot, not contenting themselves with the yearly revenues and profits that were wont to grow to their forefathers and predecessors of their lands, . . . leave no ground for tillage; they enclose all in pastures; they throw down houses; they pluck down towns (=villages), and leave nothing standing but only the church to make of it a sheepcote.'

On the whole subject see G. Baskerville, *English Monks and the Suppression of the Monasteries* (Cape, 1937), and the *Eynsham Cartulary,* edited by H. G. Salter (Clarendon Press), especially his summing-up on p. xx. See also Tawney, *Agrarian Problems in 16th Century,* pp. 382–83; A. Savine, *English Monasteries on the Eve of the Dissolution* (Clarendon Press); R. H. Snape, *English Monastic Finances* (Cambridge Press); Leadam, *Domesday of Enclosures* (Royal Hist. Soc.); Tanner, *Const. Documents,* pp. 50–57, and H. A. L. Fisher, *Political History, passim.* All these must be compared to Cardinal Gasquet's *Henry VIII and the English Monasteries.* A more general review of monastic and ecclesiastical estate policy in relation to the peasants in Europe throughout the Middle Ages will be found in G. G. Coulton's *Mediæval Village* (Cambridge Press, 1925), and his *Five Centuries of Religion.*

CHAPTER FOUR

Interludes, Protestant and Catholic

KINGS: Edward VI, 1547–53, and Mary I, 1553–58

The patient craft of Henry VII and the imperious vigour of Henry VIII had laid the foundations of modern England. Order had been restored, the nobles and their retainers had been suppressed, royal government through Council and Parliament had become a reality in every corner of England and even of Wales,[1] the Royal Navy had been founded, the independence of the country had been established in the face of Europe, secular and spiritual, and the lay revolution in the relations of Church and State had been carried through. But all this, though accomplished, had not been secured. When Henry VIII died, the State was heavily in debt, the coinage had been debased, and the religious feuds which he seemed to have suppressed by violence were bound to break out afresh with increasing fury. The work of the Tudors might yet be ruined, unless the country could be governed on a method at once effective and cheap, and unless a form of religion was found for the new State Church sufficiently acceptable to prevent civil war leading to anarchy or counter-revolution. These problems were eventually solved by Elizabeth, a wise woman and something of a sceptic. But in the dozen years between her father's death and her own accession, government remained in the hands of fools and adventurers, foreigners and fanatics, who between them went near to wrecking the work of the Tudor monarchy, and who actually reduced England to a third-class power, torn by religious feud, a mere appanage of Spain on land and sea.

And yet this inglorious period was by no means barren of results. Religious parties and issues became more clearly

[1] For Henry VIII's settlement of the Welsh problem see pp. 124–25, below.

defined. It was demonstrated that Henry's half-way tabernacle was not permanently habitable where he had pitched
it, but that the country must choose between reunion with
Rome and further advance in a Protestant direction. At
the same time the national resistance to the Pope became
identified in the popular mind with another issue—independence of Spain. The Prayer Book under Edward and
the Protestant martyrology under Mary raised the English Reformation onto a new intellecutal and moral plane,
and rendered it possible for Elizabeth in 1559 to make a
permanent settlement of religion, a feat that no human
wisdom could have achieved in the drifting chaos of
opinion that still obscured the land a dozen years before.

Edward VI [1547–53.], son of Henry VIII and Jane Seymour, was nine years old at his accession. He was an invalid child, intellectually precocious, earnest and severe,
with more conscience than his father but scarcely more
softness of heart. So far as we can judge of one who died
before he was sixteen, he might, if he had lived longer,
have ruined the Reformation by overdriving, much as his
half-sister Mary ruined the Catholic cause. So long as he
lived, two men in turn guided the State in his name. First
his uncle Seymour, the Protector Somerset, a rash idealist;
and after him John Dudley, Earl of Warwick and Duke
of Northumberland, a man of no principle at all except
selfish ambition.

But Edward's reign was saved from futility by the two
dominating figures of its religious life. The first of these was
Archbishop Cranmer, whose Prayer Book, based largely on
his translations from late Latin into the purer English of
the Tudor age, harmonized the old and the new, and
appealed successfully to the temperament and higher emotion of large sections of the population who without this
rallying point might have flown off into mutually hostile
factions. Henceforth the Church of England was something more than a remnant spared by the royal and anti-
clerical revolution: it had found what it so sorely needed—
a positive religious atmosphere of its own. The final triumph
of the Prayer Book was postponed till Elizabeth's reign,

but it made its first voyages on the stormy seas of opinion under Edward. Cranmer, timid and time-serving at the Council Board, as soon as he took his pen in his hand in the freedom of his own study was like a man inspired.

Very different was his friend, Hugh Latimer. He did not resume the episcopal office which he had been obliged to relinquish on account of his Protestantism in Henry's reign, but remained as the free lance of the Reformation under Edward, free even to 'cry out against covetousness' in the Lords of the Council. Preaching at St. Paul's Cross to the citizens and in the King's garden to the courtiers, Latimer, by his rough, homely sermons, set the standard of that English pulpit oratory which, together with the Bible and the Prayer Book, effected the conversion of the people to Protestantism in the course of the next hundred years.

Meanwhile he did his best to redeem the crimes of the Royal Reformation by the honesty with which he denounced them. Edward's reign opened with the completion of Henry's plan for the robbery of the guilds and chantries, ostensibly for the sake of putting down 'superstition' and paid prayers for the dead, but trespassing far outside these limits in order to load the courtiers with fresh spoil; the schools attached to the suppressed corporations were in the first instance abolished and were not in all cases re-established as 'King Edward Grammar Schools.' To Latimer and his contemporaries education was a part of religion, and he saw that without education Protestantism could never take root. The learning for which the English Church became afterwards so distinguished, the long array of divines and scholars from Jewel and Hooker to Westcott and Hort, were yet in the future, while in the present the sharers of chantry lands 'crammed their rich thievery up,' they cared not how.

Schools are not maintained (cried Latimer). Scholars have not exhibition, the preaching office decayeth. Men provide lands and riches for their children, but this most necessary office they for the most part neglect. It will come to pass that we shall have nothing but a little English divinity that will bring the realm into a very barbarousness and utter decay of learning. It is not that, I wis, that will keep out the supremacy of the Bishop of Rome. Here I will make a supplication that ye would bestow so much to the finding of scholars of good wits, of poor men's sons, to exercise the office of salvation, in relieving of scholars, as ye were wont to bestow in pilgrimage matters, in trentals, in masses, in pardons, in purgatory matters.

It was because many of the middle classes learnt this new conception of piety and good works that the rapacity of the courtiers was made good in the course of years, and the land saved alike from 'barbarousness' and from 'the Bishop of Rome.' Yet the great chance for endowing education from the confiscated lands had been let slip, because England was then neither democratic nor in love with learning.

The Protector Somerset, in spite of the protests of Cranmer, had pushed on the spoliation of the guilds and chantries largely for private interests; he had secured his own share of the spoil, out of which the original 'Somerset House,' too princely for a subject, rose on the banks of the Thames. He aimed at monopolizing power to an unwise degree for a statesman who had at his back no monarch of age and authority to support him against a revolt of his fellow-Councillors. Nevertheless he was a strange mixture of pride and humility, selfishness and pure public spirit. He was more honest, humane and democratic in sympathy than the other politicians of that time.[2] He believed in toleration in both Church and State. He encouraged Parliament to repeal the oppressive laws of Henry's later regime, the Statutes of Treason and Act of Six Articles. [1547.] Under his influence Parliament legitimized the marriage of clergy in response to their petition, and issued the first edition of Cranmer's Prayer Book,

[2] The extraordinarily low level of the past in humanity and decency is often forgotten by controversialists who judge it as if it were a struggle under modern conditions between the well-behaved sects and parties of to-day. In the last year of Henry VIII's reign Wriothesley, the Lord Chancellor, and Rich, the Solicitor-General, with their own hands turned the screws of the Tower rack while torturing the Protestant lady, Anne Askewe, in hope of extorting confessions. Her shattered body was afterwards tied to the stake at Smithfield and burnt.

which was enforced by the mildest Act of Uniformity ever issued by a Tudor Parliament. [1549.]

Somerset persecuted neither Catholics nor Protestants on account of their opinions, and permitted free discussion of religious differences. The result was not altogether encouraging. The moment the heavy hand of government was raised, the religious parties everywhere flew at one another's throats. 'Hot gospellers' matched against 'suppressed' monks and friars led on the rival crowds. Brawling in church and street over the removal or the non-removal of images, the reading of Mass or Prayer Book, Protestant preaching or Catholic processions, seemed the prelude to civil war.

There were serious disturbances in Oxfordshire, put down by the hanging of priests. The North was fairly quiet, perhaps because the Catholics there had not recovered from the severity of the repressions that followed the Pilgrimage of Grace a dozen years before. But only in the extreme South-West did anything that could be called a religious rebellion come to a head. The men of Cornwall still spoke their old Celtic language, and of two services in unknown tongues preferred the sound of the familiar Latin to the 'Christmas play,' as they termed it, in English. In Devon also the peasantry rose under their priests, but the mariners rescued Sir Walter Raleigh's father out of their hands, and the citizens of Exeter stood a six weeks' siege on behalf of Protestantism. In Elizabeth's reign the squires and the new clergy succeeded in bringing round the peasants to the point of view of the seaman and townsfolk, in that shire which more than any other was to challenge Catholicism upon the high seas.

Elsewhere the numerous local risings that disturbed Somerset's Protectorate were not religious but agrarian. Times were bad, Henry VIII had debased the coinage and the consequent rise and uncertainty of prices caused great distress. The most formidable outbreak was in Norfolk, where the Reformation was generally popular, but where the landlords' excessive sheep-farming on common lands had caused discontent. The armed commonalty, under their leader Kett, captured Norwich and camped outside its gates upon Mousehold Heath, afterwards so famous a spot in English landscape. [1549.] There they slaughtered and devoured 20,000 of the offending sheep! Their spirit was democratic, not unlike that of John Ball's men in 1381, or of the German peasants who rose in Luther's time. One of their demands was the emancipation of all who were still villeins—an aspiration that was fulfilled in the reign of Elizabeth, who characteristically compelled all the villeins she could find on her royal estates to purchase their freedom at a swingeing rate.

Like all unassisted risings of peasantry, that of 1549 was soon put down by the better organized classes. Its chief result was a reaction in favour of 'strong government' and the fall of the too liberal Somerset, who had sympathized with the popular complaints. Under the influence of Latimer and the party of social reform known as the 'Commonwealth's men,' the Protector had endeavoured to induce Parliament to pass effective statutes to control enclosures, but members elected on the strictly limited franchise of that day[3] were too deep in the business themselves, as also were many of Somerset's colleagues on the Council. It was easy for them now to lay at the Protector's door the blame for Kett's rising and the similar troubles elsewhere. He had, moreover, alienated the magnates of the City, though he was popular with the mob of the London streets. The affection of the peasantry stood him in little stead in a struggle for power. A combination of the Catholic and Protestant parties in the Council effected his overthrow, after he had made a wild appeal to the people to rise on his behalf against 'the great.' [1549.]

The Catholic party looked to benefit by the change which they had helped to bring about, but they found themselves deceived. Somerset's supplanter, Dudley, Earl of Warwick and afterwards Duke of Northumberland, had no sincere religious opinions of his own, but he elected to work with the Protestants, and the Reformation was pushed on with greater vigour and less discretion than before. Toleration in Church and State, and popular sympathy in social questions had been tried by Somerset and found a

[3] See Vol. I., p. 338 for the disfranchising Act of 1430.

failure by the upper classes. Encouraged by the set of opinion in Parliament, Dudley revived some of the harsher methods of Henry VIII, but this time in connection with a more advanced Protestant doctrine. No one indeed was put to death for religion, except Joan Bocher who denied the humanity of Christ and a Dutchman who denied His divinity. But some leading Catholics were deprived and imprisoned.

The Prayer Book was reissued with Protestant emendations—nearly in its present form (1925). Since Lutheranism had gone to sleep in the arms of the German Princes, Strasburg and Switzerland were the hearth of the Protestant flame, and the gathering places for English religious exiles, whence many now returned to speed the work at home. A breath from the lands on which the Alps look down began to make itself felt in England. As yet that influence came from the milder Zwingli of Zurich rather than from Calvin of Geneva, but both of these reformers were democrats, as anyone appealing to the Swiss must needs be. German Protestantism had become official and princely, but Swiss Protestantism always strove to arouse a lively sense of religion in the common people, whether in Holland, Scotland or England. It thereby contributed a useful element to the English Reformation, which went on its course gathering fruit off many trees old and new, but never entirely pleasing anyone outside its native island.

[1549–53.] The ascendancy of Dudley, who became Duke of Northumberland in 1551, was as unpopular as it deserved to be. It was the high-water mark of corruption and greed among courtiers with the country in their power and no King to keep them in order. Northumberland, a purely self-seeking man, built his schemes of ambition on the narrow basis of personal influence over a dying boy, who took him for an earnest Protestant. But outside the King's sick chamber, people of all religions soon recognized that Dudley rang as false on the counter as one of the bad coins issued by his government. The Protestants of London and East Anglia liked him as little as the Catholics of the North and West. In warfare and in political intrigue he had both skill and courage, but these availed little to save a man without statesmanship, whom all detested. For he had not even the art, by which many political adventurers have prospered, to arouse the devotion of a small personal following, and in the day of crisis Northumberland found himself deserted by all.

On the death of Edward VI he sprang his audacious plot to exclude both of Henry VIII's daughters, Mary and Elizabeth, and to place on the throne a distant heir, Lady Jane Grey, his own daughter-in-law. He had induced the dying Edward, by fears of a Catholic reaction under Mary, to sign a will to that effect, and the Council was terrified into lending it a certain measure of support. The plot had been well staged, but London and all England rejected it with scorn, and Northumberland himself was fain to throw up his cap with a hoarse cheer for Queen Mary. [JULY 1553.]

That did not save him from the axe on Tower Hill, after a public recantation of Protestantism as insincere as his original adherence, and as vain to achieve its purpose as all the clever schemes he had spun. The vision of Northumberland kneeling on the scaffold, looking round vainly for the reprieve he had purchased by apostasy, and at the last flinging himself down with a gesture of irritated despair, remains in dramatic contrast to the dignified resignation of Lady Jane Grey, the modest and studious girl of sixteen, whom he had inveigled into a false position. Her execution six months later aroused in the people of England exactly opposite feelings to those aroused by the death of her father-in-law. As learned as any of the Tudor sovereigns, this gentle Grecian had a more perfect character than the best of them; but whether she could have borne the weight of sovereignty as well as Elizabeth may well be doubted.

Mary, through the mistakes and violence of her enemies, began her reign [1553–58.] in an atmosphere of popular enthusiasm, which she dissipated almost as quickly as James II, when he sacrificed a like initial advantage on the same altar of fanaticism. But in character Mary was the superior of James. She showed the high Tudor courage in time of danger, and she had no personal vindictiveness; if she had been a sceptic or even a moderate in religion she might in after years have been remembered as Mary the Humane. But the narrow understanding of the daughter of Catherine of Aragon had been educated by brooding in secret, a neglected girl, over her mother's wrongs and her mother's religion, while her mother's Spanish origin drew her affections with fatal magnetism towards Southern Europe. She had no national pride on behalf of the country she ruled. She cared only for the souls of the English, and believed they would be safer in Italian and Spanish hands. From her chapel she had as little vision of the real England as her brother from his sick bed. Wrapt in doctrinal studies or religious ecstasies, neither brother nor sister had an eye for the great outlines of Tudor policy, for the broad prospect of England's ploughlands and pastures, thronged marts and manor-houses, and England's ships tossing on distant seas; no instinct told them what all those busy far-scattered subjects of theirs were thinking and needing day by day. But that vision and that instinct were the secret of all successful Tudor rule, and never deserted Elizabeth in her closest councils of State, in her devotions or her studies of theology, in her interviews with flattering foreign envoys, or even in the more dazzling presence of favourite suitors.

Identification with the Pope and Spain soon clouded the fortune that had seemed to shine upon the Catholic cause while Mary was being welcomed as Queen by the shouting 'prentices of London. On that day the Protestant cause had been associated in men's minds with violence and unrest. The robbery of the guilds and chantries, the continuous troubles of Edward's reign, above all Northumberland's headlong career ending in treason and crowned by apostasy, made the new religion for a while odious and despicable to the great body of floating opinion. It would have been safe and popular for Mary to return to the religious compromise of her father, to restore the Latin Mass, and discreetly to burn a dozen Protestants a year. If she had been content that England should rest there, at least for a while, there would have been no such re-

vulsion to heresy as actually took place in the decisive
first year of Elizabeth. But when Mary insisted on marrying Philip of Spain [1554.] in flat disregard of her subjects'
wishes, making England the cockboat tied to the stern of
the great Spanish galleon, when she insisted further on reviving that Papal jurisdiction over the realm which even
Gardiner and Bonner had helped Henry to abolish, she
twice challenged the national pride in a way her father and
sister would never have dared. [1555.] And when, to crown
the work, she burnt 300 Protestants in four years, she made
the old religion appear to the English as a foreign creed,
unpatriotic, restless and cruel, an impression more easily
made than eradicated. [1555–58.]

It is common to speak of the 'Tudor despotism,' but the
English were never 'mutes and audience' to the acts of
their sovereigns, as the French were to the doings of Louis
XIV. Henry VIII's policy had been in touch with general
opinion and particularly with those parts of it which were
represented in Parliament. In Edward's reign Parliament
had played an independent if not a popular part, for Somerset's government had been foiled in its endeavour to
carry democratic agrarian legislation through the Houses.
And now popular acclamation had vetoed the will and
testament of Edward VI and the action of the Council,
and had prevented the substitution of the Dudley line for
the Tudors. What would happen next? For Mary's policy
of submission to Spain and Rome was contrary to the
wishes both of Parliament and of people.[4]

[4] In the first Parliament of Elizabeth's reign John Story,
an active persecutor under Mary, 'being at the Parliament
House, did with great vehemency speak against the Bill
that was there exhibited for the Restitution of the Book of
Common Prayer, and said these words, "I did often-times,
in Queen Mary's time, say to the Bishops that they were
too busy with chopping at twigs, but I wished to have
chopped at the root; which if they had done, this gear had
not now come in question," and herein most traitorously he
meaned the destruction of our dear and sovereign lady
Queen Elizabeth. For which words spoken, in such an
audience and in such a vehement manner, there was no
honest nor true heart that heard him but did utterly abhor
him.'–State Trials and Strype, I. i. 115.

Parliament had no constitutional power to prevent the Queen from marrying whom she would, and the Commons' address against the Spanish match was therefore unavailing. The Kentish rising under Wyatt [1554.] gave expression to the national feeling against a Spanish King, but though Wyatt obtained popular sympathy he missed popular approval, for men regarded rebellion as the sin of witchcraft. The horror of armed rising against the Crown was stronger in London and the South than in the wild North and West. Nor had Mary yet dissipated the personal popularity with which Northumberland's crime had endowed her. Protestant London refused to join Wyatt's forces when they cut their way along Fleet Street to Ludgate; he was overpowered, captured and executed.

Wyatt had intended to place Elizabeth on her sister's throne. But the young princess had already learnt the lesson of caution from some harsh personal experiences in girlhood, which had taught her that there were tricks in the world. With regard to Wyatt's rebellion, nothing could be proved against her, for she was innocent. Her sister was not wicked. The nation was on her side. After long weeks of anxiety in the Tower, during which Renard the Spanish ambassador clamoured for her blood, she was at length released, to the lasting regret of some in after years. The Catholic prelate and statesman Gardiner, though he had opposed the Spanish match, would have had Elizabeth excluded from the succession, for he suspected the quality of her devotion as she knelt at the Mass. But Parliament protected her reversionary claims, and in the matter of the succession its constitutional rights were undeniable and its will prevailed. People and Parliament stood by Elizabeth against Spanish ambassador and Catholic Bishop. She silently took note where her strength lay.

[1555–58.] With Philip of Spain husband to a doting queen, England was for three years vassal of the great Spanish monarchy.[5] So long as Mary lived and loved, all thought of a foreign policy anywhere opposed to Spain must be set aside, together with all hope of trade with

[5] In 1556 Philip succeeded his father, Charles V, as King of Spain.

America—which Philip strictly denied to his island subjects
—and all dreams of colonization or sea power. The terms
of the royal marriage were most injurious to England, and
the Venetian envoy declared that Mary was bent on
nothing but making the Spaniards masters of her kingdom.
Only revolution or the Queen's death could open England's
path to the freedom and greatness that awaited her upon
the sea.

[1555.] The next step was reunion with Rome. The experience of Edward's reign had convinced Bishops Gardiner and Bonner that Catholic doctrine could not be safe
under the Royal Supremacy, and Mary, as her mother's
daughter, had always been a Papalist. A new Parliament
yielded to the pressure of Crown and Privy Council, while
imposing restrictions and conditions that bitterly galled the
devout Queen. It was indeed an ignoble compromise. Matters of faith and spiritual jurisdiction were restored to
Rome, but the material interests of the lay revolution were
saved entire. Title-deeds of monastic lands, tithes and all
Church properties that had found their way into the coffers
of warm gentlemen were to lie there untouched, while the
Queen had her way about Papal jurisdiction, and while
the revived heresy laws allowed the spiritual courts and
the Privy Council to burn alive believing Protestants at their
pleasure. While cobblers and clergymen died in agonies for
their faith, none of the well-born among the laity suffered
in Mary's reign. The lay beneficiaries of the 'great plunder'
conformed to the service of the Mass, to save their skins
and their lands. But they began to perceive that both
would be more safe under a thorough change of system.
'God save the Princess Elizabeth' became the prayer of
many a squire, dreaming on things to come. The Venetian
envoy wrote home that, 'with the exception of a few most
pious Catholics, none of whom are under thirty-five years
of age, all the rest make this show of recantation yet do
not effectually resume the Catholic faith.' The opportunity
that Mary's State action gave to the old religion was lost
for want of a corresponding religious revival to support it
among the rising generation.

When Mary's Parliament consented to the revival of the

Bible, the Prayer Book and loyalty to the Queen. The contest finally resolved itself into a maritime war against Spain as the head of the Catholic reaction in Europe and the monopolist of the ocean routes to the New World. In the heat of that struggle English civilization was fused into its modern form, at once insular and oceanic, distinct from the continental civilization of which the Norman Conquest had once made it part.

Not only was modern England created, but the future of Great Britain was mapped out. The exigencies of the struggle for island independence against the Catholic powers of the continent put an end to the long hostility between the peoples of Scotland and England, while the same causes dictated the ruthless and ill-fated conquest of Catholic Ireland.

Amongst the Elizabethan English, by land and by sea, individualism became the ally of nationalism on free and equal terms, for the national State could not afford to pay for an army and a bureaucracy to bend the individual to its will, like the France and Prussia of later days. The poverty of the Elizabethan State explains many of its worst failures and meanest shifts, and not a few also of its greatest merits and noblest attitudes. A Queen whose revenue in war time did not reach half a million pounds a year must needs be 'niggardly'; but since her subjects would not be taxed to give her adequate supply, she was fain to appeal to their free loyalty to fight her battles and to wear themselves out in her service for love. They gave her their lives and affections more readily than their cash. For the rest, her great object, as defined in a political poem she herself wrote,[1] was 'to teach still peace to grow,' till men treasured the life of their Queen because it meant for them peace and prosperity at home while the neighbour nations were ablaze with religious war. Many who disliked her ecclesiastical compromise as being too Protestant, or not Protestant enough, accepted it as the condition of tran-

[1] 'The Daughter of Debate, who discord eke doth sow, / Shall reap no gain where former rule hath taught still peace to grow.'

The 'Daughter of Debate' is Mary Queen of Scots.

quil government, which in an age of rival fanaticisms seemed, and perhaps was, a miracle of statecraft.

When Elizabeth became Queen at the age of twenty-five the country was in no condition to resist a foreign invader. [NOV. 1558.] Not only was it divided by fierce religious feuds such as opened contemporary France to the foreigner, but it had for several years been treated as an appanage of Spain; its financial credit, its warlike stores and its militia, were at the lowest ebb, and if there were any men capable of leading it in peace or in war, it was left to this young woman to find them out. It was rumoured in the Spanish Embassy that the coming man was Sir William Cecil, a politician of the rising middle class of smaller gentry, a pestilent heretic at heart, the more dangerous because he was no zealot but had, like Elizabeth herself, deemed life to be well worth a Mass.

Yet Philip of Spain protected the new Queen's accession and extended his protection for years after she had fulfilled his worst fears on the score of religion. For the next heir to the English throne was Mary Queen of Scots, a devout Catholic indeed, but married to the Dauphin of France. Throughout Elizabeth's reign it was the rivalry of the two great Catholic powers, France and Spain, that saved the heretic island from conquest, till it was too strong to be conquered. Neither rival could allow Britain to be subdued by the other. The rebellion of the Netherlands against Spain and the religious wars in France were further safeguards, and Elizabeth frequently sent men and money to keep both movements alive. But in the early years of her reign the Netherlands were not yet in open revolt and her part was still to cajole Philip. This she did by holding out hope that she would marry either him or a man of his choice, though she had no real intention of slipping any such noose over her head.

Yet anxious as she was to stand well with the Spaniards, she would not allow their ambassador to say that she in any degree owed her life, liberty or throne to the goodwill shown her by his master in Mary's latter days. She owed all, she said, to the English people. If this was not the whole truth, it was the part of the truth that mattered most. It was one of those lightning flashes of sincerity that so often burst from the cloud of vain and deceitful words in which Elizabeth loved to hide her real thought and purpose. Sometimes, indeed, she lied for amusement rather than in hope of deceiving, as when she told the envoy of Spain 'she would like to be a nun and live in a cell and tell her beads from morning to night,' on which his only comment was 'this woman is possessed by a hundred thousand devils.'

To her own people she boasted on her accession that she was 'mere English.' Her mother had been no foreign princess but an English flirt, and her father, the founder of England's Navy and of England's religious independence, had possessed a sixth sense whereby he understood the English people, even in the highest rages of his tyranny. She inherited from both, but most from her father in whose steps it was her ambition to walk. If she was heir to her mother's vanity and coquetry, she heeded the warning of her fate; and her own bitter experiences as a girl,—disgrace, imprisonment and danger of death,—had taught her, as Frederic the Great was taught by similar experiences in boyhood, that private affections and passions are not for Princes. She had learnt every lesson that adversity had to teach, and she would leave it to her rival to lose the world for love.[2]

There was in her a certain hardness and coarseness of fibre, necessary perhaps for her terrible task in life. As a private person she would scarcely have been lovable, perhaps not even very admirable. But lonely on the throne she knew all the arts to make herself adored by her Court and her people. Without ceasing to be a woman, and while loving life in all its fullness, she made everything subservient to purposes of State. Her learning endeared her to the Universities, her courage to the soldiers and

[2] It is possible, though not certain, that Elizabeth knew she was incapable of child-bearing, and never had any real intention of marriage, or desire for anything beyond flirtation. It would have been characteristic of her to guard this invaluable political secret like death—even from Cecil.

sailors. Her coquetry became a means of keeping her
nobles and courtiers each in his place, and exacting
from each one the last ounce of personal devotion in the
public service. Leicester's neck might be tickled by the
royal hand, but his rival Cecil would be trusted in matters
of high policy. And Cecil too might serve her the better
for a shrewd spasm of fear that she would marry the worthless and intriguing Leicester, who, though sometimes posing as patron of the Puritan party, had offered Philip to
restore the Roman Church in England if Spain would secure his marriage with Elizabeth. Her love of hunting and
dancing, masque, pageantry and display, was used to
strengthen the wider popularity which was her ultimate
strength; her public appearances and progresses through
the country, which she thoroughly enjoyed, were no dull
and formal functions, but works of art by a great player
whose heart was in the piece, interchanges of soul between
a Princess and her loving people.

Her speeches to Parliament were very different from
the official 'King's Speech' of our modern constitution.
'Though I be a woman,' she told a deputation of both
Houses who had come to urge measures about the Succession, 'I have as good a courage answerable to my place as
ever my father had. I am your anointed Queen. I will
never be by violence constrained to do anything. I thank
God I am endued with such qualities that if I were turned
out of the realm in my petticoat, I were able to live in any
place in Christendom.'

Men, they say, have been worn out by high office in a
few years or even months; this heroic woman was her own
Prime Minister in war and peace for forty-five years, most
of them fraught with danger both to the State and to her
own much threatened life. And all the time she was an
invalid—suffering, and subject to moods, caprices and nerve-
storms that shook her but never shook her from her course.
It may be true that her heart was cold, but it was a heart
of oak.

'Mere English' as she was, her education had been the
broadest that modern and ancient Europe could afford.
She discoursed in Greek and Latin to the Universities of

Oxford and Cambridge, and in fluent Italian to the natives of the land of Machiavelli. Her enemies might have called her, in the phrase of that day, '*Inglese Italianata*,' though she never in her long life quitted the English shore. She had been influenced by the Italian heretics, such as Vermigli and Ochino, who were more philosophers than zealots. She was a child of the Renaissance rather than of the Reformation, so far as the two movements could any longer be distinguished. She approached religion in the modernist spirit of Colet and Erasmus; but two generations after their time, to a mind of their disposition, Rome of the Jesuits was abhorrent and transubstantiation incredible. The Church of Geneva attracted her as little, with its usurpation of the province of the State and its democratic republicanism. If it was left to her successor to say 'No Bishop, no King,' she had thought it and acted on it long before.

Sceptical and tolerant in an age of growing fanaticism, all English in feeling but pan-European in education, she was born and bred to re-establish the Anglican Church, and to evade religious war by a learned compromise between Catholic and Protestant that would leave Crown and laity masters in their own island. She regarded her action as a revival of her father's policy, but changed times demanded a larger infusion of Protestantism, for the Jesuit propaganda and the spearmen and sailors of Spain were not to be conquered save with the help of men who regarded the Pope as anti-Christ and the Mass as an abomination. Cranmer's revived Prayer Book was the golden mean. It served well on board Drake's ships before and after battle with the idolaters, and in parish churches where Bernard Gilpin and other earnest Protestant clergy laboured to instil the new religion into rustic ignorance. Yet the concealed Catholic, doubtfully attending church to avoid the twelve-penny fine, was often less shocked than he feared, and could remind himself that they were still the old prayers, though in English. The book was a chameleon which could mean different things to different people—an advantage in the eyes of this wise young woman, who herself had as many different explanations of her policy as she had dresses in her wardrobe, and loved to display them all in turn.

The Parliament of 1559 restored the Reformation in its Anglican form by passing the Act of Supremacy which abolished the Papal power, and the Act of Uniformity which made the Prayer Book the only legal form of worship. These Statutes represented the will of Crown and House of Commons. The Queen was a restraining force on the zeal of her faithful Commons, as for instance in declining to adopt for herself in full the title of Supreme Head of the Church, although she assumed the name and function of its Supreme Governor. The House of Lords was with difficulty brought to accept extensive changes in ritual and doctrine. The lay peers, lukewarm and divided on the religious issue, attempted in vain to induce the Commons to accept large amendments in a Catholic sense. But the victory lay with the Lower House and the classes it represented, who were already more important in the State than the nobility, and were in this matter acting in concert with the Queen and her Council.[3]

The Bishops in the Upper House were against all change, but were voted down, partly because an unusual number of sees happened to be empty. Outside Parliament, the Convocation of the Clergy of the Province of Canterbury reaffirmed the supremacy of the Pope and the doctrine of transubstantiation. Their will was overridden and their protest ignored by Parliament.

The Reformation was in short a lay revolution carried by Crown and Parliament—more specifically by Crown and Commons—against the will of the Church authorities. But it was not therefore contrary to the will of the religious-minded laity who had no representation in Church assemblies; and out of 8000 beneficed clergy at least 7000 acquiesced in the accomplished fact, some gladly, some

[3] This House of Commons was not packed. There is evidence that the elections were at least as free as those for the parliaments of Elizabeth's father, brother, and sister Mary. See *English Hist. Review,* July and October 1908, Mr. Baynes' articles.

with indifference, some in hopes of another reaction that never came; whereas there had been as many as 2000 deprivations of obstinately Protestant clergy under Mary. But with one exception the whole bench of Bishops refused to conform to the Elizabethan settlement and were deprived. In the reigns of Henry VIII and Edward VI the Bishops and the Convocations of Clergy had acquiesced in the changes made. The increased stubbornness of official clerical opposition in the first year of Elizabeth may be ascribed to two causes: in the age of the Jesuits and Council of Trent the parties of Reformers and Romanists were becoming more distinct and mutually exclusive, even in the remote island of compromise. Furthermore Queen Mary had weeded out the Protestants from the official body of the Church. The Convocation of 1559 gave no fair representation to the large and active Protestant body among the priests. It followed that the Parliamentary proceedings of that year, even more than those under Henry VIII, wore the appearance of a coercion of the clergy by the uprising of lay opinion.

But in England the laity did not proceed, after the manner of the contemporary Scottish reformers, to secure lay representation in the ecclesiastical assemblies and to associate the clergyman in every parish with a board of lay 'elders.' The internal organization of the English Church was left in its mediæval form, entirely clerical in composition. For this very reason it was felt to be the more necessary to subject the Church to the external control of Crown and Parliament. The bulk of the clergy loyally accepted that control from outside as the necessary condition of the large franchises still left to them, among others the national monopoly of all religious rites, which the Crown and Parliament secured for them at the expense of all would-be Dissenters, Romanist or Puritan. No one dreamed of permitting a variety of religions. No one therefore could reasonably deny to the nation the right of deciding in Parliament what its one and only religion was to be.

This external control by the laity was applied to the Church through laws passed in Parliament defining doctrine and ritual, and through Commissioners and Bishops appointed by the Queen who inspected and administered the Church according to her orders. Towards the end of her reign, and still more under her two successors, the Puritan party in the Church appealed to Parliament for help, and the Anglican party to the Crown. Neither school of thought attempted to take up the high religious ground of the Scottish Church, which claimed to be entirely autonomous, and even to dictate on matters of policy to the feeble Scottish Parliament and to 'God's silly vassal,' the King.

Rome and Geneva, Loyola and Knox, claimed for the Church freedom and even superiority in relation to the State, the claims of Rome resting on sacerdotal authority, those of Geneva on religious democracy. The English Church made no such claims, for in England the days of sacerdotal authority were numbered in a land where men had learned to think for themselves, and the spirit of democracy, so far as it yet existed, found its expression and organ in the House of Commons and not in any assembly of the Church. The arrangement suited the Tudor English well, for they were interested in many other things besides religion; when in succeeding centuries the spirit of democracy required expression in religion, it found it in the safety-valve of the Non-conformist sects. The Elizabethan religious settlement, tempered by successive doses of Toleration, has held a permanent place in the institutions and still more in the spirit of modern England.

If the year 1559 is to count as the first of modern England, it is still more decidedly the birth year of modern Scotland. The precise coincidence in time of the final breach with Rome to north and to south of the Border, though largely accidental, was of great consequence. The double event secured the unbroken permanence of the Reformation in both countries, and drew English and Scottish patriotism, which had hitherto thriven on mutual hostility, into an alliance of mutual defence. In both countries the Reformation meant release from continental dominion, secular no less than spiritual. In the autumn of 1558 England was a Roman Catholic country virtually subject to Spain, and Scotland was a Roman Catholic country virtually subject to France. Two years later each was a Protestant country cleared of foreign soldiery and rulers, and closely identifying its newly chosen religion with its national independence. The double rebellion succeeded because Spain and France remained rivals, while England and Scotland became friends for the first time since the reign of Edward I. In the stress of that twofold crisis the foundations of Great Britain were laid by William Cecil and John Knox.

England approached the Reformation through the Renaissance; Scotland approached the Renaissance through the Reformation. Catholicism as a religion had meant less to the Scots, for with them the Church was more corrupt and inefficient as a spiritual power than to the south of the Border. After the slaughter of so many leading nobles at Flodden in 1513, the secular power in Scotland was wielded more than ever by the prelates, cadets of noble families, living like laymen and fighting each other with sword and gun for the abbeys and benefices of the Church. The vernacular poetry of Sir David Lyndsay and other makers of 'godly ballads' prepared the way for the Reformation by holding up to popular contempt the lives and pretensions of the Churchmen.

It is the less surprising that Protestantism obtained under the leadership of Knox the same hold on the intelligence and moral feeling of the common people in Scotland, as it obtained more gradually in England by the middle of the following century. In England the Reformation was promoted by the Crown and its satellites, while the old feudal nobility were lukewarm or hostile; in Scotland the opposite was the case. But in both countries the genuine core of the movement lay in the burghers, yeomen and artisans and in the smaller landed gentry—the squires of England and lairds of Scotland.

It was only in the years immediately preceding 1559 that the Protestant party in Scotland had the advantage of figuring as patriots. In the 'forties it was the Catholic party that led the national resistance to English interference. For Henry VIII, though wisely aspiring to the union of

the whole island through the marriage of his son Edward
to the infant Mary Stuart, Queen of Scots, foolishly sought
to force the policy on Scotland by the sword. Destructive
raids in the valley of the Tweed and in the Lothians made
the Scots curse the English tyrant and heretic, and frown
upon his supporters in their own midst. [See Map 13, Vol.
One.] When Henry died, the Protector Somerset carried
on the same disastrous policy in the campaign of Pinkie,
a dire defeat for Scotland, but a still worse blow to Somerset's prophetic daydreams of a united Great Britain, 'having the sea for wall and mutual love for its garrison.'
[1547.] To keep Mary Stuart out of the way of this rough
and pertinacious wooing on behalf of Edward VI, the Scots
sent the impressionable little girl to the court of Valois
France, to learn in that most unsuitable atmosphere the
art of governing their dour and stubborn selves. [1548.]

But the insolence of the French army of occupation,
which was the price of the French alliance, did not long
suit the proud stomach of the Scots. Gallic domination became as unbearable in Scotland as Spanish domination
in contemporary England. In her sixteenth year Mary
Queen of Scots was married to the Dauphin of France,
and became party to a secret compact whereby her native
country was to go as a free gift to the French King in
case of her death without heirs. [1558.] The able Regent
who governed Scotland in her absence, Mary of Guise,
relied on French troops, and thought of the land of Bruce
as a Protectorate to be administered in the interests of
France. In these circumstances the Protestants in their
turn became the champions of national independence,
while the Catholic party became unpopular as the catspaw of French aggression. Under Mary of Guise and Mary
Tudor both North and South Britain lay beneath the
'monstrous regiment (rule) of women,' which Knox be-
wailed all too loudly, improvident of his future relations
with Elizabeth.

[1557.] In these circumstances a section of the Scottish
nobles, accustomed in that land of feudal anarchy to form
'bands' for the coercion of the Crown, formed a 'band' to
protect the new religion. The confederates were bound to-

gether by the first of Scotland's many 'covenants' with God. This 'Congregation of the Lord,' as it styled itself, was organized as an assembly of estates, in which each Protestant notable took his place as minister of religion or as noble, laird or burgess. It was more representative of the political forces of the country than Scotland's Parliament, which was feudal in its form and served for little more than a court of registration. The 'Congregation of the Lord' was army, Church and political assembly in one. It formed the transition stage between Scotland's feudal warrior past with its 'bands' of rebel nobles, and her democratic religious future with its Kirk Assembly. Nobles, styled 'Lords of the Congregation,' were its leaders, but the popular and religious elements were heard in its counsels, especially as they spoke through the voice of John Knox.

The Moses of Scotland was a very rare combination of genuine prophet and successful statesman. He who 'never feared the face of man' could calculate chances and consider ways and means as the utterly fearless and the 'God-intoxicated' are very seldom able to do. He had been hardened by grim servitude and meditation at the oar of a French galley, and had since been founding Church congregations all over Southern Scotland. He knew the people well and saw that the hour had come to strike.

In 1559 a democratic religious revolution, preached by Knox and accompanied by image-breaking, swept through the Scottish burghs, beginning with Perth. It was thus that Calvinist revolutions began, whether in the Netherlands or in French-speaking countries, but they were as often as not suppressed with fire and sword. In Scotland, however, the 'Congregation of the Lord' came with arms in their hands to defend the insurgent populace from the French troops and from Mary of Guise. There followed a spasmodic and ill-conducted war, in which little blood was shed; it was going ill for the Scottish Protestants when it was decided in their favour by the intervention of England. Cecil had persuaded Elizabeth to take one of the few great initiatives of her reign. The English fleet appearing in the Firth of Forth, and an English army joining the Scottish Protestants before Leith, saved the cause of the

Reformation. This *coup de théâtre* being followed by the death of Mary of Guise, led to the evacuation of Scotland by the French troops in accordance with the terms of the Treaty of Edinburgh. [JULY 1560.]

The Scottish Reformation was singularly bloodless, in spite of the violence of the language used on both sides. Very few Protestants had been burnt, and no Catholic was executed on account of his religion. Continental Europe, and even England in Mary Tudor's reign, presented a far bloodier spectacle of religious fanaticism.

Another Catholic force soon landed from France to take the place of the Regent and the soldiers. Mary Queen of Scots herself and a train of pleasure-loving ladies and favourites came over to try issues with that harsh land of old feudal power and new popular theology. [1561.] An able, energetic and attractive widow, Mary Stuart was little likely to submit her royal will to Knox and the Lords of the Congregation. They had many enemies in the land —personal, political and religious—who would rally to the banner of the young Queen. Moreover, her eager eyes scanned horizons far beyond the borders of barren Scotland. The Catholics of Europe looked to her as their chosen champion to win back Britain to the faith. France and Rome were at her back. A great party in England hoped and intrigued to see Britain united by a counter-revolution, which should dethrone the illegitimate daughter of Henry VIII and place the English crown on the head of the rightful heir, Mary Queen of Scots.[4]

HENRY VII.

Arthur = Catherine
died   of Aragon.
1502.
	Margaret = James IV
	          of Scotland,
	          killed at
	          Flodden,
	          1513.
		HENRY VIII

James V,
died
1542.

	(by Catherine of Aragon) MARY TUDOR.	(by Anne Boleyn) ELIZABETH.	(by Jane Seymour) EDWARD VI.

1. Francis II = Mary Stuart,
   of France,   Queen of Scots,
   died 1559.   born 1542,
2. Ld. Darnley. deposed 1567,
3. Earl of   executed 1587.
   Bothwell.

(by Darnley)
JAMES VI of
Scotland, 1567,
and I of England.
1603.

The Protestant party in Scotland could not therefore afford to quarrel with Elizabeth, nor she with them. Little as she wished to abet feudal nobles and Calvinist peasants in resistance to their lawful sovereign, that sovereign was her open rival for the throne on which she sat. The situation was the more dangerous because the Catholic and feudal part of England lay precisely in the moorland counties nearest to the Scottish Border. Catholicism and feudalism were so strong to the north of the Humber that early in her reign Elizabeth was fain to employ the Catholic grandees of that region as her officials, in which capacity the Percys, Dacres and Nevilles continued to exert their old feudal influence and to thwart the policy of the government they served. 'Throughout Northumberland,' it was reported, 'they know no other Prince but Percy.' Bernard Gilpin, a mild and Anglican John Knox, was indeed busy helping the new Bishops to found the Protestantism of North England. But for many years there was the greatest danger of a feudal and Catholic reaction uniting all Britain north of the Humber in a single Kingdom governed by Mary Stuart. Northern England, like Scotland, was inhabited by a race of hardy and lawless fighters, bred to Border war, not easily kept in order by a distant government that had no army. But, fortunately for Elizabeth, Northern England, like Scotland, was very thinly inhabited and very poor. Until the Industrial Revolution, wealth and population were concentrated in the South, and most of all in and near London.

Grave as were her motives for dreading any increase in the power of Mary, Elizabeth was too cautious and too short of revenue to involve herself deeply in Scottish politics. For six years of high romantic history, the struggle for power between Mary, Knox and the nobles continued with little interference from England. [1561–67.] There was no organ of constitutional opposition to the Catholic Queen, for the Scottish Parliament, after putting the Reformation into legal shape in 1560, had sunk back into a negligible quantity, a mere court of record once more. Mary might therefore have triumphed over the feudal aristocracy, divided as it was on the religious issue in spite of its firm adherence to the abbey lands, had not John Knox and his party created other organs of national life, and put a new spirit into the educated middle class which inspired it to compete with the old feudal power. In parish after parish arose a democracy of laymen, who elected their own minister and found a nucleus for self-expression in the Kirk Session of the parish. Nor was a national organization lacking for long: in the General Assembly of the Church, ministers and lairds sat side by side, representing clerical and lay forces of a very different social class from the high-born prelates and noblemen who had ruled Scotland for centuries past. The General Assembly of the Church became the centre of Scottish life almost to the extent to which Parliament was the centre of English life, and the Church became the focus of resistance to the Crown.

The Church brought Scotland freedom and bondage in one. A spirit not of sacerdotal but of democratic tyranny strove to dictate the dogma and discipline of the new religion to the government of the land, to the peasant in his cottage and to the laird in his hall. This zealous and uncompromising spirit was intolerable to many; it was a chief cause of the factions and blood-feuds of Scotland for a hundred years to come. In the end the power of the Church was subordinated to that of the State, but not before it had wrought a remarkable change. It transformed the lowland Scot from a fierce feudal vassal, ignorant of all save sword and plough, into the best educated peasant in Europe, often plunged in solitary meditation and as often roused to furious argument on points of logic and theology which few Englishmen had the mental gifts or training to understand. Times and the Church had changed, but the intellectual and moral vantage-ground won by the Scot in that hard school has not yet been lost.

But the making of modern Scotland had only begun when Mary reigned at Holyrood, and she might perchance have stopped it all at the outset by winning her battle against Knox, if she had been as ready as Elizabeth to control her private passions in deference to her public policy. But her marriage with Darnley, his murder by

Bothwell at the Kirk of Field, and her too hasty marriage with the murderer, led her subjects to suppose her pre-cognizant of the deed. True, assassination was still a custom of the country. Knox had not disapproved the slaughter of Cardinal Beaton, and Darnley had conducted the tragedy of Rizzio. But people had a prejudice against the killing of husbands by their wives. Innocent or guilty, Mary had by her marriage with Bothwell delivered her reputation and her kingdom into her enemies' hands. After some confused fighting and some romantic and luckless adventures, she was obliged to fly from Scotland. [1568.] She elected, whether from rashness or from necessity, to take refuge with Elizabeth whose throne she challenged and endangered. What did she expect? If she looked for romantic generosity she had come to the wrong door. Or did she trust her own sharp wits to fool her rival?

From the moment that Mary made herself Elizabeth's captive, the politics of England, and indeed of all Europe, turned on the hinges of her prison door. Since she had thrown away her own liberty and her own power of initiative, Philip began to think that she might be used to serve the purposes of Spain instead of those of France. Urged by the Pope, Spain, and the Jesuits, the more extreme English Catholics laid plot after plot to place her on Elizabeth's throne, through assassination, rebellion and foreign conquest. The first great crisis was the 'Rising of the Earls' of Northumberland and Westmorland, followed by Dacre's rebellion. [1569, 1570.] The Catholic feudal chiefs of North England, the Percys, Nevilles and Dacres, took up arms on behalf of Mary and the Mass, calling on the Catholic nobles of Scotland to cross the Border and join them. The crusaders marched under the banner of the Five Wounds of Christ, and tore up the Bible and Prayer Book in Durham Cathedral. But the Scottish government prevented the Scottish Catholics from crossing the Border, and South England rose eagerly to defend Elizabeth. The feudal spirit was no longer sufficiently sure of itself to look the national spirit in the face on the field of battle. Even the borderers were no longer at ease in following the modern

Percy against the Crown, as their forefathers had followed Hotspur. A single skirmish sufficed to disperse the feudal and Catholic armies.

Instead of being thankful for a victory which demonstrated to a surprised world the solidarity of her position in her subjects' hearts, Elizabeth took a cruel vengeance on the feudal tenantry, of whom 800 were executed. But she was wise in her further arrangements. The problem of North England was liquidated at last. The Council of the North[5] and the Wardenships of the Marches could now be manned entirely by loyal officials; it was no longer necessary to defer to territorial magnates who were rebels at heart. The cessation of Border war with Scotland created new conditions of life that enabled government in the coming epoch to wean the North from its military and feudal traditions. The great-hearted but tragic society of Border ballad and blood-feud was gradually transformed into that of the law-abiding and Bible-reading shepherds who peopled the moorlands in the days of Thomas Bewick and Walter Scott.

The internal unity of the new England had been demonstrated by the failure of the Northern rebellion, and foreign dangers might now be faced with a good courage. They came thick and fast. In 1570 Pope Pius V excommunicated Elizabeth and the Jesuit mission was launched on England. In 1572 the Duke of Norfolk was executed for plotting with the agents of Philip, Alva and the Pope to set Mary on the throne, this time as the puppet not of France but of Spain. She was to have Norfolk for her husband, the Pope undertaking to divorce her from Bothwell. The assassination of Elizabeth was henceforth a customary part of these discussions among the secular and religious chiefs of continental Europe, to whom the murder of heretics seemed a holy work.

The execution of Norfolk, the greatest nobleman in the land, following close on the fall of the Northern Earls, marked the final victory in England of the new regime over the old feudalism. It was indeed a changing world. In the

[5] For the Council of the North, see p. 24, above.

same year the Massacre of St. Bartholomew, which crippled but did not destroy the Huguenot cause in France, was counterbalanced by the effective rebellion of the seamen and towns of Holland against the cruelties of Philip of Spain. [1572.] The Commons of England, full of rage and fear, were petitioning for the execution of Mary Queen of Scots as though she had not been anointed with oil. For fifteen years longer Elizabeth, obeying her pacifist and royalist instincts, stood between her people and Mary's life. She liked not the killing of Queens, and the deed would mean formal war with Spain. So long as Mary was her next heir, she might hope that Philip would bear yet a little longer with her and her seamen. But if Mary disappeared, Philip might claim England for himself and launch the invasion. Only sixty miles lay between the shores of Kent and the yet unvanquished veterans of Alva in the Netherlands. Fortunately those miles were of salt water, and turbid salt water was an element of increasing importance in this new age so disrespectful to the feudal past and to all the chiefs of chivalry.

CHAPTER SIX

The Origin of English Sea-Power

Which of the Kings of this land before her Majesty had their banners ever seen in the Caspian Sea? Which of them hath ever dealt with the Emperor of Persia, as her Majesty hath done, and obtained for her merchants large and loving privileges? Who ever saw, before this regiment, an English Ligier (Ambassador) in the stately porch of the Grand Signor of Constantinople? Who ever found English Consuls and Agents at Tripolis in Syria, at Aleppo, at Babylon, at Balsara, and, which is more, who ever heard of Englishmen at Goa before now? What English ships did, heretofore, ever anchor in the mighty river of Plate? Pass and repass the impassable strait of Magellan, range along the coast of Chili, Peru and all the backside of Nova Hispania further than any Christian ever passed?—*Hakluyt*.

Throughout ancient and mediæval times Britain was cramped onto the edge of the *Mappa Mundi*. Since there was nothing beyond, every impulse of private adventure and national expansion on the part of the islanders had to expend itself upon Europe. Yet old Europe was no longer malleable stuff and could take no impress of British language and customs, even from the most vigorous efforts of young England, as the barren close of the Hundred Years' War had very clearly shown. And now the gate of return that way was bolted and barred by the rise of the great continental monarchies, so that Englishmen seemed shut in upon themselves, doomed for ever to an insular and provincial existence, sighing in old manor-houses for the departed glory chronicled by Froissart, and the spacious days of Harry the Fifth.

But it was the most unexpected that occurred. Gradually, during the Tudor reigns, the islanders became aware that their remote situation had changed into a central post of vantage dominating the modern routes of trade and colonization, and that power, wealth and adventure lay for Englishmen at the far end of ocean voyages fabulously long, leading to the gold-bearing rivers of the African anthropophagi, to the bazaars of jewelled Asia, and to the new half-empty continent which was piecing itself together year by year under the astonished eyes of men, upsetting all known ideas of cosmogony and all customs of commerce.

In mediæval, as formerly in ancient times, the great trade of the world and the centre of maritime power had lain in the Mediterranean Sea. The external trade of Europe, which in modern times traverses the ocean in European vessels, was formerly carried overland by caravans across the heart of Asia, or was taken by Oriental shipping up and down the Persian Gulf and the Red Sea. The precious goods from China and India and the Spice Islands were dumped off the backs of camels onto the wharves of Levantine ports for shipment in Italian vessels to Venice and Genoa, whence they were distributed to the rest of Christendom.

Neither the Venetian traders, nor the Romans and Phœnicians before them, had been obliged to cross the ocean at any point. Ships were only required to traverse the Mediterranean waters, and to coast along round Spain and France to the ports of England, Flanders and Northern

Germany. The navies, whether commercial or military, consisted chiefly of oared galleys. This state of things lasted from prehistoric times till the latter part of the Fifteenth Century. Then the discovery of the Cape route to India and the revelation of the American continent destroyed the trade and the maritime supremacy of the Italian cities. Thenceforward Europe went round by sea to fetch its Asiatic, African and American goods, and on those ocean voyages the oared galley would be useless. The contest for commercial and naval leadership under the new conditions would clearly lie between Spain, France and England; each of them faced the Western ocean which had suddenly become the main trade route of the world, and each of them was in process of being united into a modern State, with aggressive racial self-consciousness under a powerful monarchy.[1]

Spain and her small neighbour, Portugal, were the first to exploit the new situation on a great scale. They led the way in discovery along the African and American coasts. They planted South and Central America with their own people, enough at any rate to close them to Anglo-Saxon settlement, so that the English, when their turn came to colonize, would have to be contented with the colder and

---

[1] See pp. 44–45, above. It is not safe to assert, as has often been done, that the Portuguese and Spanish discoveries were due to 'the closing of the mediæval trade routes by the barbarous Turks.' On this subject see Mr. Lybyer's article in the *Eng. Hist. Rev.*, 1915. The Turk, though less liberal than the Tartar who had controlled the central Asiatic route in the time of Marco Polo, by no means stopped all commerce with and through Europeans in the Fifteenth Century. The trade by way of Egypt was flourishing until the Cape route supplanted it. The Cape route in ocean-going ships could take bulky goods on a much greater scale than any of the mediæval routes. Mediæval Europe was being constantly denuded of precious metals because she had to pay for Asiatic spices etc. in gold and silver, for the camels could not carry back Europe's bulky goods. Relief came, none too soon, when the American mines produced abundance of gold and silver, and at the same time the ocean routes to the Eastern markets rendered it possible to send thither bulky articles in the holds of sailing ships.

less envied climates to the north, where the white man must dig with his own arms, and not for gold.

France seemed half-inclined to follow the suit of Spain, and compete for supremacy at sea and in America. But already, by the time of Columbus, her efforts were distracted by preoccupation with European conquest towards the Rhine and beyond the Alps. England, on the other hand, had learnt the lesson of the Hundred Years' War, for the glories of which she had been punished by a long period of anarchy and weakness. She steadily refused to be drawn again down the blind alley of continental ambition. From Tudor times onwards, England treated European politics simply as a means of ensuring her own security from invasion and furthering her designs beyond the ocean. Her insularity, properly used, gave her an immense advantage over Spain and France in the maritime and colonial contest.

The other distraction which impeded France in the race for the New World was religious war, raging in her midst during the precious years when Elizabeth kept England free from that blight. The French Huguenots, like the Protestants of Holland and England, were the commercial and sea-going folk. If they had won, they might have made France mistress of the ocean. But Admiral Coligny and his followers were massacred on St. Bartholomew's Day, while Francis Drake and the Protestant sailors whom he led became the servants of the English monarchy and the heroes of the English people, turning England's main thought and effort to the sea.

The square, unbroken mass of rural France, with its long land frontiers, rendered it inevitable that the old feudal life should be the prevailing social element, and set the fashion for the territorial activities of the new national monarchy. But in England, with its narrow, irregular outline, almost surrounded by a well-indented coastline, at peace at last with her only land neighbour the Scot, well supplied with harbours great and small thronged with mariners and fishermen, the State was subjected to the influences and ideas of the commercial and naval men, who formed one society with the best county families in seaboard shires like Devon. The old song expressed a feeling very general among our ancestors:

We care not for your martial men
   That do the State disdain.
But we care for your sailor lads
   That do the State maintain.

Indeed England's success against Spain after the defeat of the Armada was limited not so much by want of naval power as by want of military organization and tradition to seize the opportunities created by the Senior Service.

Since no point in England is more than seventy miles distant from the coast, a large proportion of her inhabitants had some contact with the sea, or at least with seafaring men. Above all, London herself was on the sea, while Paris lay inland and Madrid was as far from the coast as it was possible to be. London was Protestant, while Paris was enthusiastically Catholic. And London was so great in population and wealth as compared to the rest of the country that she gave the lead to all England. La Rochelle, the seaport of the Huguenots, was insignificant compared to a dozen great cities of the French interior. For these and other reasons France, in the Sixteenth Century, failed to compete in earnest for maritime supremacy. The best part of her sea-force acted in religious and political alliance with the English and Dutch in preying on the Spanish ships as they passed between Cadiz and the Netherlands.

If France was more feudal than England, Spain was yet more feudal than France. Spain, indeed, when she had annexed Portugal [1580.], was almost as much surrounded by the sea as England, and she had, moreover, a war fleet with a naval tradition. But it was a fleet of slave-rowed galleys and its traditions were those of the Mediterranean. The fleet that triumphed over the Turks at Lepanto [1571.], with the tactics of Salamis and Actium, would be of little avail against Drake's broadsides; it could not cross the Atlantic and would be of limited use in the Bay of Biscay and the Channel. Spain had, indeed, her ocean-going vessels sailing up and down the Pacific coast of America, or crossing the Atlantic between Cadiz and the Spanish Main.

They served to carry out emigrants and to bring back silver
and gold, but they were not warships, and therefore fell
an easy prey to the English pirates. Spain, in fact, began to
build ships capable of fighting England only on the very
eve of the outbreak of regular war. The Armada was not
the last but the first of her oceanic fighting fleets. [1588.]
The English, on the other hand, though their total population was small compared with French or Spaniards, had
a large sea-going community, accustomed for centuries to
sail the stormy tidal ocean of the North. And ever since the
reign of Henry VIII they possessed a royal fighting
navy built and armed on modern principles, which gave a
professional stiffening to the warlike efforts of private merchants and pirates. When Philip married Mary it had been
his policy to rely on the English war navy because he
could not hope to get its equal from Spain.[2]

Naturally, the Spaniards, even when they came to build
an ocean-going war-fleet in earnest, were hampered by
the feudal and military ideals that permeated their social
life, and by the Mediterranean traditions of their navy,
adorned with the fresh laurels of Lepanto. Whether on
oared galley or on wind-driven galleon, the instinct of the
Spaniard at sea was to sail or row straight in, get to close
quarters and either ram or board the enemy. The Spaniards,
in short, like the Greeks, Romans and Venetians before
them, wanted to make sea warfare as much like land
warfare as the elements would permit. They stowed their
ships with soldiers, who despised the sailors and ordered
them about as if they too had been galley slaves. The

[2] For Henry VIII's navy, see pp. 46–48, above.
   Sir William Monson, the great Elizabethan naval authority, wrote: 'To speak the truth, till the King of Spain
had war with us, he never knew what war by sea meant,
unless it were in galleys against the Turks in the Straits or
in the islands of Terceras (Azores) against the French,
which fleet belonged to him by his new-gotten kingdom of
Portugal. The first time the King showed himself strong
at sea was the year 1591, when the *Revenge* was taken.'
Philip annexed Portugal, its navy and its overseas possessions in 1580. It remained attached to the Crown of Spain
till 1640; after that it maintained its recovered independence, often through alliance with England.

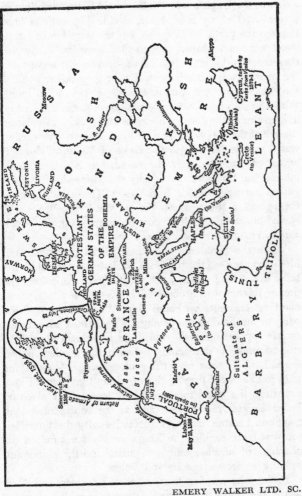

EMERY WALKER LTD. SC.

Map 3   Europe in the time of Elizabeth

'mariners,' said one who knew, 'are but as slaves to the
rest, to moil and toil day and night, and those but few
and bad and not suffered to sleep or harbour themselves
under the decks.'

It was the English who led the world in the evolution of
a new kind of warfare at sea, decided by cannon fired
through the portholes in the side of the ship. Drake's guns
were not much smaller, though they were less numerous,
than those on board Nelson's three-deckers. To serve them
the seaman was more important than the soldier, because
the success of the cannon-fire depended on manœuvring the ship into favourable positions to rake the enemy,
and on aiming the guns with a sailor's instinct for calculating
the roll of the two vessels. To Sir Francis Drake the warship
was a mobile battery; to the Duke of Medina Sidonia it
was a platform to carry the swordsmen and musketeers
into action. English naval history tells, indeed, of many a
gallant boarding episode, from those of Drake and Hawkins
themselves to Nelson at St. Vincent and 'brave Broke who
waved his sword'; yet it was not the boarder but the broadside that made England mistress at sea.

While the Spaniards with their feudal prejudices and
Mediterranean methods of sea-warfare subordinated the
sailor to the soldier even when afloat, Drake worked out the
proper relation to be observed between the military and
maritime elements on board ship. When he quelled the
party of insubordination among the gentlemen adventurers
on his voyage round the world, he laid down his golden
rule to prevent 'stomaching between the gentlemen and
the sailors':—'I must have the gentlemen to hale and draw
with the mariner.' [1578.] Starting from that point of new
departure the 'gentlemen' gradually learnt their place on
board English men-of-war, and in the course of a long
evolution became 'mariners' themselves. By the time Nelson was born, each of the King's naval officers united the
character of 'mariner' and 'gentleman,' and the sailing and
fighting service was one and indivisible.

Drake, who was first the greatest of privateers and afterwards the greatest of Royal Admirals, established as no
one else could have done a complete understanding between the Royal Navy and the merchant adventurers who
carried on the unofficial war against Spain. The Spaniards
had slaves to row their galleys and magnificent soldiers
to fight from their ships, but for the more indispensable

supply of mariners they had no large and energetic class of private merchants and seamen, such as those who were the wealth and pride of England.

For indeed the technical differences between the personnel and tactics of a Spanish and an English ship represented something more profound—the difference of social character between Spain and the new England. Private enterprise, individual initiative and a good-humoured equality of classes were on the increase in the defeudalized England of the Renaissance and Reformation, and were strongest among the commercial and maritime population. The most energetic spirits of the gentry, the middle and the lower classes were taking to the sea together in a rough *camaraderie,* for purposes of war and of commerce. In Spain the ideas and manners of society were still feudal, though in politics the King had become absolute. Discipline, as Drake well knew, is needed on board ship, but not feudalism and class pride. The hierarchy of the sea is not the same as the hierarchy of the land.

The Spaniards at the height of their power were great soldiers and colonists, less great sailors, unenterprising merchants, execrable politicians and rulers. Catholic enthusiasm drove them to expel or kill out from their own peninsula just those classes and races which might have enabled them to seize their new commercial opportunities. No country could flourish for ever on the importation of gold and silver from the American mines, even if the English did not waylay the cargoes. Furthermore, in their zeal for religion, the Spaniards murdered the prosperity of the great cities of Flanders, which might otherwise have been England's rivals in the new age. The mariners of Holland, who inherited the commerce lost by the Flemish merchants, were compelled by Spanish cruelty to become England's allies. If ever there was a victory of the spirit of social and intellectual freedom over its opposite, it was the maritime victory of England and Holland over Spain.

The success alike of maritime warfare under Elizabeth and of colonization under the Stuart Kings rested on the growth of English commerce. For lack of a native commerce to feed it, the Spanish marine power, for all Philip's

political and military strength and his empire over un-
counted millions scattered round half the globe, went down
before the attack of a small island State and a few rebel
towns among the mudflats and sand dunes of Holland. For,
unlike the Spaniards, the English and Dutch learnt how
to trade with the newly discovered regions of the world.

To find vent for the new cloth manufacture[3] the Merchant Adventurers of England had from the beginning of
the Fifteenth Century onwards been vigorously searching
for new markets in Europe, not without constant bloodshed
by sea and land in an age when piracy was so general as
to be scarcely disreputable, and when commercial privileges were often refused and won at the point of the sword.
Under Elizabeth they went further afield to find new markets in Africa, Asia and America.

Hakluyt laboured to inspire the English with a consciousness of their country's destiny at sea, by patiently recording
the stories that the survivors of each notable voyage had
to tell. His book serves to remind us that, side by side with
the more warlike enterprises of Drake in robbing the Spaniards and opening trade with their colonies at the cannon's
mouth, there was much traffic of a more peaceable character in Muscovy, Africa and the Levant. Besides Hawkins
and those who dealt in the slave-trade, other English merchants preferred to develop the Guinea trade by giving
the negroes fairer treatment than they got from the Portuguese and by trying to avoid unnecessary conflict with
either black or white.

Yet it is impossible to draw a clear line between the
peaceful and the warlike traders, because the Portuguese
attacked all who came near the African and Indian coasts.
They were no less determined than the Spaniards in America to exclude all foreigners, especially heretics, from the
lands and seas which the Pope had assigned to them for
ever.[4] Not seldom the African Gold Coast re-echoed to
the noise of battle between English interlopers and Portuguese monopolists, and by the end of Elizabeth's reign

[3] See pp. 27–30, above.
[4] See pp. 45–46, above.

the same sounds were already breaking the silence of the Indian seas and the Malay Archipelago. A sea fight with a pirate or a foreign rival was an unavoidable incident in the life of the most honest trader, whether in time of peace or in time of war. Companies were formed in the City to bear the expense and the risks of necessary hostilities, and were granted charters by the Queen giving them diplomatic and military authority on the other side of the world, where neither royal ships nor royal ambassadors ever came. Private English merchants, travelling on their lawful occasions, were the first men to represent their country at the Court of the Czar at Moscow and of the Mogul at Agra.[5]

Commerce was the motive of exploration as well as of warfare, and all three were combined in some of the greatest deeds of that generation. Romance and money-making, desperate daring and dividends, were closely associated in the minds and hearts of men. There was no line drawn between the bread-and-butter facts of life, and the life of poetry and imagination. The transactions of the money market and the war plans of sober statesmen turned on expeditions resembling those which in our own day explore Everest and the South Pole for naught save honour. Partly for that reason the Elizabethan age aroused the practical idealism of the English genius to its greatest height. Drake, Sidney, Spenser, Raleigh, and Shakespeare himself passed their lives among men to whom commerce was a soul-stirring adventure of life and death—

As full of peril and adventurous spirit,
As to o'erwalk a torrent, roaring loud,
On the unsteadfast footing of a spear.

To the men of London and of Devon the unmapped world beyond the ocean seemed an archipelago of fairy islands, each hiding some strange wonder of its own, each waiting to be discovered by some adventurous knight vowed to

[5] The 'Chartered Companies' formed to develop the interior of Africa in the later Nineteenth Century were a revival under somewhat similar circumstances of the powers of the Elizabethan Muscovy Company, Levant Company, and East India Company.

leave his bones far away or to come back rich and tell his tale in the tavern.

To such a generation of men it seemed a light thing to find a passage through the Arctic seas by which the markets of India might be reached behind the backs of 'Portugalls' and Turks. Sebastian Cabot in his old age revived the idea in English minds in the reign of Edward VI, and in 1553 Richard Chancellor sought the North-East Passage by the White Sea, and found instead the Czar keeping barbarous state over fur-clad tribes at Moscow; returning, he revealed to his countrymen the possibilities of a great Russian trade, and three years later perished on a second voyage. And so in Elizabeth's time the English Muscovy Company were the first Westerners to organize trade with the interior of Russia, though early in the following century they lost it for a while to the Dutch. The corresponding attempts of Frobisher [1576–78.] and of Davis [1585–87.] to reach India by the North-West Passage led to the Hudson's Bay fur trade of Stuart times, one of the main streams of British Canadian history.

Neither did Elizabethan merchants hesitate to traverse the Mediterranean in spite of the war with Spain. The Levant Company traded with Venice and her Grecian isles and with the Mahommedan world beyond. Since the naval enemies of the Turk were the Venetians and Spaniards, the Sultan welcomed the heretic English at Constantinople. But on the way thither they had to defend themselves against Spanish galleys near the Straits of Gibraltar and 'Barbary pirates' off the Algerian shore. Such were the beginnings of English sea-power in the Mediterranean, though it was not till Stuart times that the Navy followed where the merchant service had already fought many a battle.

While the Armada was attacking England, one of these Turkey merchants named Ralph Fitch was travelling in the Far East, having started from Aleppo overland to India. After eight years of wandering he brought home reports on the Persian Gulf, Hindoostan and Malacca, which greatly encouraged the promoters of the East India Company. They obtained a Charter from Elizabeth in 1600, and proceeded to trade in the Indian seas by rounding the Cape of Good Hope in tall ships laden with goods and well armed to defend themselves against the 'Portugall.' Not lust of conquest but vent of merchandize first drew our countrymen to the great peninsula which their descendants were destined to rule. Hakluyt already had his patriot's eye on lands still further afield:

Because (he wrote) our chiefe desire is to find out ample vent of our wollen cloth, the naturall comoditie of this our Realme, the fittest place which in all my readings and observations I find for that purpose are the manifold islands of Japan and the Northern parts of China and the regions of Tartars next adjoining.

All these trade routes and distant markets, sketched out by the daring of the Elizabethan merchants, led in Stuart times to an immense volume of commerce, particularly in the export of cloth. The Queen and her ministers understood the mercantile community and served it well. Unlike her brother and sister, Elizabeth was in close touch with London opinion, a condition of successful rule in Tudor England. She and Cecil were both personal friends of Sir Thomas Gresham, the founder of the Royal Exchange. She used him to raise State loans at home and abroad, and took his advice on financial questions. The chief of these was the difficult problem of the recoinage, which she effected at the beginning of her reign, successfully relieving her subjects of the burden laid on every-day life by her father's wanton debasement of the currency.

Elizabeth's financial difficulties were increased by the continued fall in the value of money. Prices had been rising all through Tudor times, especially after Henry tampered with the coinage. And just when his daughter had applied a remedy to that, the flow of silver and gold into Europe from the Spanish-American mines began to act as a further cause of high prices. This may not have been bad for the merchant, but it was bad for hired labour, and for the Queen in whose revenue many of the items were fixed amounts. Even in war time barely a quarter of the royal income was derived from extra taxation put on by Parliament; the Parliamentary 'subsidy' was assessed in such a manner as to produce sums altogether incommensurate with the increasing wealth of the nation. The art of taxing the subject was not taken seriously in hand until Parliament had to find the sinews of its own warfare against Charles I.

Some historians, in their imperialist or Protestant zeal, have blamed the Queen for her parsimony, and have wondered why she did not send more men to the Netherlands, to France, to Ireland; why she lied and prevaricated so long instead of challenging Philip to open war early in her reign; and why, after the Armada, she did not seize the Spanish colonies and strike down the Spanish power. The royal accounts give a sufficient answer. The year after the Armada her total revenue was less than £400,000, of which the sum of £88,362 came by way of Parliamentary taxation. In the last five years of the war and of her reign, her average annual revenue was still well below half a million, the 'subsidies' voted by Parliament still bearing the same small proportion to the whole. If anyone is to answer at the bar of history for Elizabeth's 'parsimony,' Parliament and the taxpayer must take their place there beside the Queen and her Ministers. What little money her subjects allowed her, she laid out with great wisdom for their safety and benefit. Because she refused to crusade hastily on behalf of Protestantism abroad, she was enabled to save the Reformation. Because she was a 'little Englander' and an economist in the day of small things, she laid the sea-foundations of the Empire, on which those who came after her could build.[6]

Regular war between England and Spain was postponed until the eve of the sailing of the Armada, because Philip and Elizabeth were both of them cautious and pacific by temperament. Yet both were inflexibly set upon policies that could not fail to end in war. Philip held to the right of excluding all foreigners from approaching the newly discovered shores of Asia, Africa and America, assigned by the Pope to Spain and Portugal. He held to the right of handing over English merchants and sailors in his domin-

[6] See note, pp. 122–23, below, for Elizabeth's revenue and war expenditure.

ions to the Inquisition. Nor would he tolerate an England permanently severed from Rome, though he was prepared to wait long in hopes of the death of Elizabeth, and artifically to hasten that event. Within a dozen years of her accession he was discussing plans of assassination and invasion against her, and thenceforward more and more assumed the role of executor of the Pope's decree of deposition. Yet his temperamental hesitation long restrained him from declaring open war, and compelled him to swallow many affronts and injuries at the hands of Hawkins, Drake, and the Queen herself. Probably he hoped each year that the resistance of the Dutch under William the Silent would collapse, and that then Elizabeth would become submissive or England fall an easy conquest.

The Queen saw that this delay was to her advantage, because each year made England stronger and more united. But she traded somewhat boldly on Philip's unwillingness to fight. On one occasion she laid hands on the pay for the Spanish troops in the Netherlands when the ships that carried it sought shelter in English ports [1569.]; three years later she secretly connived at the capture of Brill by the Sea Beggars that founded the Dutch Republic,[7] and she permitted English seamen to assist the rebels. [1572.] [SEE MAP 4.] In those early days the effective resistance of the Dutch was not in the open field, but on water and in the heroic defence of their amphibious walled towns like Haarlem and Leyden. [1573–74.]

Above all, Elizabeth abetted the piratical attacks of Hawkins and Drake on the Spanish ships and colonies, by which the fighting power of England was trained during the years of public peace and private war. The chief scene of these irregular hostilities was Spanish America. Its ports were officially closed to foreign trade, but its inhabitants were not unwilling to purchase, under a show of compulsion, goods with which Spanish merchants were too unenterprising to provide them. Besides more innocent traffic,

[7] Motley, who is often very unfair to the English, mistook Elizabeth's part in the Brill episode. See Pollard, *Pol. Hist.*, pp. 331–32.

Dutch Republic *(Seven United Provinces and Their Territories)*
Spanish Netherlands

EMERY WALKER LTD. SC.

Map 4   Spanish and Dutch Netherlands

Hawkins dealt with them largely in negroes whom he had kidnapped in Africa. It would have been difficult to find anyone in Europe to condemn the slave-trade from the point of view of its victims, and for two hundred years England, being the most energetic maritime community, took as much the leading part in the development of this curse of two continents as she finally took in its suppression.

Drake was less interested in the slave-trade, but he attacked and robbed Spanish ships, towns and treasure caravans, along the American coasts. His proceedings were much in accordance with the practice of European sailors of all countries in days before the growth of international law. But they were disapproved on moral and prudential grounds by some of Elizabeth's advisers, especially by

Cecil,[8] though he himself had seized the Spanish treasure in the Channel.

In one sense England was the aggressor. But if England had not taken the aggressive she would have been forced to accept exclusion from the trade of every continent save Europe, to abandon her maritime and colonial ambitions, and to bow her neck to reconquest by Spain and Rome as soon as the resistance of Holland collapsed. A world of sheer violence, in which peaceful Englishmen were liable to be imprisoned or put to death in any Spanish possession, the world of the Inquisition and the Massacre of St. Bartholomew, of Alva's appalling devilries in the Netherlands, and the Pope's deposition of Elizabeth which Catholic Europe was preparing to enforce, left no place for nice standards of international conduct.

It was Sir Francis Walsingham who urged upon the Queen that her throne could be saved from the slow closing of the Spanish net only if she encouraged the lawless acts of Drake and his companions. A share in their plunder was a strong additional argument to a ruler with an insufficient revenue. The influence of Walsingham was rising at Court, not like Leicester's as a star hostile and co-rival to Cecil's, but as the complementary influence of a younger man who supports his elder but sees some things that the older man cannot see. Walsingham carried weight, for the system of spies he had organized repeatedly saved the Queen's life from the assassins set on by Philip and the Jesuits, who destroyed William the Silent for want of such a guard. [1584.] Walsingham, inspired by a Puritan zeal against the Catholic reaction then raging on the continent, was impatient with the greater caution of the Protestant Nationalist Cecil and the 'mere English' Queen. He was ever for action, at all risks and at all expense of treasure. If Elizabeth had taken Walsingham's advice on every occasion she would have been ruined. If she had never taken it she would have been ruined no less. On the whole she took what was best in the advice of both her great Ministers.

[8] William Cecil became Lord Burleigh in 1571, but I continue to call him Cecil for the sake of clearness.

The situation reached its crisis over Drake's voyage round the world. Cecil was an enemy to the expedition, but Walsingham had persuaded Elizabeth secretly to take shares in the greatest piratical expedition in history. [1577.] 'Drake!' she exclaimed. 'So it is that I would gladly be revenged on the King of Spain for divers injuries that I have received!' She had applied to the right man.

Since Magellan had discovered a way round the southern end of America [1520.], the passage had been generally avoided as too stormy and dangerous for the tiny vessels of the day. The Spanish ships on the Pacific coast were built *in situ*, and communication with the Atlantic went overland by the isthmus of Panama. When therefore Drake appeared from the south upon the coast of Chile [1578–79.], he seemed 'like a visitation from heaven' to the secure and lightly armed Spaniards, who had learnt to think of the Pacific as an inland lake closed to the shipping of the world. Although he had less than a hundred men in the *Golden Hind,* which alone of his tempest-tost squadron had held right on past the Horn and the Straits of Magellan, it was the easiest part of his task to rob the long coast-line of its fabulous wealth, and ballast his little bark with the precious metals. Then he turned homewards across the Pacific Ocean, bound for the Cape of Good Hope.

Such was the importance attached in Spain and England to these proceedings, of which word came to Europe by Panama, and so loud was the outcry raised by the Spanish ambassador, that if Drake had failed to return home safe and rich, the victory at court might have rested with Cecil's more timid policy, and the victory in the world-contest might have fallen to Spain and Rome. Drake had told his companions that if they failed in their venture 'the like would never be attempted again.' When the *Golden Hind* grounded on a shoal in the uncharted Molucca Sea and hung for twenty hours on the edge of apparently certain destruction, to glide off safe into deep water at the last moment, vast destinies depended on the relation of a capful of wind and a tropical sandbank to a few planks of English oak.

[1580.] As Drake entered Plymouth Sound after nearly

three years' absence from Europe, his first question to some
passing fishermen was whether the Queen were alive and
well. Yes, in spite of all her enemies, she was still alive, and
well enough to come next year and knight him on board
his ship at Deptford. It was the most important knight-
hood ever conferred by an English sovereign, for it was a
direct challenge to Spain and an appeal to the people of
England to look to the sea for their strength. In view of
this deed, disapproved by her faithful Cecil, who shall
say Elizabeth could never act boldly? Her bold decisions
are few and can be numbered, but each of them began an
epoch.

After the accolade at Deptford, events drifted towards
open war as fast as Philip's slow spirit could move. England's final act of defiance to all comers, the execution of
Mary Queen of Scots [1587.], was the volition of the people
rather than of their sovereign. Elizabeth long resisted the
outcry, but her subjects forced her hand when the discovery
by Walsingham of Babington's plot to murder her revealed
Mary as acquainted with the design. Mary's prolonged existence raged like the fever in men's blood, for if she survived Elizabeth, either she would become Queen and the
work of the Reformation be undone, or else there would be
the worst of civil wars, with the national sentiment in arms
against the legitimate heir backed by the whole power of
Spain. The prospect was too near and too dreadful to leave
men time to pity a most unhappy woman. Parliament, people and Ministers at length prevailed on Elizabeth to au-
thorize the execution. Her attempt to avoid responsibility
for the death warrant by punishing her Secretary Davison
was in her worst manner, as the knighting of Drake was in
her best.

Mary's execution made it certain that Spain would at
once attack England, but it united England to resist. Moderate Catholics who might have drawn sword for Mary as
being by their reckoning the legitimate sovereign, stood for
Elizabeth against Philip of Spain when he claimed the
throne for himself. Nor had Elizabeth driven moderate
Catholics to despair. Beyond fines for non-attendance at

church, irregularly levied, she had not persecuted the Catholic laity for their opinions.[9] A more ultra-Protestant Prayer-Book or a harsher persecution of 'Popish recusants,' such as her Parliaments demanded, might well have led to civil war in face of the Spanish attack. As it was, a united people faced the storm of the Armada. For the Puritans, whatever they on their side suffered from Elizabeth in Church and State, would fight for her among the foremost.

The crews who manned the Invincible Armada, collected from half the sea-going populations of the Mediterranean, were many of them novices in the management of sailing ships in the open Atlantic, and acted as mere underlings of the soldiers, whom it was their privilege to carry from Spain to England. Very different was the opposing fleet. In those days the Lord High Admiral must needs be a great nobleman, but Lord Howard of Effingham, a Protestant though related to the Duke of Norfolk, was a fine sailor like his father before him, and well knew the value of the group of great seamen on whose services he could rely. Like Hawkins and Frobisher, he looked without jealousy on Drake as the master mariner of the world, who only the year before had 'singed the Spanish King's beard,' destroying with his broadsides the finest war galleys afloat, in the harbour of Cadiz itself.

The numbers of the rival fleets under Howard and Sidonia were not unequal. The English, combining their Royal Navy with their armed mercantile marine, had an overwhelming mastery in weight of gun-metal, as well as in seamanship and the art of gunnery. The Spaniards were superior only in the tonnage of their secondary craft and in their soldiers, who stood ranked on deck, musketeers in front of pikemen, waiting in vain for the English to draw near according to the ancient rules of warfare at sea. But

[9] On the question of the treatment of Catholic 'Recusants' see Mr. Merriman's article in the *American Hist. Rev.*, April 1908, and W. P. M. Kennedy, *Elizabethan Episcopal Administration*, Alcuin Club, 1924. The 12*d*. fine of 1559 for non-attendance at church was often exacted, but the ruinous fine of £20 a month ordained by later statutes of 1581 remained *in terrorem*, a dead letter. For the persecution of the Jesuit missionaries, see p. 130, below.

as the English preferred that it should be a duel between
artillery and infantry at range chosen by the artillery, small
wonder that the Spaniards, as they passed up the Channel,
underwent terrible punishment. Already demoralized when
they reached Calais roads, they mishandled their vessels in
face of Drake's fire-ships, and failed of any attempt to
embark the waiting army of Parma in the Netherlands.
[SEE MAP 3.] After another defeat in the great battle off
Gravelines [JULY 29, 1588.], they were thankful to escape
total destruction on the Dutch sand-dunes owing to a
change in the wind, and ran before the tempest, without
stores, water or repairs, round the iron-bound coasts of
Scotland and Ireland. The winds, waves and rocks of the
remote North-West completed many wrecks begun by
the cannon in the Channel. The tall ships, in batches of
two and half-a-dozen at a time, were piled up on the long
lee-shore, where Celtic tribesmen who knew little and cared
not at all what quarrel of civilized men had flung this
wreckers' harvest on their coast, murdered and stripped by
thousands the finest soldiers and proudest nobles in Europe.
Out of 130 great ships scarce the half reached home.

Profoundly moved by a deliverance that perhaps only
the seamen had confidently expected, the English took for
their motto '*He blew and they were scattered,*' ascribing
to the watchful providence of God and His viewless couriers
a result that might without undue arrogance have been in
part attributed to their own skill and courage at sea.

The first serious attempt of Spain to conquer England was
also her last. The colossal effort put forth to build and equip
the Armada, the child of such ardent prayers and expecta-
tions, could not, it was found, be effectively repeated,
although henceforth Spain kept up a more formidable fighting fleet in the Atlantic than in the days when Drake
first sailed to the Spanish Main. But the issue of the war
had been decided at its outset by a single event which all
Europe at once recognized as a turning point in history.
The mighty power that seemed on the eve of universal
lordship over the white man and all his new dominions had
put out its full strength and failed. One able observer, Car-

dinal Allen, was quick to recognize in the Armada campaign the ruin of his life's work, to which he had sacrificed the ordinary feelings of patriotism by urging on the invasion of England. When, some years later, the traveller Fynes Moryson entered Rome in disguise to view its antiquities, he found that the Cardinal had ceased to persecute his Protestant fellow countrymen who visited the city, having changed his conduct in this respect 'since the English had overthrowne the Spanish Navy in the yeere 1588, and there was now small hope of reducing England to papistry.'

The defeat of the Armada ensured the survival of the Dutch Republic and the emancipation of France under Henri IV from Spanish arms and policies. Less directly it saved Protestant Germany, whose Lutheran Princes, at this crisis of the onslaught made by the organized and enthusiastic forces of the Counter-Reformation, had shown themselves more interested in persecuting their Calvinist subjects than in helping the common cause.

The fate of the Armada demonstrated to all the world that the rule of the seas had passed from the Mediterranean peoples to the Northern folk. This meant not only the survival of the Reformation in Northern Europe to a degree not fully determined, but the world-leadership of the Northerners in the new oceanic era.

The regular war between England and Spain continued till the death of Elizabeth in 1603. She regarded it as a first charge on her slender war-budget to see that French and Dutch independence were maintained against Philip. This was secured, partly by English help and by the holding of the seas, and partly by domestic alliance of the Calvinists with Catholic *'politiques'* averse to Spanish domination; it followed that an element of liberality and toleration very rare in the Europe of that day made itself felt in France and in Holland in a manner agreeable to Elizabeth's eclectic spirit.

The fine English regiments in Dutch pay, led by 'the fighting Veres,' helped to defeat, in the battles of Turnhout and Nieuport, the infantry of Spain, till then unconquerable in the open field. [1597, 1600.] Under Prince Maurice of Nassau, the son of William the Silent, the Dutch army was becoming a school of scientific warfare for all Europe, and these Englishmen in that foreign service have some claim to be regarded as founders of the modern military traditions of their native land.[10]

What martial force Elizabeth herself could afford to pay, was for the most part sunk in the Serbonian bog of the Irish tragedy. Partly for this reason it was impossible, in spite of our naval supremacy, to dismember the Spanish empire or even to release Portugal from Philip's grasp. There were fine episodes, like the last fight of the *Revenge* off the Azores, which poetry has not greatly exaggerated, and the plunder of Cadiz, the maritime base of Spain. But England made no permanent conquests, such as were won for her by the United Services in the wars of Marlborough, Chatham and Napoleon. The war party led by Drake had saved England and much else besides, but in the day of their apparent triumph they found themselves in eclipse. The regular war, for which they had waited and wrought so long, brought them, when it came, grave disillusionments.

England had yet to evolve a financial and a military system adequate to support her new-born naval power. Nor at the end of Elizabeths reign, with scarce five million inhabitants, was she wealthy and populous enough to seize Spanish possessions or to found a colonial empire of her own. Even Raleigh's plantation at Virginia was premature in 1587. When in the Stuart epoch England's accumulated wealth and superfluous population enabled her to resume the work of colonization in time of peace with Spain, the path of the Puritan and other emigrants led necessairly to the Northern shores of America where no Spainards were to be found. That way the greater future lay before Anglo-Saxon colonization than if the Elizabethans had risen to

[10]Three fine old ballads, printed together in Percy's *Reliques—Brave Lord Willoughby, The Winning of Cales* (Cadiz) and *The Spanish Lady's Love,* will give the reader an idea of the national spirit in this war and of the ideal of conduct in the English soldiery. Vere's *Commentaires* give the spirit of the English regiments in the Dutch service; the 'Buffs' trace their regimental traditions to Nieuport and Vere's campaigns.

the opportunity offered by the war to annex the tropical settlements of Spain and Portugal, and had thereby directed the stream of English emigration into those deeply demoralizing climates. Here too Elizabeth's 'little Englandism' served the future of the Empire well. The limitations imposed on the scope of the war, against which Drake and Raleigh fretted, may be counted among the blessings of a reign on which Englishmen have reason to look back as the most fortunate as well as the most wonderful in their history.

NOTE (see p. 112, above)

Elizabeth's Revenue and Expenditure: For the year Michaelmas 1588 to Michaelmas 1589 the Queen's total *ordinary* receipts were £294,819, including the fines and ancient customs and imposts, which increased somewhat with the trade of the country; to this was added extraordinary Parliamentary taxation of £88,362 by 'subsidies,' besides £4410 by benevolences and £4878 for 'prizes.' The average annual revenue for the last five years of the reign and the war was:—

£	
360,519	Ordinary revenue
125,000	Subsidies and tenths
£485,519	Total

See pp. 516–17, W. R. Scott, *Joint Stock Cos. to 1720* (Cam. Press, 1911).

The following is a table of extraordinary war expenditure throughout the reign, drawn up by officials in 1603:—

£	
178,820	Leith, in Scotland, 1559–60
246,380	Newhaven (Havre), 1562
92,932	Rebellion in the North, 1569
230,440	Shane O'Neill's rebellion, 1573
254,961	Desmond's rebellion, 1579
1,924,000[11]	Tyrone's rebellion, etc.
1,419,596	Netherlands, 1585 to 1603
297,480	Aid of the French King, 1591 and later
161,185	Spanish Armada, Tilbury Camp
172,260	Voyages to Cadiz and the Islands

[11] Such is the sum in the original MS., misprinted as 192,-400 in the *Cal. St. Papers, Dom.*, 1603.

Besides these sums, ordinary recurrent expenses, including upkeep of the fleet, were to be met out of the permanent sources of royal revenue not voted by Parliament like the subsidies, but including the ancient customs and imposts. The total sum obtained throughout the reign by extraordinary Parliamentary taxation in subsidies and fifteenths was about 3½ millions (spread over more than forty years); this went to meet the extraordinary war expenses tabled above.

CHAPTER SEVEN

The Great Elizabethan Era. Wales. Ireland. Religion. The Boundaries of Elizabethan Freedom. The Bible, Poetry and Music. Apprenticeship and Some Conditions of Industry. The Gentry and Parliament

Forward from the time of Elizabeth, warfare against some great military empire is a recurrent *motif* of British history, but because such warfare was conducted from behind the shield of the sea and the Royal Navy, the island never became the scene of foreign invasion, nor until the novel circumstances of 1914–18 was it ever found necessary to sacrifice a large part of the manhood of the country abroad, or to interrupt the usual course of business and pleasure at home. Such continuous security, a privilege usually confined to countries either very humble or very remote, but enjoyed in this case by a Great Power on the very highway of the world's affairs, is the secret of much in British character and institutions. It enabled us to evolve Parliamentary government and the freedom of the subject before any other great country, and even to pride ourselves on a diversity of eccentric opinions and habits of life in our midst. Its first good gift was the rich harvest of the Elizabethan Renaissance.

The advantage of the 'moat defensive to the house' was fully understood by Shakespeare's contemporaries. During fifteen years of open war with Philip [1587–1603.], his veteran infantry were unable to cross from Antwerp to London, and England enjoyed greater security from 'foreign levy' and 'malice domestic' than during the three decades of troubled and dangerous peace with which Elizabeth's reign had begun. Nor did the state of war involve anything serious in the way of increased taxation or economic disturbance. A comparison may be made with the situation during the struggle with Napoleon: that later period was indeed a golden age in England for landscape-painting, poetry, novel-writing, boxing, hunting and shooting, but it was a dark time for the mass of people owing to the economic reactions of the war, and during it the seeds were sown of future social cleavage. But during the Elizabethan war the social and economic problems of the Tudor period continued to grow less acute. Since employment increased side by side with population, it was possible for Parliament, Privy Council and Justices of the Peace to cope with the problem of public provision for the poor. In the last year of the war a foreign traveller observed with surprise the absence of the plague of beggars which infested continental countries, and which had so gravely disturbed England in the earlier Tudor reigns.[1]

One cause of Elizabethan security and well-being was the fact that the outline of a united Great Britain had at length been drawn. There was lasting peace on the Scottish Border and a friendly State beyond it, as there had never been since the days of Edward I. And the Tudors had solved the problem of Wales, by which the mediæval

[1] *Diary of the Duke of Stettin's Journey*, 1602 (R. Hist. Soc., 1892), pp. 11–12. 'It is a pleasure to go about [at the Royal Exchange] for one is not molested or accosted by beggars, who are elsewhere so frequently met with in places of this kind. For in all England they do not suffer any beggars except they be few in number and outside the gates. Every parish cares for its poor. Strangers are brought to the hospital, but those that belong to the Kingdom or have come from distant places are sent from one parish to another, their wants being cared for, till at last they reach their home.'
This would not be worth quoting if it did not bear out what we know from other sources as to the working of the Elizabethan Poor Law and compulsory Poor Rate, in which England was ahead of other countries. See pp. 32–33, above.

English had been baffled only less completely than by the Irish question itself.[2]

In dealing with Wales, Henry VII [1485–1509.] had begun with two great advantages. First, he was a more powerful Marcher Lord than any of his predecessors, uniting in his own person the Marcher Lordships of the Houses of York and Lancaster to the number of some fifty. In the second place, he was a Welshman educated in Wales and retaining all his life a love of Welsh poetry and tradition. His fellow-countrymen considered that they had recovered their independence by placing one of their own Princes on the throne of England at Bosworth Field, and they flocked to his court as the Scots a century later to the court of James Sixth and First. With these advantages the prudent Tudor King was able to introduce a little order into the bloodstained anarchy of Wales, and his son completed the work.

Henry VIII [1509–47.], who mishandled Scotland and Ireland, understood Wales and solved its problems by a policy which combined repression of disorder with justice to the Celtic population. Rowland Lee, Bishop of Lichfield, the energetic President of the Council of the Marches, hanged thieves and murderers without mercy, and made the King's authority feared by great and small, Saxon and Celt. His methods would shock us to-day, but he gave peace to a land that had never known it before. Like many great administrators he had little faith in the future of the rude people he kept in awe, and it was contrary to his advice that Henry VIII incorporated Wales in England on equal terms. [1535.] This bold measure was the first and not the least successful Act of Union in British history. Henry abolished both Principality and Marcher Lordships, dividing the whole land into twelve counties, to be governed like English counties through the Justices of the Peace, subject to the orders of the King's Council and the laws made in Parliament. [See Map 1.] The Welsh shires and boroughs were henceforth represented in the English House of Commons. The authority of the King's Council,

[2] See Vol. I., pp. 275–83, for mediæval Wales.

very necessary in those disturbed districts, was brought to bear through its local offshoot the Council of Wales and the Marches, a body corresponding to the Council of the North.[3]

Thus supported by the strong arm of the central government, the Justices of the Peace were able to rule in the wild hill region where tribalism and feudalism had run riot for centuries. These magistrates, under the system inaugurated by Henry VIII, were not Englishmen imported to hold down the natives, but Welsh gentlemen who were the natural leaders of the people. In Wales the English government made friends with the native upper class, instead of destroying it as in Ireland.

The sight of the House of Tudor occupying the English throne enabled Celtic pride to accept union on these terms, and kept Wales loyal throughout the dangerous storms of the Tudor period. When Shakespeare represents Captain Fluellen boasting of the Welsh birth of the hero King Henry V, we suspect that the poet had overheard some honest Welshman boasting in similar terms of the racial origin of Queen Elizabeth. It was well that the Celtic population had this personal feeling for the House of Tudor, for a great strain was put on their loyalty by the English Reformation. It is true that, after the Methodist revival, Wales became the most Protestant part of Britain, but in the Sixteenth Century this was far from being the case. Protestantism under the Tudors first came to Wales in an official Anglican dress, with a Prayer Book and Bible in a tongue as little known to many Welshmen as the Latin of the Mass. And the new religion was preached at first by an alien official clergy, many of whom were absentees and sinecurists. It was a great opportunity for Rome to capture the Celtic nationality and temperament in Wales, as she was doing so successfully in Ireland under very similar religious conditions. But the Jesuit missions in Elizabeth's reign neglected Wales, partly owing to a fierce domestic quarrel between the Welsh and English in the continental seminaries.

Thus left to themselves, the Welsh people regarded the

[3] See pp. 23–24, above.

Reformation changes with apathy. While their educated and landlord classes were becoming English in speech and habits of life, while their native language was discouraged in Church and State, intellectual torpor settled down for awhile on the quick-witted mountain peasantry. But though the Celtic language was neglected as an instrument of education, it survived among them more than among the Irish. At length in the Eighteenth and Nineteenth Centuries there was a great revival of national feeling and culture in connection with Puritan religion, education, music and Celtic poetry. In the history of the Welsh people the tribe has died, but the bard still reigns. Fortunately this later Celtic renaissance did not, like the contemporary movement in Ireland, take a form hostile to England. Henry VIII's Act of Union had been justified by leading to a union of hearts.

Very different was the outcome of Tudor policy in Ireland, inspired by an ignorance of local conditions comparable to that of Philip in his dealings with the Netherlands. In the Fifteenth Century, Ireland had been governed on the principle of 'aristocratic Home Rule' through the great Anglo-Irish families, particularly the Fitzgeralds of Kildare. But the system had begun to break down in the reign of Henry VII,[4] and it came to a violent end when Henry VIII hanged the Earl of Kildare and his five uncles at Tyburn. [1537.] No other system of government was immediately substituted. Although the Earl of Surrey reported to Henry that English conquest and colonization had become indispensable, that dread alternative was not seriously applied before the later years of Queen Elizabeth.

Henry VIII, however, contributed something to the development of the Irish tragedy besides the hanging of the Fitzgeralds. He subjected Ireland, as a matter of course, to the religious revolution that he had devised to suit conditions in England. At first, indeed, the abolition of Papal Supremacy meant little to the Celts, to whom Rome had always remained a somewhat alien power, more closely allied to the Anglo-Irish nobles than to the people at large.

[4] See Vol. I., p. 274.

The simultaneous abolition of the monasteries destroyed centres of culture more valuable to Tudor Ireland than to Tudor England. For though many of the Irish monks were as worldly and useless as the Bishops and parochial clergy, they were certainly no worse, and what little education there was in the island owed much to monastic centres. Popular religion was maintained chiefly by the itinerant friars, who also fell under Henry's ban. The English brought nothing that could effectively replace that which they destroyed. They founded no University and no schools to replace the monasteries.[5] Henry's English Bible and Edward's English Prayer Book were in a tongue then unknown to the Celt, who had moreover stood outside the current of the European Renaissance and the New Learning. But the old religion too was decadent, and there was little active resistance made to the official acts of the Reformation, until the Jesuits from abroad came to the aid of the wandering friars, whom government might proscribe but could not suppress.

Largely owing to the activity of the Jesuits, who turned to full account the English 'lack of governance' secular and spiritual in Ireland, the situation became full of danger to Elizabeth. 'Ireland hath very good timber and convenient havens,' it was observed, 'and if the Spaniard might be master of them, he would in a short space be master of the seas, which is our chiefest force.' The Pope himself sent armed invaders to Ireland bearing his commission, six hundred of whom were captured and massacred by the English at Smerwick. [1580.] Ireland was the danger point in Elizabeth's dominions, and when her enemies attacked her there she was compelled most reluctantly to undertake its conquest. Because her military and financial resources were inadequate to the task, her lieutenants used great cruelty in destroying the people by sword and famine, and in making a desert of districts which they had not the power to hold.

At the same time the policy of English colonization was

[5] Trinity College, Dublin, was not founded till late in Elizabeth's reign.

favoured by government as the only means of permanently holding down the natives, who were growing more hostile every year. This opened the door to a legion of 'gentlemen-adventurers' and 'younger sons' from the towns and manor-houses of England. It has been said that the Elizabethan eagles flew to the Spanish Main while the vultures swooped down on Ireland; but they were in many cases one and the same bird. Among the conquerors and exploiters of Ireland were Humphrey Gilbert, Walter Raleigh, Grenville of the *Revenge,* and the high-souled author of the *Faerie Queene.* They saw in America and Ireland two new fields, of equal importance and attraction, where private fortunes could be made, public service rendered to their royal mistress, and the cause of true religion upheld against Pope and Span-iard. When Raleigh and Spenser were stone-blind to the realities of the Irish racial and religious problem under their eyes, it was not likely that the ordinary Englishman at home would comprehend it for several centuries to come.

And so, in the last thirty years of Elizabeth's reign, Irish history, till then fluid, ran into the mould where it hardened for three hundred years. The native population conceived a novel enthusiasm for the Roman religion, which they identified with a passionate hatred of the English. On the other hand the new colonists, as distinguished from the old Anglo-Irish nobility, identified Protestantism with their own racial ascendancy, to maintain which they regarded as a solemn duty to England and to God. Ireland has ever since remained the most religious part of the British Islands.

In such circumstances the Irish tribes finally became welded into the submerged Irish nation. The union of ha-tred against England, and the union of religious observance and enthusiasm became strong enough to break down at last the clan divisions of dateless antiquity, which the Eng-lish also were busy destroying from outside. The abolition of the native upper class to make room for English land-lords, begun under the Tudors and completed by Crom-well, left this peasant nation with no leaders but the priests and no sympathizers but the enemies of England.

The conversion of England to Protestantism, which can be

traced to origins in the time of Wycliffe, was substantially
effected during the long reign of Elizabeth. When she came
to the throne, the bulk of the people halted between a
number of opinions, and the anti-Catholic party still consisted of anti-clericals as much as of Protestants. When she
died, the majority of the English regarded themselves as
ardent Protestants, and a great number of them were living
religious lives based on Bible and Prayer Book.

There were two stages in the home policy of Elizabeth's
reign. During the first dozen years, although the Prayer
Book was the only ritual sanctioned by law, Roman Catholics were not persecuted except by moderate fines irregularly exacted.[6] No one in that period was put to death on
account of religion, and a great deal of private Roman
Catholic worship was winked at by the authorities, even
among persons in high State employ. But when in 1570
the Pope excommunicated the Queen, and absolved her
subjects from their allegiance, the second period begins,
and soon we breathe a harsher air. Jesuits from abroad
travel through the island, passed on in disguise from hall
to hall, hiding in 'priest-holes' behind the wainscot, infusing
into the quiescent body of old English Catholicism the new
zeal of the European Counter-Reformation. They checked
the peaceful process by which the Catholic squires were
gradually becoming habituated to the English ritual. The
Jesuits' mission was religious, but, if it should succeed, its
political consequences must be the deposition of the Queen
and the end of everything on which the new England had
set its heart, at home or beyond the seas. The Jesuits
preached spiritual obedience to the Pope-King who was
at war with Elizabeth, and who invaded Ireland with his
own armed forces. Crown and nation struck back savagely
at his missionaries, who were hanged as traitors to the
English State, but were regarded by their co-religionists as
martyrs to the Catholic Church. Of the two most noted
leaders of the Jesuit mission in England, Campion, who
cared more for religion than politics, was unfortunately
caught and hanged [1581.], while the indubitable traitor

[6] See p. 118, above, and note.

Parsons escaped abroad to work for a Spanish invasion.[7]

On the average, four Catholics suffered for every year of Elizabeth's reign, as against 56 Protestants for every year of Mary, and the charge was no longer heresy but treason. It was a tragic business, and no doubt many English Catholics who would fain have been patriotic and loyal, but who craved for the offices of their own religion, were ground small between the upper millstone of their spiritual lord, the Pope, and the lower millstone of their temporal lord, the Queen. Both sides had declared the two loyalties to be incompatible one with the other. There were many innocent victims of this tremendous conflict, wherein for the moment no compromise was possible. In the middle of Elizabeth's reign England was in a state of siege, and adopted something of the discipline of a besieged town. Until the Roman Church throughout the world ceased to use the methods of the Inquisition, the Massacre of St. Bartholomew, the deposition and assassination of Princes, the States which she had placed under her formidable ban did not dare to grant toleration to her missionaries. To do so would have been to invite defeat by pitting a naked man against a fully armed and ruthless warrior.

Under these conditions the propaganda of the Protestant religion in England went forward apace. It was favoured by the alarmed authorities; and it was identified in the minds of Englishmen with patriotism, with defiance of Spain, with sea power and Drake's American adventures, with the protection of the life of the Queen from assassins. The remodelled Grammar Schools familiarized the young with the Classics taught in the spirit of Erasmus and Colet, and with the Bible and Catechism, and so produced the men of the new English Renaissance in literature, and the champions of Protestant Anglicanism in religion. During

[7] Parsons, debating the use to be made of the conquest of England, queries 'What form or manner of Inquisition to bring in, whether that of Spain (whose rigour is misliked by some) or that which is used in divers parts of Italy (where coldness is reprehended by more).' The Catholic Bishops were to have the power to negative or confirm elections to the House of Commons.

the death-struggle with Rome, Anglo-Catholicism could not
flourish, and the new generation of clergy and scholars
were ardent Protestants.[8]

The Puritans were most of them inside the Church, using
it to convert the country to Protestantism and hoping ere
long to change the Church's ritual and government more in
their own direction. Elizabeth indeed had difficulty in getting Bishops who were not too rigidly anti-Catholic for her
own instincts and policy, until she made the able Whitgift
Archbishop of Canterbury, and with his help took a firm
stand against the Puritanizing of the Church. [1583.] Whitgift indeed was on many doctrinal points a Calvinist, but he
opposed the democratization of Church government and
stood stiffly for the Royal and Episcopal power as against
Parliament, laity and Presbyterian clergy.

In her double resistance to returning Romanism and
encroaching Puritanism, Elizabeth employed the power of
the old Church courts and authorities, backed by the High
Commission, a kind of ecclesiastical Star Chamber, by
which the novel control of the Crown over the Church was
very effectually maintained. Though an offshoot of the
Privy Council, the High Commission represented the Queen
rather than the generality of her Councillors. Indeed many
of them, like Cecil himself, disliked its procedure of cross-
questioning the accused under oath as redolent of the
'Romish inquisition,' and saw danger to the State in its
policy of persecuting too ardent Protestants. But the Queen

[8] The following account of the English parish churches
early in Elizabeth's reign is by Harrison (*Holinshed*, II.1):
'Whereas there was wont to be a great partition between
the choir and the body of the church, now it is either very
small or none at all: and to say the truth altogether need-
less, sith the minister saith his service commonly in the
body of the church, with his face toward the people, in a
little tabernacle of wainscot provided for this purpose; by
which means the ignorant do not only learn divers of the
psalms and usual prayers by heart, but also such as can
read do pray together with him: so that the whole congregation at one instant pour out their petitions on to the
living God for the whole estate of his church in most earnest
and fervent manner.' Such at any rate was the ideal aimed
at in many churches, increasingly as the reign went on.

held on her way in spite of the advice of her Councillors and the votes of her faithful Commons, and so preserved the Anglican character of the Church at a time when popular forces bade fair either to carry it into the full stream of the European and Scottish Reformation, or haply to tear it asunder by fresh divisions.

There were Protestant as well as Catholic martyrs under Elizabeth's State-Church. Puritan controversialists like Penry, author of the 'Marprelate' tracts, made their violent attacks on the Bishops at their peril. In the Queen's eyes, to attack Episcopacy was a political offence, because it endangered the delicate balance of her establishment in Church and State. Even the more decorous Presbyterian propaganda of Thomas Cartwright angered and alarmed her. Cartwright was imprisoned, and Penry, Barrow and Greenwood were hanged as seditionists. [1590, 1593.]

There were other martyrs of conscience who had no great party at home or abroad to pity their fate or commend their fortitude, but who were more clearly innocent of all offence against the State than either Jesuit or Puritan. Several persons in East Anglia were burnt for 'diverse detestable heresies,' because they had scruples as to the orthodox doctrine of the Trinity. For such men, neither Catholic, Calvinist nor Anglican had in that age any mercy. They were the victims, not of reasons of State, but of intolerant religious prejudice and the still surviving habits of the mediæval heresy-hunt.

The Crown in Parliament, the modern State omnicompetent within its own borders, did indeed wield terrific powers after the Tudor monarchy had subdued the Church to its will. Such powers were perhaps needful to save the country from Spanish conquest, but they set a limit to the otherwise steady growth of individual liberty. Economic and intellectual freedom had enlarged their borders by the disappearance of the mediæval system. But in religion and politics the new State for awhile imposed fetters scarcely less galling than those which had been broken. The right of Catholic and Puritan to worship God each according to his own conscience was not conceded. And in politics no opposition was allowed; no one might criticize the government. Even loyal John Stubbs, for writing a pamphlet advising the Queen not to marry the French Prince, Alençon, had his right hand cut off by the hangman. [1579.] Waving the bloody stump he cried from the scaffold 'Long live the Queen!' Such was the relation of that strange, subtle woman to her simple-hearted subjects. She had never had the remotest intention of marrying Alençon, but no Puritan squire was to be allowed to interfere with the mystifications of high female diplomacy.

As yet there was neither political nor religious liberty for the individual, but a split between Crown and Parliament might produce both. For England was not a despotism. The power of the Crown rested not on force but on popular support. The people still wished the Crown to exercise these coercive powers in the public interest. But it was significant that the Parliament men, while not denying the Queen's ecclesiastical authority which they themselves had restored in 1559, criticized the use she made of it against the Puritans. The English State had won control of religion from the mediæval Church only by an alliance with the rights of private judgment and the forces of free speculation; it could not permanently deny the moral origin of its new-gotten authority. Puritan and Catholic might for awhile be a danger and might for long be an embarrassment to statesmen. But their claim, in the name of the higher law of conscience, to challenge the religious decrees alike of the Crown and of Parliament must carry weight in the end. Since the appeal to private judgment had triumphed in England over the vast organization and immemorial prestige of the European Church of the Middle Ages, how much more certainly would it prove stronger in matters of religion than the secular authorities of the island State. And so, after another century of faction, persecution and bloodshed, the attempt to force all Englishmen inside the doors of a State Church would be abandoned, and a larger liberty would be evolved than any dreamt of by Penry or Parsons, Whitgift or Cecil.

But outside the politico-religious sphere, intellectual and poetic freedom had already reached their fullest expansion

by the end of Elizabeth's reign. The Renaissance, with its
spirit of enquiry and its vision of the ancient freedom of
Greek and Roman thought, had been transplanted from
Italy, where it was fast withering away under the hands
of Spaniards and Jesuits. It bloomed afresh in England,
tended by poets who grafted it on English trees in the
Forest of Arden. There the imagination was free indeed,—
freer than in our own day, when it is burdened by too
great a weight of knowledge, and hemmed in by the harsh
realism of an age of machinery. Shakespeare and his
friends, standing as they did outside the dangerous world
of religious and political controversy, enjoyed in their own
spacious domains a freedom of spirit perhaps irrecoverable.

But though Shakespeare may be in the retrospect the
greatest glory of his age, he was not in his own day its
greatest influence. By the end of Elizabeth's reign, the
book of books for Englishmen was already the Bible, although the Authorized Version that is still in use was only
drawn up by James I's Bishops in the years immediately
following her death. For every Englishman who had read
Sidney or Spenser, or had seen Shakespeare acted at the
Globe, there were hundreds who had read or heard the
Bible with close attention as the word of God. The effect
of the continual domestic study of the book upon the national character, imagination and intelligence for nearly
three centuries to come, was greater than that of any lit-
erary movement in our annals, or any religious movement
since the coming of St. Augustine. New worlds of history
and poetry were opened in its pages to a people that had
little else to read. Indeed it created the habit of reading
and reflection in whole classes of the community, and
turned a tinker into one of the great masters of the English
tongue. Through the Bible, the deeds and thoughts of men
who had lived thousands of years before in the eastern
Mediterranean, translated into English during the period
when our language reached its brief perfection, coloured
the daily thought and speech of Britons, to the same degree
as they are coloured in our own day by the commonplaces
of the newspaper press. The Bible in English history may
be regarded as a 'Renaissance' of Hebrew literature far

more widespread and more potent than even the Classical Renaissance which, thanks to the reformed Grammar Schools, provided the mental background of the better educated. The Bible and the Classics together stimulated and enlarged the culture of the British, as their ocean voyages stimulated and enlarged their practical outlook on life.

Another source of popular inspiration and refinement in the great age that lies between the Armada and the Civil War, was music and lyrical poetry. They flourished together: many of the best poems, like the songs in Shakespeare's plays, were written to be sung. Europe recognized Elizabethan England as the country of music *par excellence.* German travellers noted with admiration how they 'heard beautiful music of violas and pandoras, for in all England it is the custom that even in small villages the musicians wait on you for a small fee.' Throughout Tudor times, fine Church music was written in England, indifferently for the Roman Mass or the Anglican service, while the Renaissance inspired non-ecclesiastical music with a fresh spirit, so that it reached its zenith under Elizabeth. The genius of Byrd [b. 1538, d. 1623.] adorned impartially the religious and the profane sphere, and whole troops of able composers flourished in that great age of the madrigal. The arena of Tudor and Stuart music was not the concert-hall but the domestic hearth. In days when there were no newspapers, and when books were few and ponderous, the rising middle class, not excluding Puritan families, practised vocal and instrumental music assiduously at home. The publication of music by the printing-press helped to diffuse the habit, and Elizabeth set the example to her subjects by her skill upon the virginals.

Music and song were the creation and inheritance of the whole people. The craftsman sang over his task, the pedlar sang on the footpath way, and the milkmaid could be heard 'singing blithe' behind the hedgerow, or in the north country crooning the tragic ballads that told of Border fight and foray. The common drama was a poetical drama, and in that age was popular because it appealed to the imaginative faculties. Poetry was not an affair solely of intellectual circles, nor was music yet associated mainly with foreign composers. It was no mere accident that Shakespeare and Milton came when they did. Among a whole people living in the constant presence of nature, with eyes and ears trained to rejoice in the best pleasures of the mind, the perfect expansion of Shakespeare's poetic gifts was as much a part of the general order of society as the development of a great novelist out of a journalist would be to-day. And in the life of John Milton, born five years after Elizabeth died, we read clearly how the three chief elements in the English culture of that day—music, the Classics and the Bible—combined to inspire the 'God-gifted organ-voice of England.'

From the age of Elizabeth down to the industrial changes in the reign of George III, the economic conformation of society was in certain respects very fortunate. The English were still country folk, not yet divorced from nature, but they were already to some degree relieved from the harsh poverty and ignorance of the mediæval peasant.

In the country towns and villages where the industry as well as the agriculture of the country was carried on,[9] a considerable proportion of the inhabitants were trained craftsmen. Apprenticeship was the key to the new national life, almost as much as villeinage had been to the old. The apprentice system was no longer left to local usage and municipal enforcement, but was controlled on a uniform national pattern for town and country by Elizabeth's Statute of Artificers, which remained in force with little modification for over two hundred years. [1563.] No man could set up as master or as workman till he had served his seven years' apprenticeship. In that way the youth of the country obtained technical education and social discipline that went some way to compensate for the unfelt want of a universal system of school education. Youth was under control of a master, in some cases until the age of twenty-four.

Industry was conducted in the home of the employer, who worked in the same shop and usually dined at the same board with his paid journeymen and his bound ap-

[9] See pp. 27–30, above.

prentices. The happiness of the manufacturing household depended, not on factory laws or trade union rules, but on the temper and character of the inmates. There was often harsher dealing than would be tolerated to-day, for conscious and organized humanitarianism is of no earlier date than the Industrial Revolution. Under the old system the men slept heaven knows where, under the rafters or in the cupboards. Masters were expected to beat their apprentices and often laid angry hands on their journeymen. But there was probably more kindness than severity, for the relation was closely personal and few people like discontent in their own home. The distinction between master and man was one of rank only, not of class; indeed, as old plays remind us, the London apprentice who happened to be cadet of a squire's family often plumed himself on being the better 'gentleman' of the two.[10]

The work of the skilled craftsman was a joy to him, and called out the artist latent in man more than the specialized functions of modern industry, which so often consist in watching some purely mechanical process. For this reason the objects in common use—the ship, the cart, the house, the chair, and all the utensils of the field and the home— bore the impress of beauty and of individual workmanship, lacking to the machine-made article of to-day. Work was more popular then than now, partly because much of it was educative of man's best talents.

But there was another side to the life of the pre-mechanical ages which is often forgotten by those who too indis-

[10] Carey's 'Sally in our Alley' portrays some of the realities of prentice life, which were just the same under Elizabeth as under Queen Anne:—
When she is by, I leave my work, / I love her so sincerely; / My master comes like any Turk / And bangs me most severely. / My master carries me to church / And often am I blaméd / Because I leave him in the lurch / As soon as text is naméd. / My master and my neighbours all / Make game of me and Sally, / And but for her I'd better be / A slave and row a galley. / But when my seven long years are out / O then I'll marry Sally, / O then we'll wed, and then we'll bed, / But not in our alley!

criminately praise the past. Besides the skilled labour, there remained a heavy weight of hard muscular toil to be done, which modern mechanism has greatly relieved. In the saw-pit, at the plough's tail, in quarrying, in moving of heavy material, man still paid very severely in his own person for the conquest of nature. The exposure and hardship which were the lot of the poorer agriculturists were terrible. The proportion of dangerous trades was great. And in cottage industries parents often employed their small children for very long hours. In the Eighteenth Century the public conscience began to be disturbed by numerous cases of cruelty to apprentices and children leading to death at the hand of their masters, and earlier generations had certainly not been more gentle.

But the Elizabethan child, when not engaged in industry, had the freedom of the fields and woods, denied by the circumstances of our modern civilization. It is small wonder if in those days he 'crept unwillingly to school,' for outside the school doors lay a world full of freedom and delight, and in school cruel flogging was still considered, by all save a few enlightened pedagogues and parents, to be an essential part of education.

Although warmth, clothing and food were more available in the Elizabethan village than in the mediæval manor, they were more often lacking than in our day. A bad harvest still meant shortage of food. Washing of clothes and person was much neglected, especially in winter. Conveniences which we consider necessities did not exist. The death-rate even in upper class families was very heavy, and the poor only expected a slender proportion of their numerous progeny to survive. Medicine was in its infancy. The aged, the sick, the debtor, and all who fell foul of the law suffered martyrdoms which were regarded as an inevitable part of human fate and fortune. If life was more full of beauty, it had less certainty and comfort than to-day, and the number of persons alive in Elizabethan England was about a seventh of the present population.

Much that would now be regarded as intolerable seemed no hardship because formerly things had been still worse. Elizabethan writers noted as innovations the use of glass instead of horn in the windows, chimneys to draw the smoke out of the poor man's cottage, and flock-beds instead of straw mattresses for some at least of the common folk.

The leading class in England was the landed gentry or squires. They were no longer a feudal or a military class, and when civil war broke out in 1642 had to be taught the art of soldiery from the beginning. So far as it is possible to define the important and recognized distinction between 'gentle' and 'simple' in the new England, the 'gentleman' was a landowner who could show a coat of arms, and who had the right when he wished it to wear a rapier and to challenge to the duel any other 'gentleman' from a Duke downwards. But yeomen and merchants were constantly finding entrance into this class by marriage and by purchase of lands, and the younger sons of the manor-house normally passed out of it into trade, manufacture, scholarship, the Church, or military service abroad, in some cases carrying with them their pretension to gentility, in other cases tacitly abandoning it.

There were infinite gradations both of wealth and rank in this peculiar upper class. At the top of the scale was the great noble, with his seat in the House of Lords, keeping semi-regal state in his castle of Plantagenet stone or his palace of Tudor brick, which served as a school of elegant accomplishments to young gentlemen pages in training for careers at Court. Broken meats were daily distributed to a crowd of poor at the great gate. In the hall, on the dais, sat his lordship with his lady and chief guests, while half a hundred hungry clients and led captains feasted at the lower tables off silver and Venice glasses, and an army of serving-men and gamekeepers caroused off pewter in the ample regions of the kitchen. At the bottom of the scale of gentry was the small squire who farmed his few paternal acres, talked in dialect with his yeomen neighbours as they rode together to market, and brought up, with the help of his hard-working wife and the village schoolmaster, a dozen sturdy, ragged lads and lasses, who tumbled about together in the orchard round his 'hall,' a modest farmstead not seldom converted by posterity into a barn.

Between these two extremes, every variety of Tudor and Stuart manor-house arose, built, according to the materials of the country-side, in stone, in new-fangled brick, or in old-fashioned half-timber. These manor-houses and their inhabitants, together with the village industries, kept the country-side in touch with the central life and thought of the new world. Shakespeare's England was rustic without being backward or barbarous, and whatever London generated the rural parts in due course absorbed.

The Tudor is the great period of domestic architecture. The Renaissance had this in common with the Middle Ages as distinguished from later times, that the investment of money with a view to its mere increase, though more possible than before, was not so customary, easy and safe as it became later on, and that wealthy persons normally put their wealth as it accumulated into art and ostentation—jewels, plate, beautiful clothes and above all beautiful buildings,—thereby adding to the pride and pageant of life. But whereas the Middle Ages had been the period of church and castle building to the relative neglect of the common dwelling house, the Tudor time brought the mansion to its perfect glory, and began to cover the English landscape with gabled farmhouses, very different from the hovels of the mediæval villein. The fine old farms which we admire in so many different parts of England were a product of modern change, improvement, cloth trade and enclosure.

The squires or smaller country gentry acquired a new importance under the Tudors. It was not merely that many of them had purchased the monastic lands at an easy rate. They were in a new social position, because the Barons and Abbots who had lorded it over them so long had been brought low. They themselves, whether as Ministers of the Crown or as local Justices of the Peace, became the mainstay of the government, the leaders of the House of Commons, the real rulers of the countryside. It was the squires, principally, who in the Stuart era led both the Cavalier and the Roundhead party.

Under the Tudors they were preparing earnestly for their new role. Some gentlemen sent their sons to travel abroad, or to study law at the Inns of Court, in order to fit them to be leaders in Parliament or magistrates in their own shires. The New Learning of the Classical Renaissance was also much to their taste. In the Middle Ages education had been sought by poor scholars destined to be clergy, while the lay upper classes had despised learning. But in Elizabeth's reign country gentlemen's sons formed an important element not only in the Grammar Schools but at the Universities, where their numbers filled the room of the departed friars and monks. There was indeed some justice in complaints that began to be heard, that the well-to-do were encroaching on educational endowments previously reserved for the humble. The movement had its scandalous side, yet it is well that the governors of a land should receive the best education that the land can give. In the Middle Ages the aristocracy had thought it enough if their secretaries came from Oxford and Cambridge, while they themselves had been schooled in the castle and the tiltyard.

Parliament represented not unfairly the opinion of those classes which took an interest in politics or showed any desire to be heard in the counsels of the nation.

The House of Lords provided seats for the nobility, both the remnants of the old feudal baronage and royal servants of recent creation like Burghley, Leicester, and Russell, Earl of Bedford. The Bishops as nominees of the Crown added to the official vote in the Upper House. The Abbots were gone, and the independent feudal power of the great nobles was gone too, after Elizabeth's victory over the Northern Earls and the Duke of Norfolk.[11] [1569–72.] In the latter part of her reign the House of Lords, however dignified, was less important as a force in politics than at almost any time before or after. The Tudors were not democrats, but they had prepared the way for middle-class power, because in the State refashioned by their hands

[11] See pp. 97–98, above.

there was no independent authority left between Crown and people.

The growing strength of the landed gentry, backed by that of the merchants and yeomen, found expression in the House of Commons. The elections were no longer regarded as a burden imposed by the Crown on the local bodies, but were valued as a means of gaining influence over the national policy. The local gentry competed with one another to secure the election of themselves or their friends to Parliament, for boroughs scarcely less than for shires, since there was no feeling of antagonism between town and country in England. The numerous Cornish boroughs, enfranchised by the Tudor monarchs, fell into the hands of the squirearchical Puritan opposition, and returned critics of government like Paul and Peter Wentworth under Elizabeth, and in subsequent reigns Sir John Eliot, Hampden and many others of that party.[12]

Both as supporter and as critic of government, the House of Commons was beginning to take an initiative of its own. In face of Spain and the Pope, it was more Elizabethan than the Queen herself. Members were in a perpetual fever of loyalty, urging her to more vigorous measures in self-defence—to get married, to name her heir, to execute the Queen of Scots, to persecute the Catholics more and the Puritans less—everything in short except raise higher taxes, which both Queen and members knew would be dangerous. She thought the House over-zealous, over-busy. In the earlier Tudor reigns the Crown, without packing Parliament at election time, had relied safely on the desire of the country and its representatives to follow as far as possible the lead of the King and Council even in matters of religion. Under Elizabeth the increasing Puritanism of the squires introduced a new element. The fear and love of God began to strive with the fear and love of the Queen in the breast of the Parliament men like Peter Wentworth. Protestantism and Parliamentary privilege were already

[12] The best authorities differ as to whether or not the creation of the Cornish borough seats was intended to increase the power of the Crown in Parliament. If it was so intended, it failed.

closely connected, before ever the first Stuart came to trouble still further the seething waters.

But the House of Commons was not yet, as James I soon made it, essentially an opposition. So long as some of the ablest Privy Councillors had seats in the chamber and were responsible there for the principal legislation of each session, a close link existed between executive and legislative, which only the negligence of Elizabeth's successor permitted to lapse.

So long as the Queen was alive, the personal factor postponed the irrepressible conflict. In spite of her irritation with much that was done and said in the House, she respected its privileges, for she knew what the Stuarts never learnt, that her strength lay not in 'right divine' but in the loyalty of these hot-headed, self-sufficient squires, and the unseen millions, far-scattered at their toil over land and sea, with whom these men were in more direct contact than herself or her courtiers. To the last she was supreme in the art of managing the other sex, even members of Parliament. Two years before she died, her gracious manner of withdrawing the unpopular trade 'monopolies' regained their affection at a stroke. Honourable members wept for joy, and in that melting mood were summoned to Whitehall by their mother and mistress, who told them what had indeed been the secret of her long reign now drawing to its close: 'Though God hath raised me high, yet this I count the glory of my crown, that I have reigned with your loves!'

BOOKS FOR FURTHER READING: See lists of books, pp. 36–37, above. See also:
GENERAL:—Creighton, *Queen Elizabeth*; Neale, *Queen Elizabeth*; Pollard, *Political History*, 1547–1603; Conyers Read, *Mr. Secretary Walsingham*, 3 vols.; J. B. Black, *The Reign of Queen Elizabeth (Oxf. Hist. of England)*, 1936; L. Strachey, *Elizabeth and Essex*; Milton Waldman, *Raleigh* and *Elizabeth and Leicester*.
PARLIAMENT:—Articles on Peter Wentworth by J. E. Neale in *E. H. R.*, 1924.
RELIGION:—*Cam. Mod. Hist.*, II., Chap. XVI., for Maitland on *The Anglican Settlement and the Scottish Reformation*; Bayne, *Anglo-Roman Relations*, 1555–1565 (Oxford, 1913); W. P. M. Kennedy, *Elizabethan Episcopal Admin-*

istration (Alcuin Club, 1924); Gee, *Elizabethan Clergy* (Oxford, 1898); E. L. Taunton, *The Jesuits in England*; Scott Pearson, *Thomas Cartwright and Elizabethan Puritanism* (Cambridge, 1925).

THE SEA:—Sir Julian Corbett, *Drake and the Tudor Navy*, 2 vols., and *The Successors of Drake*; Sir Walter Raleigh, *English Voyages in the Sixteenth Century*; Prof. Callender, *The Naval Side of British History*; J. A. Williamson, *The Age of Drake* (1938).

SCOTLAND:—*C. M. H.*, II., Chap. XVI., as above; Hume Brown's and Andrew Lang's *Histories*; R. S. Rait, *The Parliaments of Scotland*; W. L. Mathieson, *Politics and Religion in Scotland, 1550–1695.*

WALES:—W. Ll. Williams, *The Making of Modern Wales.*

IRELAND:—Bagwell, R., *Ireland under the Tudors*, 3 vols.; Stephen Gwynn, *History of Ireland.*

BOOK FOUR

The Stuart Era
Parliamentary Liberty and
Overseas Expansion

INTRODUCTION

The Tudor period made, it is probable, more difference to
the Englishman's outlook and habits of life than the Stuart
period that followed. But the Renaissance, the Reformation, and the development of oceanic adventure, which
changed so much for the Tudor English, had been world
movements in which other countries took an equally
active part. In the Stuart era the English developed for
themselves, without foreign participation or example, a
system of Parliamentary government, local administration
and freedom of speech and person, clean contrary to the
prevailing tendencies on the continent, which was moving
fast towards regal absolutism, centralized bureaucracy,
and the subjection of the individual to the State. While
the Estates General of France and the Cortes of Aragon
and of Castile were ceasing to exercise even their mediæval functions, while the political life of Germany was
atrophied in the mosaic of petty Princedoms that constituted the Empire, the House of Commons, under the
leadership of the squires and in alliance with the merchants and the Common Lawyers, made itself the governing organ of a modern nation. This it achieved
by developing inside itself an elaborate system of committee procedure, and by striking down the royal power
in a series of quarrels of which the chief motive was
religious and the chief result political.

English freedom, being rooted in insular pecularities,
required, if it was ever to reach its full growth, a period

of isolation from European influences and dangers. Elizabeth and Drake had rendered that isolation possible. Circumstances abroad, of which the Thirty Years' War was the chief, enabled England, behind the shield of her Navy, to work out her domestic problems undisturbed by any dread of interference by her neighbours.

It was only when the period of internal evolution had resulted in the settlement of 1688-89, that the new Parliamentary England, based on freedom in religion and politics, was matched under William III and Marlborough against the new type of continental autocracy personified in the all-worshipped Louis XIV, Grand Monarch of France. That struggle freed Europe from French domination, and left the English fleet for the first time unrivalled mistress of all the seas of the world. The wars against Louis may be regarded as the ordeal by battle which demonstrated the greater efficiency of the free community over the despotic state.

This result greatly astonished and impressed a world that had up till that time held a diametrically opposite theory of power. Despotism, it had been thought, was the secret of efficiency; freedom was a luxury to be enjoyed by small communities like the Cantons of Switzerland and the Seven Provinces of Holland—and Holland's power after a short period of glory was waning fast before the rising might of the French King. The victory of parliamentary England over despotic France was a new fact of the first order; it was the prime cause of the intellectual movement abroad against despotism in Church and State which marked the Eighteenth Century, from the time of Montesquieu onwards. The British Navy and Marlborough, the battles of La Hogue and Blenheim, gave to Locke and the other English philosophers a vogue on the continent seldom enjoyed by English philosophy in its own right. English institutions for the first time became an example to the world, though they remained somewhat of a mystery and were very imperfectly understood.

Britain's successes in the reigns of William and Anne surprised men all the more, because, prior to the Revolution of 1688, the rivalry of Parliament with the regal executive had been a cause not of efficiency but of weakness to England as a member of the European polity. Under James and Charles the First, and again under Charles and James the Second, the balance between King and Parliament made England of little account abroad.

The exception that proved the rule was the period of national efficiency under the Puritan Commonwealth. Then indeed the Parliamentary, or at least the Roundhead party, was supreme. Legislature and executive were united; and so, both before and during the period of Cromwell's personal rule, the Commonwealth Government wielded powers of taxation and of military and naval preparation which no Stuart King enjoyed. Then indeed the voice of England was heard and feared abroad. But the concentration of power in the hands of the Roundhead party was a temporary phenomenon, because it was based not on agreement but on force.

In 1660 the nation restored the balance of power between King and Parliament, between executive and legislative, in which Clarendon rejoiced as the perfection of our mixed constitution. And with this perfect balance returned financial inability to meet our engagements, national disarmament and divided counsels, making us the mock of our enemies and the despair of our friends. This balance of the constitution, more than the wickedness or carelessness of Charles II, lay at the root of the disasters of his reign. No country can remain half monarchical and half parliamentary without paying the penalty in want of power.

It was the Revolution of 1688 that gave to Great Britain freedom and efficiency together, because it tipped the balance of power permanently on to the side of Parliament, not as forty years before by the victory in arms of one party in the State over another, but by an agreement of Whigs and Tories, thrown into each other's arms by the fortunate folly of James II.

Thenceforward there was agreement in general policy between executive and legislative, between King and Parliament, as formerly under the Tudors; but this time it was Parliament that led and the King who had to follow.

Then and then only was it possible to reorganize the taxation and the credit of the country on a modern basis, to keep a small standing army on foot as well as a large fleet permanently afloat, to develop the organization necessary for a great empire, without giving rise to the jealousies which had frustrated similar attempts by Strafford and by Cromwell. Then and then only was it possible to induce the Scots to accept freely a legislative union with England, such as Cromwell had presented to them at the sword's point. At the same time, the attempt to force all Englishmen through the doors of a single State Church, the cause for so many generations past of faction and bloodshed, was at length abandoned as impracticable by the Toleration Act of 1689. The new era of latitudinarianism and religious peace greatly strengthened Britain's commercial, military and colonizing power as against that of France, then engaged in casting out the pick of her industrial population, the Huguenots, to aid the rising manufacturers of England, Holland and Prussia.

It is during the Stuart period that we emerge from the arena of English history into the ampler spaces of British history in its largest sense. The modern relations of England to Scotland and to Ireland respectively had been outlined under Elizabeth. Under the Stuarts they were deeply engraved on the imagination of posterity by a series of dramatic events. After many vicissitudes, we reached, in the reigns of William III and Anne, a defined and permanent relation of England to Scotland which still gives satisfaction to-day, and a relation of Britain to Ireland that fixed the lines along which all subsequent misfortunes developed.

In the same Stuart period, England planted populous and self-governing communities in North America. Englishmen began to live on the other side of the world, but under the English flag and under free English institutions. Before the Seventeenth Century closed they were learning so to adjust these institutions in New York and elsewhere, that Dutch and other foreigners were happy to live under the English flag. Already we see the germ of a free Empire, of a widespread Commonwealth of many races and religions, the ideal which both the United States and the British Empire of to-day realize in two different ways but in a kindred spirit. At the close of the Seventeenth Century, the colonies of other European countries were developing on very different lines. Neither religious nor political freedom existed in French Canada or Spanish America; the Dutch colonies in Africa had no political freedom, and in America relatively little. It was England who first planted the flag of liberty beyond the ocean.

The toleration of varieties in religion, though not admitted within England herself until 1689, was part of the very liberal practice both of the Stuart Kings and of their Parliamentary enemies in colonial affairs throughout this period. Anglican, Puritan or Roman Catholic, if discontented with his lot in the old country, could go to America with the good will of government and pray there according to his own fancy, but still under the old flag. Those who were regarded as troublesome at home, would be a strength and glory to England—on the other side of the ocean. This relatively liberal principle gave England a great advantage in the race for colonial supremacy.

Another reason why the governments of the Stuart epoch favoured the planting of colonies even by their political enemies, was the increasingly commercial and industrial character of the English polity at home. Massachusetts, New York, Virginia and the West Indian Islands were valued as important markets for English manufactures, at a time when the Parliamentary regime was bringing commerce more and more to the front as a prime consideration in domestic and foreign policy.

The Revolution of 1688 established the supremacy of the House of Commons, but left it handicapped with the system of 'rotten boroughs' which were bound to grow more unrepresentative as years rolled by. The idea of redistributing Parliamentary seats in accordance with the movement of population was buried in the grave of Cromwell. It followed that the House of Commons and the government which it controlled became increasingly iden-

tified with the landlord class who were able to control
the 'rotten boroughs.' If the Roundhead party had been
able to come to terms with the rest of the nation, a considerable element of democracy might have been introduced
into the English State. But after 1660 the democratic
spirit disappeared until the industrial changes of the
following century gave it a new form of life. The Revolution of 1688, though Parliamentary and liberal, was not
democratic. Partly for that reason the nascent democracies
beyond the Atlantic became increasingly out of touch
with the aristocratic Parliament at home, a difference ac-
centuated by differences in the prevalent form of religious
observance in old and New England.

The downfall first of King Charles, then of the Puritan
Commonwealth, and finally of James II in consequence of
attempts to override the squirearchy and the chartered
corporations, left the State weaker than it had been under
Elizabeth in its relation to the local government of the
countryside. The kind of control that Cecil and Walsingham had exercised over the doings, economic and other,
of the Justices of the Peace, was on the decline throughout
the Stuart era, and was conspicuously absent under the
early Hanoverians. The struggle of Parliament against
Crown had, indeed, from the first been rooted in a struggle
for local independence against the centre, a rebellion of
the squires against the Court and the Privy Council. In
that contest the yeomen and townsfolk had supported the
squires, especially that section of squires that was most
opposed to the Crown. The victory of Parliament, though
it made England more united and efficient for action
abroad, meant the subordination of the central authority
to the will of the localities as regards their domestic affairs.
And owing to the failure of the Puritan Revolution, the will
of the localities from 1660 onwards meant the will of the
squires.

The political victory over the House of Stuart finally
rested with the Whigs—the section of the squires who
were in alliance with London and the merchant community in matters of national policy. But the social power remained with the Justices of the Peace and the whole

body of the squires who as a mass were less Whig than Tory.

The political and religious tyranny of the monarch had been effectively curbed. The State Church no longer pretended to be co-extensive with the nation. The individual was protected in freedom of speech and person by Parliament victorious over the Crown, and by the Common Lawyers victorious over the Prerogative Courts. Henceforth, so far as the government was concerned, 'a man might speak his mind' as nowhere else in Europe and as never before in England. To abolish social tyranny was more difficult. But until the advent of the Industrial Revolution the need of social emancipation from the squirearchy was not seriously felt. Under the first two Georges Englishmen regarded human freedom as a science which they had perfected. That view, partly inspired by national pride in contemplation of a continent still domineered over by Kings, priests and nobles, was indeed erroneous. And yet it may fairly be doubted whether any set of men, since the victors of Marathon and Salamis, had done as much to establish human freedom on a practical basis as the Roundheads and Cavaliers, the Whigs and Tories of the Stuart Parliaments.

CHAPTER ONE

James I. Parliaments, Puritans and Recusants. Decline of English Sea-Power. The Spanish Match. Buckingham and the Thirty Years' War. Charles I. The King, Parliament and the Common Law. Coke and Eliot. Laud and Strafford.

KINGS: James I, 1603–25 (James VI of Scotland, 1567); Charles I, 1625–49

The keynote of Tudor government had been King-worship, not despotism. Monarchs without an army at the centre or a paid bureaucracy in the countryside were not despots, for they could not compel their subjects by force. The beefeaters of the Palace could guard the barge in which a rebellious nobleman or a fallen Minister was rowed from Whitehall steps to Traitors' Gate in the Tower, because the London 'prentices never attempted a rescue on the way. But they could not coerce a population of five millions, many of whom had sword, bow or bill hanging from the cottage rafters.

The power of the Tudors, in short, was not material but metaphysical. They appealed sometimes to the love and always to the loyalty and 'free awe' of their subjects. In the century that begins with Sir Thomas More and ends with Shakespeare, 'the deputy elected by the Lord' walks girt with a sunlike majesty. In his presence rank, genius and religion vail their pride, or lay their heads resignedly upon the block if the wrath of the Prince demands a sacrifice. In the following century genius and religion were to show a less obliging temper.

English King-worship was the secret of a family and the spirit of an age. It owed much to the political talents of the two Henrys and Elizabeth, and yet more to the need for national leadership in the period of transition from the mediæval to the modern world. When, after the death of the last Tudor, James I in his pedantry tried to materialize English King-worship into the political dogma of divine hereditary right, he spilt its essence in the dust.

England had found in the Tudor monarchs adequate representatives of her own spirit and policy; but the Stuarts, while claiming yet greater powers from a higher source than English law and custom, adopted policies at home and abroad which were in some of their main lines opposed to the wishes of the strongest elements in English society. The situation thus created forced to the front claims on behalf of the House of Commons which were as new to the constitution as the claims of divine hereditary right and autocratic power on behalf of the Crown.

Whether the conflict would have come to blows without the complication and inspiration of the religious question in a religious age, may perhaps be doubted. And certainly the novel claims on behalf of the Lower House would never have been advanced, still less made good, without the preparatory work of great constitutional law-yers like Coke and Selden, and great Parliamentarians—a new profession—like Eliot, Hampden and Pym. In the reigns of James and Charles the First the manor-houses of England produced a famous breed of men to sit in Parliament. Antiquarians in learning, and devotees of law, custom and precedent, they persuaded themselves and their countrymen that they were only claiming ancient privileges, and carrying out the spirit and even the letter of Magna Carta.[1] Historical science was yet in its infancy, for in fact they were innovators, unconsciously groping after a form of government new to England and new to the world. These men were not adventurers or self-seekers, and had more to lose than to gain by quitting their broad acres and private gardens; for Parliament was then the road not to power but to prison. The earnest personal character of their Protestant religion was combined with the cultured habit of mind and manner of gentlemen who were the ripe products of the English Renaissance. Only with the breach in the Parliamentary party in the second session of the Long Parliament [1641–42.] did these two elements begin to divide, and to form the Roundhead party on the one hand and the Constitutional Royalists on the other.

When James VI of Scotland, the comic offspring of the tragic union of Mary Queen of Scots with Darnley, succeeded to Elizabeth's throne as James I, the English rode in from far and near to catch a glimpse of their new sovereign on his slow progress from Edinburgh to London. [1603.] Those whose rank gave them access through the throng in the Midland market towns, found themselves in the presence of the good-natured, conceited, garrulous King, wise in book-learning but a poor judge of men, and so ignorant of England and her laws that at Newark he ordered a cut-purse caught in the act to be hanged without trial at a word from his royal mouth. Scotland indeed he knew and in part understood, but that knowledge

[1] See Vol. I., p. 231.

would be of less than no use to him in deciphering the political map of his southern kingdom.

His new subjects, however, were in no mood to be critical. For forty years and more they had lived in the black shadow of the question 'What will befall us when the Queen dies?' That anxiety had been aggravated and prolonged by Elizabeth's half-politic, half-coquettish dislike of the topic, and her irritation at the demand for an acknowledged heir, who might, she feared, divide the loyalty of her servants before she herself had finished with them. But Robert Cecil, wise son of a great father, had negotiated with James and smoothed the way for his undisputed accession. The relief felt by the English people at the peaceful continuity of things after Elizabeth's death is enshrined in the hyperbolical language of the Preface to the Authorized Version of the Bible.

Since infancy, James had reigned in Scotland as his mother's supplanter. He was in no sense her avenger or the successor to her policy. He came to England on the implied condition that he should continue the Elizabethan regime, and so he did, in so far as he was capable of understanding its true nature. Robert Cecil remained chief Minister and became Earl of Salisbury. Francis Bacon acted as another advisor to James, though his sage counsels of toleration in Church and State were too often neglected. Only the Elizabethan 'men of war' were discarded, and Raleigh was mewed up in the Tower, to gaze over the battlements of his terrace walk at the masts in the Thames below, and listen, sick with memory, to the sounds and songs of the mariners at their work.

The new sovereign brought with him one good gift that was personal to himself—the union with Scotland. Now that both crowns were set on one head, the long, romantic story of the Border came to an end. The moss-trooper's occupation was gone; he yielded place, on the moors that had known him, to the shepherd, who could now drive the flocks in security to the very ridge of the Cheviots and to the heart of the Debatable Land. But there was no union of the Parliaments, Churches or laws of the two Kingdoms, and the Scots were disliked by their fellow-subjects as proud, beggarly rivals for the royal favour. Not till the Eighteenth Century did the Empire begin to draw its full increase of strength from the union. But the close reactions of English upon Scottish and of Scottish upon English affairs make up a great part of the tangled and sanguinary skein of politics and religion under the Stuarts.

Scotland, in losing the presence of her King, who now became a mighty potentate at four hundred miles' distance from Edinburgh, was thereby subordinated to royal power as she had never been before. [1603.] From Whitehall the sixth James could keep the Scots nobles in awe, and at the same time prevent the Kirk from domineering over the State. To achieve the latter end, he successfully aroused the jealousy of the nobles against the small lairds and ministers who were laying hands on power through the medium of the ecclesiastical organization. He had established some humble and ill-paid Bishops, whose functions he gradually increased at the expense of the democratic Assemblies and Synods. In so doing he was protecting moderate and liberal elements in the religious life of Scotland, and preventing clerical tyranny, but he was also thwarting the only form of self-expression that was then open to the Scottish people. He did not, however, attempt to destroy the Presbyterian organization in the parishes, or to impose the English service book on the Scottish congregations. He would never have become the dupe of the strange delusion which betrayed Laud to his undoing, that there was 'no religion' in Scotland! There was a great deal more of it than James liked, and his only desire was to keep it in its place. He knew Scotland as he never knew England, and as his son Charles never knew either the one land or the other.

Not only did England remain *terra incognita* to James, but he never became aware of his ignorance. His mind was already formed when first he came to reign in Whitehall, and the flattery he received there confirmed his good opinion of his own penetration. Was not politics a science he had mastered? He was perpetually unbuttoning the stores of his royal wisdom for the benefit of his subjects, and as there was none who could venture to answer him to his face, he supposed them all out-argued. In Scotland he had had no experience of anything analogous to the English House of Commons. The Scottish 'Parliament' was in effect a court of record, and he could not appreciate the much higher position of the body bearing the same name in England. In Scotland the only opposition came from feudal Barons on their estates and Presbyterian preachers in their pulpits. Who then were these squires and lawyers in the House of Commons, with their talk about 'privilege' and 'precedents,' and 'fundamental laws of the realm,' refusing to let him raise money from his subjects except on their conditions, and striving to dictate to him on the weightiest affairs of ecclesiastical and foreign policy? He condescendingly pointed out to them their folly, and, when they disregarded his lectures, fumed over in angry words and deeds.

The relation of the House of Stuart to the Puritan movement in England was decided by one of the first acts of the new reign. The Church of England was then the principal arena of Puritan activity, and some leading clergy of the Establishment came to the Hampton Court Conference to beg for a legalized comprehension of men of those views within its borders. [1604.] They were in humble mood, no longer, as in the days of Cartwright and Penry, demanding the overthrow of episcopal government or the serious alteration of the Prayer Book. They knew it was impossible to capture the Church against the will of the King, but they asked for a certain permissive variety in ritual and parish work which would regulate their position.

It was a moment when a settlement might well have been made on the basis of comprehension, by a little widening of the borders of a State Church designed to be elastic, more especially since toleration outside the Church was not then regarded as permissible. To deny any legalized activity, either within or without the Establishment, to the movement which then had most influence on the laity and particularly on Parliament, was to sow the seeds of civil war. That is precisely what James did at Hampton Court. When he exclaimed 'No Bishop, no King!' he was well within his rights, but the existence of the episcopate was not then at issue. When he added in a fury 'I shall make them conform themselves or I will harry them out of the land,' he evoked a feud that cost the blood and tears of three generations, and incidentally transferred the sovereign power from King to Parliament.

The refusal of James to grant toleration either inside or outside the Establishment was not the outcome of personal adherence to High Church religion such as inspired his son Charles. He was still a Calvinist in doctrine, but he feared the political associations of the democratic and earnest type of religion of which he had seen so much more than he liked in Scotland. 'A Scottish Presbytery,' he cried at Hampton Court, 'agreeth as well with a monarchy as God with the Devil. . . . Then Jack, Tom, Will and Dick shall meet and at their pleasure censure me and my council.' Following on the abortive conference, three hundred English Puritan clergy were ejected from their livings. It was the beginning of 'non-conformity' on a large scale. Yet for another eighty-four years non-conformist worship remained illegal and subject to penalties; hence the earnestness and fury of all parties in the struggle for control of the State Church, since nowhere outside its bounds were men permitted to worship God.

Like so many who have been the cause of war and strife, James prided himself on being the 'peace-maker,' set on an intellectual eminence high above the angry passions of common men. He had tried his pacific hand on the position of his Roman Catholic subjects, promising them what he could not perform, a measure of toleration which was rendered impossible by the persecuting attitude he adopted towards Puritanism. A brief relaxation of the penal laws revealed the numbers of the crypto-Catholics and struck panic into the mass of his subjects. It was indeed a vicious circle. The Jesuit policy, aiming at the overthrow of the existing regime and the forcible extirpation of Protestantism in England, necessitated in the eyes of statesmen and people the degree of persecution customary under Elizabeth, and that persecution justified the Jesuit policy in the eyes of many Roman Catholics.

The re-enforcement of fines for 'recusancy,' after the royal promise of relief, so incensed a group of Catholic gentlemen of the Jesuit party that they formed the Gunpowder Plot, for the destruction of the King and the two Houses of Parliament together. In early Tudor times government could have been paralyzed or overturned by murdering the King; it was now felt to be necessary to murder Parliament too. The material preparations, made by men who had served as officers in the Spanish army in the Netherlands, were all complete when the conspiracy was revealed by a man of tender conscience. [1605.] 'The attempt but not the deed confounds us': it was the heaviest moral blow suffered by the Roman Catholics between the reigns of Mary Tudor and James II. Everything that had been said about the result of the Jesuit teaching seemed to plain Englishmen to be more than confirmed, and the Protestant feast of Guy Fawkes and the Fifth of November, decorously celebrated in the Church service, had democratic rites at the street corner in which the least mystical could heartily participate. Henceforth the anti-Roman passion in England remained a constant and often a determining factor in all the mazes of the long history of the House of Stuart.[2]

James disliked 'men of war' whether by land or sea. Until in his declining years he let the initiative pass to the volatile and ambitious Buckingham, he was the most thorough-going pacifist who ever bore rule in England. He wielded the sceptre and the pen, and held them both to be mightier than the sword. Of naked steel he had a physical horror, perhaps because he was born three months after the terrible day when armed men had burst in upon his mother's supper party and stabbed Rizzio under her

[2] There is direct reference in *Macbeth* (1606) to the Gunpowder Plot and the Jesuit doctrine of equivocation, which was much discussed at the trial of the Jesuit Garnet. 'Here's an equivocator, that could swear in both the scales against either scale; who committed treason enough for God's sake, but could not equivocate with heaven.' There are several similar references scattered about in the lesser dialogue of the play.

eyes. And not only was James most unwarlike in his own particular: but being a Scot of that period he had no conception of the importance of sea-power. He was the only Stuart King of England who utterly neglected the Navy.

Neglect of the Navy deprived his peace with Spain of some at least of its good effects. The terms of the treaty [1604.] that ended Elizabeth's war obtained for English merchants open trade with Spain and her possessions in Europe, and set some limit to the power of the Inquisition over them in Spanish ports. But the claims of the Elizabethan seamen to trade with Spanish America and the regions monopolized by Portugal in Africa and Asia were not mentioned in the treaty, and the enforcement of these claims no longer received countenance from the English government, which let the Royal Navy decay, while it suppressed privateering to the best of its ability.

In these circumstances, private war against Spanish and Portuguese was continued without the countenance of the State. In the American Indies, the 'buccaneers' found friends and bases in the West Indian Islands and in the New English colonies on the Northern mainland, so long as they maintained, however illegally, the interests and prestige of England against the Spaniard. But their high-seas robbery was not always directed against Spaniards alone, and before the end of the Stuart era the buccaneers had degenerated far from the traditions of Drake and Raleigh towards the melodramatic villainies of Teach and the black-flag pirates. Meanwhile the trade of South America remained, by law at least, closed to all save Spaniards; but as a result of Drake's victories, North America was in practice open to English, French and Dutch settlement.

On the coasts of Africa and the East Indies the Portuguese, then subjects of the King of Spain, endeavoured to prevent the subjects of James I from trading with the natives even in time of peace. But the English East India Company armed its ships for battle, and Captains Thomas Best and Nicholas Downton blew the Portuguese out of the water in decisive actions off Surat, and so established more regular trade with the native peoples of Asia than was as yet possible with the inhabitants of the guarded shores of the Spanish American colonies. [1611, 1614–15.]

In their hostilities against the Portuguese in the East, the English merchants had the Dutch as allies. But for the rest there was enmity between the trading communities of the two Protestant nations, which increased when the Portuguese power became of no account in the Indian seas. In the reigns of James and Charles I the merchant of the Dutch East India Company had greater resources behind him than his English rival. It was the day of the amazing wealth and power of little Holland, safe at last from Spain and not yet threatened by France. She led the world in the arts and sciences, and was mistress of the sea. The Dutch became the carriers for mankind, largely to the detriment of English shipping. They ousted the English from the Russian trade, which the Elizabethans had been the first to open. They fished where they liked, and often drove English fishermen from their own grounds. They expelled the Portuguese from Ceylon and the Spice Islands of the Molucca Sea, and in 1623 massacred the English there at Amboyna; James was helpless, and it was left to Cromwell, a generation later, to exact compensation for the long-remembered outrage.

But the English East India Company, when driven from the Spice Islands, pushed its trade on the Indian mainland. In James I's reign it founded a successful trading station at Surat, and in Charles I's reign built its Fort St. George, Madras, and set up other trading stations in Bengal. Such were the humble mercantile origins of British rule in India. But from the first these East India merchants were not mere 'quill-drivers'; they had destroyed the Portuguese monopoly by diplomacy at the courts of native potentates, and by the broadsides of their ships at sea.

Meanwhile James abandoned one by one the claims of the Royal Navy. The salute to the flag by other nations in the English seas was no longer demanded. The pirates from the 'Barbary' coast of North Africa raided in the Channel with impunity. The diplomatic protests of James about the treatment of his subjects by Dutch and Spaniards were laughed to scorn. Raleigh was beheaded to appease the Spanish Ambassador. [1618.] We were still a maritime community, but for thirty years we almost ceased to be a naval power.

One consequence was the deep and lasting resentment of the mariners and merchants against the House of Stuart, increased by the strong Protestant feeling of those who went down to the sea in ships. The new monarchy had abandoned the Elizabethan tradition at sea and in its dealings with Spain; the indignation produced by this change of attitude was not removed even when Charles I honestly appropriated the illegal Ship Money to the reconstruction of the Royal Navy which his father had allowed to decay. [1634–40.] In the hour of his need, the ships which Charles had built revolted to his enemies, and the seaports of England followed the lead of London and the House of Commons in the first Civil War with decisive effects on its fortunes. The ghost of Raleigh pursued the House of Stuart to the scaffold.[3]

James' peaceful policy was put to a cruel test by the outbreak of the Thirty Years' War. [1618–48.] At that crisis his neglect of the fighting fleet foredoomed his well-meant pacific diplomacy to failure, for why should Spain or Austria, France or Holland, listen to the man who had let England's national weapon rust, and could never prevent Spanish troops from sailing up the Channel to the Netherlands?

In its origin the Thirty Years' War was a resumption of the forward march of the great Catholic reaction to which England and Holland had set a limit in the days of Philip II. Its new protagonist was Austria, with Spain assistant. Bohemia and the Rhenish Palatinate were overrun, the

[3] The scene of Raleigh's execution in 1618, in Palace Yard, Westminster, was only a quarter of a mile from the space in front of Whitehall where Charles perished 30 years later. On the naval questions of James' reign and the peace with Spain, compare *Gardiner*, I. pp. 209–14, to Corbett, *Successors of Drake*, Chap. VII., and *England in the Mediterranean*, Vol. I., and Callender, *Naval Side of Br. Hist.*, Chap. VI.

first by Austrian arms, the second by Spaniards from the Netherlands, and cruel persecution put down Protestantism in both the conquered lands. The Prince who had been driven from these two dominions was none other than James I's son-in-law. His wife Elizabeth, and their infant children, Prince Rupert and Prince Maurice, began thus early their long life of disinherited wandering, which never undermined the great abilities and virtues of either mother or children.[4] James vainly thought to effect their restoration by ingratiating himself yet more with their enemies, by subjecting English policy more than ever to Gondomar the Spanish Ambassador, and finally by proposing to marry his surviving son Charles to the Spanish Infanta.

The Spanish match, as the English people clearly saw, would lead to Spanish heirs and Catholic Kings who would endeavour to undo the work of Elizabeth. But James in his old age and Charles in his youth were alike infatutated with George Villiers, whom they made Duke of Buckingham; and Buckingham's volatile imagination was for a time dazzled by the idea of giving peace to Europe through the Spanish match. When that dangerous project broke down after the escapade of the visit of young Charles and the favourite to Madrid [1623.], a marriage only one degree less fatal was carried through, Charles being mated to the zealous Romanist Henrietta Maria of France, destined to be the mother of many troubles to England and of more to the House of Stuart.[5]

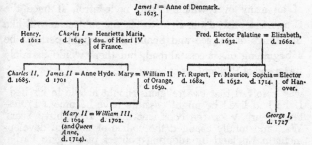

[5] Henry, Prince of Wales, who died in 1612, had told his father when he proposed to him a French marriage, that he

James I died in 1625, but his death made little difference, for Buckingham's influence was no less strong over King Charles. The fiasco of the Spanish match was followed by a period of warlike expeditions, rashly undertaken by Buckingham, who now cast himself for the part of Protestant hero abroad. [1625–28.] But armies and navies cannot be improvised, and the result was a series of disasters disgraceful to our arms. Some of these idle expeditions were directed to aid the Huguenots of La Rochelle against the France of Cardinal Richelieu. A wiser policy would have taken the Cardinal by the hand to resist the progress of the Catholic reaction conducted by the Hapsburg enemies of France beyond the Rhine. Other English expeditions directed against Spain were equally unsuccessful.

This tale of folly and disaster lowered the prestige of monarchy in England, and brought the Crown into fierce conflict with the House of Commons. The wars, such as they were, had led to unparliamentary taxation, billeting, arbitrary imprisonment and martial law over civilians, all of which were defined as illegal in the famous Petition of Right conceded by Charles to his Parliament in return for a vote of five subsidies. [1628.] Yet the Petition of Right, like the Magna Carta, was the beginning, not the end, of a struggle for the principles it enunciated.

The House of Commons was not yet strong enough to dictate the foreign policy of the Crown, but it was strong enough to be a clog on the effective conduct of war. For it could not but be jealous of the taxing power and fearful of an army over which it had no control. If once the Crown established the right to tax the subject at will like the Kings of France and Spain, there might perhaps be a beginning of success abroad, but there would certainly be an end of Parliaments at home.

was 'resolved that two religions should not lie in his bed.' If he had lived he might possibly have become a Protestant Henry V on the continent during the Thirty Years' War, and totally changed the course of political development in England by adopting policies pleasing to Parliament and so keeping it in voluntary subordination to the Crown.

The squires who composed the Lower House, no longer as in Elizabeth's reign guided by tactful Privy Councillors sitting in their midst, were becoming an opposition rather than an organ of government. Their homespun wit enabled them to understand the interests of their own country better than the courtiers, but they knew nothing of the continent, and showed little wisdom in their advice as to how the Protestant cause was to be maintained abroad. With a royal executive and a tax-granting Parliament at loggerheads and both of them grossly ignorant of foreign affairs, with no army and a diminutive Royal Navy, England was a cypher in European politics at this crisis.

Buckingham, while still preparing warlike expeditions to relieve Rochelle, was murdered by a Puritan fanatic, to the shameless joy of the common folk. [1628.] Charles, alienated from his people by the blood of his friend, soon abandoned warlike schemes that were clearly foredoomed to failure, and strove instead by rigid economy to govern without the Parliaments that he hated. In this design he was confirmed by a violent quarrel with the House of Commons of 1629; members held the Speaker down in the Chair while they passed the famous resolutions against 'Popery and Arminianism' and illegal Tonnage and Poundage, which the circumstances of the time associated together in the minds of men. No Parliament was held again for eleven years.

Contrary to the privileges of Parliament as respected by Queen Elizabeth, Sir John Eliot and his friends Valentine and Strode were kept in prison on account of what they had done in the House of Commons. [1632.] Eliot died in the Tower, refusing to obtain release by signifying his submission to these illegal proceedings, a martyr to English law and freedom; his two friends did not regain their liberty for eleven years. The hardness of Charles in his dealings with Eliot, whom he would not even suffer to be taken for burial to his Cornish home, can most charitably be regarded as a measure of his silent grief over the murdered Buckingham, for the Commons' leader had been inveterate and even furious in his eloquent attacks upon the favourite. But such a temper in Charles towards his subjects, even if humanly excusable, was very dangerous in a king who for a dozen years to come was to rule the land at his own mere will and pleasure.

By dispensing with Parliaments and by dismissing all Judges who dared to interpret the laws impartially, Charles removed every constitutional check upon his actions. None the less, the genius of the English Common Law was still the enemy of absolute regal power, and thanks to the work of Sir Edward Coke it had become the great ally of Parliament. If Parliament ever revived and conquered royal despotism, the spirit of the Common Law would revive with it and conquer the Prerogative Courts of Star Chamber, High Commission, Requests and Councils of Wales and the North. The professional jealousy felt by the lawyers in the courts where English Common Law was administered, against these Prerogative Courts dealing out a different law by different rules of procedure, had been deeply stirred by the leadership of the fierce and arrogant Coke, and had by him been closely connected with the Parliamentary party in the House of Commons. The Petition of Right, which was largely his work and expressed his doctrine, represented the spirit of the Common Law and the vigilance of Parliament combining to protect the subject of the land against arbitrary power.

The two men who had worked together to lay the foundations of Parliamentary resistance to the Crown were strangely different specimens of humanity. Eliot was the best type of well-to-do country gentleman, seeking nothing for himself, ardent and eloquent only in the public interest. Coke was an ambitious, pushing lawyer, a bully, and in his early days a sycophant. As Attorney-General to King James in 1603 he had attacked the prisoner Raleigh in a spirit worthy of Jeffreys, crying out to the lifelong foe of Spain, 'Thou hast a Spanish heart and thyself art a viper of hell!' Only one thing was dearer to Coke than promotion and power, and that was the Common Law. For it he sacrificed place and royal favour, stepping down off the Bench to make on the floor of the Lower House his alliance with the Puritan squires, a union whence sprang the liberties of England. [1616–28, d. 1634.]

In essence the quarrel was this: James and Charles held, with the students of Roman Law, that the will of the Prince was the source of law, and that the Judges were 'lions under the throne,' bound to speak as he directed them. Coke, on the other hand, in the spirit of the English Common Law, conceived of law as having an independent existence of its own, set above the King as well as above his subjects, and bound to judge impartially between them. Laws were alterable only by the High Court of Parliament. The Prerogative Courts, with their reception of Roman Law and their arbitrary procedure, belonged, he thought, to an alien civilization.

The battle between these two systems of law had to be fought out, for England could no longer, as under the Tudors, be governed by both at once. The first blood was drawn by Charles, who by packing the Bench seemed to have subjected the Common Law courts themselves to prerogative ideas. But the last word was to lie with the Long Parliament.

The English Common Law was a survival from the Middle Ages, while the Prerogative Courts and the increased deference for Roman Law had been a Renaissance product of Tudor times.[6] Coke and the Parliament men whom he schooled in his doctrines, stood therefore on conservative and national ground, against innovation of the type prevalent on the continent. Their appeal was made to the past,—to the past of England, not of the Roman Empire. Hence the antiquarian and historical character of their arguments, not always good history in detail, but consonant generally with a real English tradition down the ages. 'Coke on Littleton' and Coke's other Institutes were less universal and less forward-looking in their appeal than theories of the Rights of Man by Paine or Rousseau, but they have served to underprop a vast structure of progress and freedom in two hemispheres.

The legal issue between the King and his opponents was

[6] See pp. 24–25, above.

no less important than the financial or the religious, and in that litigious age it was well understood by the English people. The case arising from John Hampden's refusal to pay Ship Money, argued fully before the Exchequer Court, was followed in its details with intense excitement by a people better versed in legal matters than the King or his advisers were aware. [1637–38.] The ruling made by the majority of the Judges against Hampden and in favour of the levy of Ship Money without Parliamentary sanction, stood condemned by public opinion. But for a short while longer the ruling enabled the King to exact the tax and to reconstruct the fighting Navy. The object was worthy, but it was not by such expedients that English maritime supremacy could be restored and maintained by a King who had lost the loyalty of his subjects. It was a necessary part of the new royal policy to abstain from all foreign entanglements, and allow the Thirty Years' War to pass from crisis to crisis with England as a spectator, even on occasions when a mere naval demonstration would have had important results. The adherence of the sea-going population and of the Royal Navy itself to the Parliamentary side of the quarrel bore witness to the patriotic character of Hampden's refusal to pay an illegal tax.

[1629–40.] Laud and Wentworth, the two men with whom Charles' period of autocratic rule is associated, were of a very different order of character and intellect from Buckingham.

Archbishop Laud was a great churchman, who unfortunately was called upon by the then relations of Church and State to play also the part of statesman, for which he was unsuited alike by temper and understanding. His memory is cherished as the founder of the High Church party in the religious life of the Church of England. But the historian is principally concerned with the political consequences of his ecclesiastical policy, which in a Church that was then by law co-extensive with the nation could not fail to be of the utmost peril and importance. It was indeed the chief cause of the Civil War, because it provoked the furious reaction of armed Puritanism in which Laud himself perished.

If James I suffered as King of England from having been bred a Scot, Laud as Archbishop suffered from having been bred a don. He treated broad England as he had been permitted to treat Oxford, but it is easier to trim a University to pattern than a nation of grown men. The ritual side of worship in the parish churches was increased by episcopal command and visitation, while evangelical practice, preaching and lecturing were effectively prohibited within the Church. At the same time nonconformist worship outside the Church was persecuted with increasing rigour. The emigration of the Puritans to America in these years was a measure of the degree to which Laud made life intolerable to them in England.[7] Owing to his activities it became impossible for a Puritan to live in his native country and worship God freely, at a time when English Puritanism was producing men of the calibre of Cromwell and Milton, Hampden and Pym. High Anglicanism had already its men of learning and its poets, but as yet it had not won the heart of any large section of the squires, still less of the people at large. Even men like Sir Edmund Verney, Falkland and Hyde, who in time of need showed themselves ready to fight to save the Prayer Book, were hostile to Laud and his over-busy Bishops.

The zeal of the Primate roused against himself and against the King, not only the strongest religious sentiments of that generation, but the feeling, always very strong in England, that resents the interference of the religious in their neighbour's affairs. Laud, who could never be either weary or prudent in well-doing, revived the activity of the spiritual courts, and summoned influential laymen to answer for their sins before the priesthood. The Church Courts, with a truly catholic indifference, incurred the odium of the Puritan precisian, the loose-liver, and the ordinary layman who had hoped that the Reformation had delivered him from clerical control. Meanwhile Bishops

7 See Chap. V., pp. 226–27, below.

were beginning to replace nobles and commoners as the favourite councillors of the Crown. And in many parishes the new school of Laudian clergy enraged the squires by setting themselves up as rival sources of authority. The censorship of the press, which was then in episcopal hands, was busily employed by Laud to silence voices opposed to his own ideas. In everything Englishmen were to toe the line drawn by a particular school of clergy. There seemed, in short, to be an attempt on foot to restore the mediæval relation of the clergy to the laity, and such a movement gave bitter offence alike to future Cavaliers and future Roundheads. The anti-clerical feeling which in 1661 swelled the popularity of the restored Anglican Church as the alternative to 'the rule of the Saints,' in 1640 added force to the Puritan uprising against Laud's domination.

While the Archbishop persecuted the Puritans with meticulous rigour, the growing influence of Charles' French Queen stopped the persecution of Roman Catholics. The consequence was that they everywhere raised their heads: there were conversions, especially in the upper ranks of society, and Henrietta Maria's religion became fashionable at Court. Meanwhile the most determined enemies of the Church of Rome were pouring out of the country to America by thousands every year. An indefinite continuance of such a state of things must, men thought, lead to the return of England to the Papal fold. Laud did not desire that, but he applied no remedy and suffered accordingly in men's estimation.

In these circumstances the fortunes of the High Church party, a minority attempting to coerce the principal forces in the nation, became identified with the cause of personal despotism and with the royal attempt to be rid of Parliament. The Laudian clergy preached up the doctrine of divine right and prerogative power. To crush Laud's opponents, recourse was often had to the reserves of royal authority in the Star Chamber and the Ecclesiastical High Commission: the Star Chamber, once popular under the Tudors, incurred the furious hatred of the Londoners for its cruel punishment of Prynne and Lilburne. [1637.] The Puritans, on the other hand, became more than ever Parliament men, looking forward to the time when circumstances would compel Charles to summon the two Houses: all their hopes lay in the thought that—

That two-handed engine at the door
Stands ready to smite once and smite no more.

The political connection of the two religious parties with King and Parliament respectively, though dictated in each case by the pressure of circumstances, was in each case a natural alliance. The authoritarian element in religion to which Laud gave renewed prominence had affinities to regal absolutism, and Parliamentary power in the State answered to the popular control of the Church, whether Presbyterian or Congregational. Between these two parties in Church and State floated indefinite masses of moderate opinion, which were frequently to decide the balance of power in the great years now coming on.

Thomas Wentworth, afterwards Earl of Strafford, had been an active member of the House of Commons in opposition to Buckingham, whose weak and mischievous rule he abhorred. But while he felt acutely the evils of royal favouritism, he did not in his heart believe that an assembly of 500 elected persons could govern a great kingdom. Besides, he was ambitious, and thought himself more fit to rule than either Parliament or Buckingham. He who had supported the Petition of Right spent the rest of his life in trying to subvert its principles. He planned to give Britain such a royal administration as Richelieu was then giving to France and as Bismarck long afterwards gave to Germany. If this great man had been Charles' chief Minister during the years when Laud was his chief ecclesiastical adviser, he might have found means to build up an army and a bureaucracy dependent on the Crown, for lack of which the autocratic system collapsed at the first touch of determined resistance. Fortunately for the liberties of Great Britain, Wentworth only became Charles' right-hand man when it was too late, after the Scots had risen with success and Englishmen had begun to realize how unanimous was their own discontent. [SEPT. 1639.]

During the previous decade Wentworth had been employed by the King first as President of the Council of the North and then as ruler of Ireland. In these proconsular capacities he had shown a fine administrative vigour and a ruthless contempt for opinion and intolerance of all opposition; to this method he gave the name of 'Thorough,' while others called it tyranny. In Ireland such fearless disrespect of persons might have been useful as the instrument of an enlightened policy. But his policy was enlightened only on its economic side. Otherwise his injustice alienated Catholics and Protestants alike.

The native Irish, when he first came to rule the island, were already deeply embittered by the proscription of their religion and by the land policy of successive governments, who had handed over more and more of their soil to British landlords. [1632.] The great plantation of Ulster in James' reign—the only part of the English garrison system that survives to our own day—had fixed a colony of Londoners in the good town of Derry, and some thousands of hard-working Presbyterian Scots on lands whence the Irish had been cleared. [1608–10.] The Scots from across the narrow seas—some of whose ancestors had been in North Ireland long ago[8]—formed the most stable part of British colonization there, because they were prepared to till the soil themselves, and not merely to exploit and rack-rent the tillers.

Wentworth harried the Protestants of Ulster for their sympathy with the Puritans of Britain, but he had not set out to propitiate the Irish Catholics. On the contrary, he planned new plantations in Connaught to deprive the natives of the lands which previous governments had left them. The fact that he ended by raising an Irish Catholic army to subdue Great Britain, certainly did not mean that he came a step nearer to solving the Irish problem than any other statesman of that century. The native Catholic rising of 1641, a terrible event in itself and yet more terrible in its consequences and its memory, was a measure of Wentworth's failure in Ireland.

[8] See Vol. I., p. 82.

Laud and Wentworth were close friends and allies, and laboured together to set up the Prerogative and its courts above Parliament and the Common Law. Laud, on his translation to Canterbury, had written to Wentworth that the Church was overmuch 'bound up in the forms of Common Law,' and his friend had replied:

'No such narrow considerations shall fall in my counsels as my own preservation, till I see my master's power and greatness set out of wardship and above the exposition of Sir Edward Coke and his Year-Books, and I am most assured the same resolution governs in your lordship. Let us then in the name of God go cheerfully and boldly. . . . And thus you have my Thorough and Thorough.'

BOOKS FOR FURTHER READING: Gardiner's *History of England*, 1603–42 (ten vols.); Holdsworth, *History of English Law*, Vol. V. (on Coke); Figgis, *Divine Right of Kings*; Gwynn, *History of Ireland*; Bagwell, *Ireland under the Stuarts*, 3 vols.; *Archbishop Laud Commemoration*, 1895 (Essays on Laud by Creighton and others); Dowden, *Puritan and Anglican*; John Forster, *Sir J. Eliot*; Traill, *Strafford*; G. M. Trevelyan, *England under the Stuarts*.

CHAPTER TWO

> England and Scotland. The Scottish Revolt. The Long Parliament. First Session: Fall of the Prerogative System and Execution of Strafford. Second Session: The Church Question and the Division of Parties

The divergent courses which the Reformation had followed in England and in Scotland respectively, did much to complicate the politics of the succeeding era, when the rule of a single King over both countries constantly pointed towards ecclesiastical union that was, in fact, always impossible.

At the Reformation the laity on both sides of the Border had asserted their will against the mediæval clergy, but in two very different ways. In England the Church had kept the outline of its ancient organization, remaining purely clerical in its internal structure; it followed that the control of the laity over its liturgy and doctrine had to be exercised not from within but from without, through Crown and through Parliament. In Scotland, on the other hand, the laity took an active part in Church organization and government. Only so could there be any control of religion by the laity, because they had no real Parliament to speak for them, and in the days of Mary Stuart they could not trust the Crown as contemporary Englishmen trusted Elizabeth. The Scottish nobles had indeed helped to overthrow the old religion; but the new religion had been fashioned, not from outside by the Crown or nobles, but from inside the Church by a democracy of ministers and laymen.

It was natural, therefore, that the English, whether Royalists or Parliamentarians, Anglicans or Puritans, should be Erastian in the sense that they wished the State to control the Church. It was equally natural that the Scottish Presbyterian party wished the Church to control the State. In these circumstances neither the Stuart Kings nor their enemies ever succeeded in imposing a uniform religious settlement on the whole island.

In those days, when the idea and practice of representation were still at an early stage of development, the English were most nearly represented by their ancient Parliament, and the Scots by their novel Church. But this difference of the position at the two ends of the island was not understood by the rulers of Britain. James I, having been brought up in Scotland, had supposed that the English Parliament, like the Scottish, existed to obey the Privy Council. His son Charles, having been brought up in England, made the corresponding error of supposing that the Scottish Church could, like the English, be moulded by royal command. Confident in the power he had recently assumed as autocratic ruler of England, and knowing that the Parliament of Edinburgh was of no account, he deceived himself into supposing that he could act as absolute monarch in Scotland, even in matters of religion. His attempt to impose Laud's English Prayer Book on the Scottish Church at the very moment when he was trying to get rid of the English Parliament, outraged both nations at once, each at the point where it was strongest and most susceptible, and broke his power in both Kingdoms. [1637–40.]

The revolt against Charles and Laud north of the Tweed took the form of a religious Covenant, and of action by the Church Assembly; the nation had to be organized on an ecclesiastical basis, because organs of political life were lacking in Scotland. This state of things naturally tempted the Church, after she had liberated the country from a foreign yoke, to claim practical control of the State and to show a most ugly temper of interference and intolerance. This in turn enabled Charles I and Charles II after him to rally the Scottish Cavalier party, in the days of Montrose and of Claverhouse, to resist the tyranny of religion. Against it the Cavaliers of the Restoration erected the tyranny of the Privy Council. The terrible feuds of the Scottish factions went on with many vicissitudes, till the Revolution settlement of 1689 established Presbyterianism as the national religion, but made it the subordinate partner of the State.

In Stuart England, where the Church never aspired to independence of the State, the religious quarrel lay between Crown and Parliament. One part of the English people demanded, through Parliament, to have the Church made purely Protestant in its services, and more representative of the laity in its internal structure. The Crown resisted this demand, backed by another part of the nation zealous for the Prayer Book, though by no means for the whole of Laud's politico-ecclesiastical system. This situation forced to the front a question that men had begun to ask themselves under Elizabeth: if Crown and Parliament disagreed, which had the right to remodel the Church of England? That was one issue fought out in the English Civil War. The other was the purely political question—is Crown or Parliament to nominate the executive and control the armed force? In practice the two issues were inseparable; to take a side on one involved taking the corresponding side on the other.

The Scottish revolt of 1638–40 began the British Revolution. Until the Scots had successfully defied Charles, in arms upon their own Border, there had been no signs of resistance in England, though many of discontent. For Stuart England had no centres of opposition except Parliament, which was in abeyance. English feudalism was dead and buried. Harry Percy's spur was cold. The squires as a class were the most peaceful and law-abiding of men,—agriculturists, sportsmen, sometimes lawyers, but very seldom soldiers. The King, it is true, had no army to enforce his will, but the habit of obedience to the Crown was the great inheritance from the Tudor age. It had been the custom in mediæval England for districts or persons with a grievance against government to rise in arms, but that tradition had not survived the reign of Elizabeth. If, therefore, the modern English were deprived of Parliament, they would be slaves to absolute power as their ancestors had never been before.

Scotland supplied what England no longer possessed, a rough and hardy population, accustomed to take up arms in their own defence. The two nations were the complement one of the other. The Scots could boast of no independent political institutions, no habit of obedience to good laws; the English had so long enjoyed peace under Parliament and the Common Law that they were slow to defend their privileges with the sword. England was neither feudal nor democratic; the fighting spirit of Scotland was composed of both those elements, formidably interfused.

Until very recent times every burgher and peasant in Scotland had possessed weapons which he was accustomed to employ in racial war or private broil, and along the Highland Line these habits still prevailed. Everywhere the nobles and leading gentry of Scotland, like those of England in the Wars of the Roses, still had retainers and tenants accustomed to follow them to war. In 1638 these feudal chiefs stood for the Kirk against the Crown. They had been alienated by Laud, under whose influence nobles had been superseded by Bishops on the Scottish Privy Council, and lay possessors of former Church lands had been threatened with resumption. Moreover, the nobles were true Scots, and the young Montrose himself took a leading part in armed resistance to the English-hearted King and his Prayer Book.

When Parliament was not sitting, the English were like sheep without a shepherd, but in Scotland the Church supplied a ready-made organization for political activity in every parish. It was the people themselves who had made the original Reformation by the strong hand, and it was all in the national tradition to defend it now by the same means. The Covenant with God was renewed in 1638 and embraced all ranks from highest to lowest. In every parish men signed it, weeping and lifting their right hands to heaven. When the Scots display emotion, something real is astir within them. Indeed the country had not been so moved since the days of Wallace and Bruce.

[1638.] The Church Assembly at Glasgow, to which the lay members came up armed and attended, defied the King as the Long Parliament in England defied him four years later. When he dissolved the Assembly, it sat on, declared Episcopacy abolished and restored the full Presbyterian government of the Church. The action of the Glasgow Assembly was supported by the Earl of Argyle, the head of the Campbells, the most powerful fighting clan in the Highlands. That day he began the connection of his House with the Presbyterian and popular cause in the Lowlands, an alliance which for more than a century to come remained a constant and often a determining factor in Scottish history. Thenceforth till the time of Culloden the clans hostile to the Campbells gravitated for that reason towards the party of the Stuart Kings.

Not the least of the causes that wrought Charles' downfall was this: Scotland, still as poor as a thin soil and mediæval methods of agriculture could make her, and still without any considerable trade either with England or across the sea, sent forth in those days her most adventurous sons to serve abroad, not then as cashiers and foremen throughout a far-flung British Empire, but as captains and ancients in the armies of Gustavus Adolphus and other Protestant champions on the continent. These men came swarming home, eager to employ their professional skill in saving their native land from English outrage. Their leader was 'that old, little, crooked soldier,' Alexander Leslie. He and they speedily put a face of disciplined war on the enthusiasm of the Scots, and camped them advantageously on Dunse Law, ready to dispute against Charles the passage of the Tweed. [1639.]

The England of the pacific James and his son had bred few 'men of war': Englishmen lived at home on the fat of the land, or traded oversea, or emigrated to America. There was no nucleus of a standing army, and failure attended the belated efforts of Charles and Strafford to improvise, without money and from a disaffected and unwarlike people, a force to match the army of the Covenant.

Wentworth, who was at length made Earl of Strafford, had been called over to England to be his master's right-hand man at this crisis. But he did not cease to act as ruler of Ireland, where he continued to harry the Scots of Ulster with persecution to enforce on them the 'Black Oath' of passive obedience unknown to the law. At the same time he raised regiments of Celtic Irish to coerce the King's disobedient subjects in either island, the first of a series of Roman Catholic armies whose threatening shadow from oversea so often prejudiced the cause of the House of Stuart, without ever striking a formidable blow for it in Britain.

As yet the general temper of England had found no means of expression. Strafford guessed it wrongly. He advised Charles to summon Parliament, in the hope that it would tamely provide the money to subdue Scotland. The 'Short Parliament,' [AP. 13–MAY 5, 1640.] however, revealed the unanimity of English discontent, and was peremptorily dismissed, but not before Pym had spoken on the floor of the House the memorable words: 'The powers of Parliament are to the body politic as the rational faculties of the soul to man.'

For a few months longer, Strafford, though suffering from untimely illness, strove single-handed to make the system of autocracy function again. But its wheels were clogged and would no longer revolve. The recent Parliament, though it had come and gone in a breath, had lifted a curtain, and henceforth the nation knew its collective mind and strength. Strafford's desperate efforts to gather round him some reliable regiments in his own Yorkshire, were countered by the army of the Covenant which crossed the Tweed,—Montrose the foremost horseman on the English shore—and occupied Northumberland and Durham. [AUG. 1640.] There the Scots cannily sat down, demanding as the price of evacuation not only their own terms but money; for money, as they knew, was a commodity which Charles could obtain only if he submitted to a new English Parliament, certain to be more angry and more formidable than the last.

The Short Parliament had been summoned to vote taxes to fight the Scots; the Long Parliament was called to buy them out of the country. But redress of grievances would certainly have to precede supply, and in the autumn of 1640 redress of grievances meant a revolution of undefined scope in Church and State. [NOV. 1640.]

The Long Parliament was not destined to prove, as half its members hoped, a turning-point in English religion comparable to the Tudor Reformation, though it did clear the way for the great incident in English religious history— the Puritan Revolution, the parent of the Free Churches of later times. On the other hand, the Long Parliament is the true turning-point in the political history of the English-speaking races. It not only prevented the English monarchy from hardening into an absolutism of the type then becoming general in Europe, but it made a great experiment in direct rule of the country and of the Empire by the House of Commons. In the course of that experiment the Long Parliament successfully organized the largest military operations ever till then conducted by Englishmen, in a four years' war against the King. After the victory it failed to make a permanent settlement at home, but it made England feared and honoured abroad. After all those memorable years, the House of Stuart might be restored, but it would never again be possible to govern the country without the participation of the House of Commons.

In all the actions of the Long Parliament it was the

Commons who led, and the Lords who followed with ever-growing reluctance. We have then to ask, how did a debating assembly, which under the Tudors had passed the Bills drawn up by Privy Councillors of the Crown, and since Elizabeth's death had acted only as an opposition,—how did an assembly so numerous, so plebeian and so inexperienced succeed in taking hold of the helm of State and riding the most terrible storm in English history?

One reason why the House of Commons was able to assume the government of the country has, until recently, attracted less attention than its importance deserves. The late Tudor and early Stuart Parliaments had made great progress in forms of procedure, especially by developing the Committee system. In 1640 the Lower House was no mere debating society, but an elaborately organized business body of the modern type, capable of conducting affairs as no mediæval House of Commons could possibly have done. For forty years past, Parliaments had no longer been content to have their work prepared for them by Privy Councillors, but had thrashed out subjects for themselves in committee, and so learnt to produce practical Bills and policies of their own.[1]

In the second place the Long Parliament had at its doors an enthusiastic ally, London, already the first city in the world, surpassing any other English town many times over in wealth, population and mental activity. It was in the London of these eventful years that Milton, the greatest of Londoners born, had his vision of England as 'an eagle

[1] The distinguished American Historian, Professor Notestein, who has made this subject his own, writes (*Journal of Sir S. D'Ewes,* 1923, Introduction): 'It can hardly be said too often that the pre-Elizabethan House of Commons was a somewhat rudimentary body, and that the Long Parliament was in many ways a complex modern organization. A knight of the shire in 1558 who stepped into a mediæval Commons probably would not have felt much out of place, but a Commoner of 1640 would; he would be more at home at Westminster to-day. It was in the years between that the enormous growth took place,—the rapid extension of Committees and of the work of Committees; the hitting upon and utilization of that wonderful device, the Committee of the Whole,' etc.

mewing her mighty youth,' as 'a noble and puissant nation rousing herself like a strong man after sleep and shaking her invincible locks.' London was the nursery of almost every movement of that time, in whatever part of the country it had first seen light; and 'correspondency with London' was alleged as the reason why the Roundhead party dominated most of the boroughs of England during the Civil War. Some may think that the effervescence of London's wit and passion drew Parliament down strange and questionable courses, but none can deny that the protection which it gave to the Houses was faithful and effective.

And, lastly, there were upon the benches in 1640 members of old experience, who had sat with Eliot and Coke in committee and debate, some of whom chanced to be men of high ability, character and courage. Pym, perhaps the strongest Parliamentary leader in history, and Hampden, the best-beloved in that choice assembly of England's best, backed by members of the type and temper of Strode and Cromwell, were not afraid to seize and wield the power of the State. The time for mere criticism had passed, and the insufficiency of Charles' signature to Statutes had been proved. Since the struggle now was for power, these men did not shrink from evoking mob passion and armed force to protect what they did from the royal reaction which had destroyed the work of every previous Stuart Parliament.

During the first session of the Long Parliament [NOV. 1640–AUG. 1641.], Pym and Hampden worked in alliance with Hyde and Falkland, a couple not unlike to themselves in ability, character and destiny. It is hard to say which pair of friends had in the end the most influence on the evolution of modern Britain. The 'constitutional Cavaliers' of 1642 were in 1640 as determined as the future Roundheads to bring about the fall of Strafford, and to abolish the Star Chamber, the High Commission and the whole Prerogative system. All were opposed to Laud, who was committed to the Tower after impeachment by the unanimous vote of the Lower House, but members were early made aware of differences among themselves on religion, and were glad to postpone the settlement of the Church till the State had first been made safe.

The work of this session, so far as it extended, was built upon the rock. It was never undone, for it was work of Puritans and moderate Episcopalians, of Roundheads and constitutional Cavaliers acting in union. It registered the great irreversible victory of 'Sir Edward Coke and his Year-Books' over Strafford and the Prerogative courts. The Star Chamber, the High Commission, the prerogative jurisdiction of the Councils of Wales and of the North were abolished by Statute, and the illegality of Ship Money and Tonnage and Poundage without Parliamentary sanction was declared beyond all cavil. Thus was the Crown put back, to use Strafford's phrase, into 'wardship' to the Common Law, and made dependent on, though not necessarily subordinate to, Parliament. The first session struck an exact balance of the constitution, the same which was restored in 1660 by Hyde, the great Common Lawyer, who believed in a precise counterpoise of Crown and Parliament. Pym, on the other hand, believed that the essential power must pass on to Parliament, or mere confusion would prevail.

The other work of the first session was the trial, attainder and execution of Strafford. In that high tragedy, unsurpassed for historical and human interest in the political annals of any time or land, Falkland and many of the future Cavaliers acted in union with Hampden and Pym. They held it necessary that the man should die who might yet, by his vigour and genius, restore the despotic powers of the Crown. Already the King was engaged in the Army Plot to rescue Strafford and dissolve Parliament. The first thing to be expected, if Strafford lived, was that as soon as Parliament was up, Charles would let him out of prison and restore him to office. So argued the Earl of Essex, typical of many members of the Upper House who feared a restoration of Strafford's insolent personal hegemony over the nobles of the land; the Earl's conclusion was that 'stone dead hath no fellow.' It was not a policy of mean revenge, like that which four years later sent Laud to the scaffold. Strafford's enemies were in deadly earnest, because while he lived they and all they strove for were in jeopardy.

They did not scruple at the last to allow mob violence to extort Charles' signature to the Act of Attainder [MAY 1641.] by which his great servant perished.

With the Act of Attainder against Strafford, the King passed another Bill which forbade the dissolution of the existing Parliament without its own consent. These two measures, the first of them the bitterest humiliation of Charles' life, seemed to make the position of Parliament secure. And so it would have been, but for the religious difference which in the second session split into two hostile parties the hitherto solid phalanx of the constitutionalists. In the Commons the Puritans won, by small majorities, divisions in favour of the Root and Branch Bill abolishing episcopacy, and the Grand Remonstrance. [NOV. 1641.] The Grand Remonstrance demanded that the King's Councillors should be persons trusted by Parliament, and that there should be a Parliamentary reformation of the Church, on what may be described as Erastian-Presbyterian principles. It is easy now to see that the times required a compromise on religion, and that England had outgrown any orthodox strait-waistcoat which could be devised by either party. Unfortunately, it was not clear then, and no serious effort was made by Puritan or Anglican either for comprehension within, or for toleration without, the borders of the Church. Moderate Episcopalians devoted to the Prayer Book, like Falkland and Hyde, saw no way of defending their religion but to go into complete opposition to Hampden and Pym.

The religious question decided the attitude of many towards the command of the armed forces of the Kingdom—the other great problem of the second session. Was King or Parliament to control the militia of the towns and shires, and the regular army which must forthwith be raised to suppress the rebellion in Ireland? For the Catholics there had risen to recover their lands; the Ulster plantation and the whole English interest were in the direst jeopardy, and some thousands of Protestants had perished. [OCT. 1641.] Law and custom assigned the command of the armed forces to the King. But if Charles had the power of the sword and Parliament had not, how much longer would he respect the concessions he had recently made? He himself answered the question by his rash and illegal attempt to arrest Pym, Hampden, Hazlerigg, Holles and Strode on the floor of the House of Commons, which might well have been stained with blood that day by the bravoes Charles had brought with him to 'pull them out by the ears,' had not the Five Members received warning and been carried by boat from Parliament stairs to the safe shelter of the City and its trainbands. [JAN. 4, 1642.]

Charles fled to the North, leaving London and Westminster to be the focus of his enemies' power and authority. Civil war was certain, and men began to choose their side, some with enthusiasm, many with dubious sighs and searchings of heart, while the majority manifested a strong desire to remain neutral if they possibly could.

Lovers of the Prayer Book for the most part remained neutral or drew sword for the King. After the disastrous fiasco of the Five Members, Charles, for the six months before the fighting began, put his case into the wise and constitutional hands of lawyer Hyde, who issued manifestos of a moderate and legal character. [JAN.–AUG. 1642.] This and the high-handed proceedings of Pym in preparation for war won the King many friends among his late opponents; but others reflected that Charles' word was of no value, and that the moment the sword was drawn it was in the nature of war that the control of his party should pass from Hyde and the lawyers to the swordsmen and friends of despotic power, from Falkland and the moderate Episcopalians to the High Laudian and Romanist devotees. Falkland sought death in battle for the King, because he could not bear to witness either his triumph or his defeat. Among the Roundheads also were many who lived to rue the victory of their cause. Moderates may well be loath to begin wars, for it is always extremists who end them.

Was it then impossible for Parliamentary power to take root in England at a less cost than this national schism and appeal to force, which, in spite of many magnificent incidents, left England humanly so much the poorer and less noble in twenty years time? It is a question which no depth of research or speculation can resolve. Men were what they were, uninfluenced by the belated wisdom of posterity, and thus they acted. Whether or not any better way could have led to the same end, it was by the sword that Parliament actually won the right to survive as the dominant force in the English constitution.[2]

CHAPTER THREE

The Great Civil War, 1642–46

Although there were sots and swaggerers enough in the King's armies, and hypocrites and fanatics enough among those of Parliament, and plain self-seekers in both camps, nevertheless upon the whole the Cavalier, with his unselfish loyalty and careless valour, the Roundhead, with his self-discipline and steady zeal for the public cause, present a favourable contrast to the emigrant noble and the Jacobin of the French Revolution. For the English Civil War was not the collapse of an out-worn society in a chaos of class hatred and greed, but a contest for political and religious ideals that divided every rank in a land socially sound and economically prosperous.

The causes of the war were not economic, and were only indirectly social. Nevertheless the older aristocratic connection was apt to favour the King, while the world that had arisen since the Reformation was apt to favour the Parliament. The new world was centered at London, while the old was strongest in North and West at the greatest distance from the orbit of the capital.

In every shire the landlords were the leaders on both sides when the war began. The majority of the nobles fought for the King; but a body claiming to be the House

[2] In the final division of opinion on the resort to arms, the Roundhead majority in the Commons was very much larger than it had been for the Grand Remonstrance. Professor Firth calculates that in the war, 300 of the Lower House were for Parliament and 175 for the King, although only thirty Peers supported Parliament and eighty the King. Of the shire members the very great majority stood by the Parliament against the King.

of Lords still sat at Westminster to make Pym's Parliament complete, and noblemen like the Earls of Essex and Manchester, and Lord Brooke, commanded the earlier Roundhead armies. The great strength of the royal party lay in the more rustic squires of ancient lineage, who had least connection with the mercantile community, while Parliament usually received the allegiance of squires more closely connected with the world of business—some of them recently risen into the landlord class and still twitted with their plebeian origin. The towns were predominantly Roundhead, especially those connected with the sea or the cloth trade. Most cathedral and some market towns were Cavalier. The tenant farmers followed their landlords into either camp. The agricultural labourer or cottager was for all effective purposes a neutral, except when he was pressed or bought to trail a pike or carry a musket in the 'poor foot.' The freehold yeomen supplied the best and most zealous fighting stuff in the ranks of both parties, particularly in Cromwell's regiments of East Anglian horse.

The North and West were strongest for the King, except the Puritan clothing districts and seaports. Before the time of Wesley, 'the Celtic fringe' was untouched by Puritan ideals; so Charles drew his best infantry from the loyal Cornish volunteers, and filled up many of his other regiments of foot from the sturdy poverty of the Welsh hills. The South and East were firmly secured for Parliament, owing to the strength of London's arm in the Home Counties, and the activity of Oliver Cromwell in the Eastern Association of which Cambridge was the centre. But in every shire and town of the land there were two parties, and many local wars were waged more or less independent of the central campaigns. A single energetic man often determined the allegiance of a whole district, for the neutrals were many and the would-be neutrals more. Under their influence 'county treaties' were sometimes made to exclude the war from a given area, but the rising tide soon swept down these frail barriers of peace.

All the Roman Catholics were for the King, and more particularly for the Queen, who was the real head of their party. They were strong in the Northern counties and in

Lancashire, where the local civil war between feudal Catholicism and the Puritanism of the clothing districts was exceptionally bitter. Since the fines prescribed in the penal laws had been suspended during the personal rule of Charles I, the old Catholic gentry and nobles were able to pour their accumulated wealth into his empty war-chest. The Earl of Worcester, enjoying a princely rent-roll of £24,000 a year, saved the King from financial ruin in 1642 by a generosity no less princely. His castle of Raglan and the Marquis of Winchester's Basing House were strongholds of Romanism and Royalism in the war, and their fall was long delayed and widely celebrated. The Roman Catholic body was destined to suffer more serious and permanent injury in the coming strife than any other section of the community.

In the end the King lost the war for lack of money. The parts of England that owned his authority were on the average less wealthy than those which defied him. His headquarters were in Oxford, a small city more famous for learning than for wealth, a poor substitute for London left in the hands of his enemies. The rustic gentlemen who offered him their lives, their swords, their horses and their plate, could not easily realize their land until it came under the hammer within the Roundhead lines as sequestrated property. And if Charles got freewill offerings, so did Parliament. For Puritan squires and shopkeepers also had silver plate in abundance, and

Into pikes and musketeers
Stampt beakers, cups and porringers.

Parliament, no less than the King, would call on gentlemen to raise private regiments, like Hampden's Green Coats. In these appeals to individual generosity the two sides were on equal terms, and that was how the war was begun. But the Roundheads had more staying power because they could do what the King could not—negotiate loans in the City, and place regular taxes on the trade of England and on its richest districts. To pay for the Civil War, the Long Parliament introduced excise duties on goods, and an improved assessment for taxes on land and property, far more

profitable to the public and far less unjust as between
individuals than the happy-go-lucky assessment for the
old 'subsidy.' In the ordinances of the Long Parliament we
find the germ of our modern fiscal system. The resources
of England, which had been grudgingly doled out to Elizabeth and denied to James and Charles, were first exploited
by Parliament in the war fought upon its own behalf.

The sea was held by the King's enemies. The Royal
Navy revolted to 'King Pym.' The seaports made a present
to Parliament of the mercantile marine. The overseas trade
of England was carried on to increase the wealth of rebels,
while Charles had difficulty even in importing arms from
abroad. The excise levied by Parliament was largely paid
for by the higher prices which upland Cavaliers had to
find for articles that had been taxed in Roundhead manufacturing centres and seaports.

If Parliament could at once have translated these financial advantages into military terms, the war would not have
lasted long, and would have been won by the original
Parliamentary party under Pym, Hampden and Essex, without any need on their part to purchase the embarrassing
help either of Covenanted Scots or of East Anglian Sectaries. In that case the history of England would have taken
some totally different course. But it was not to be. The
Cavaliers, though starting at a great disadvantage, rapidly
improved their position, until by the end of 1643 they had
conquered the South-West and solidified their position
north of the Humber.

The King's generals won these early successes because
they had ready to their hand human material that could
be very quickly manufactured into good soldiers. In that
most civilian of societies neither side had any trained force
at the outset, for the militia could scarcely count as such.
But the hard-riding squires and their huntsmen and grooms
only wanted a soldier to teach them how to charge home
as cavalry. And there was a lad of twenty-two, the King's
nephew Rupert, who had actually seen a campaign in Germany and whose spirit burned like a fire. He saved his
uncle from desperate straits in 1642 by making for him a

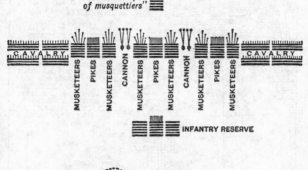

Note: *The general idea of this formation is based on the well known map-picture of Naseby in Sprigge's* Anglia Rediviva, 1647. *The precise depth of the columns–six lines for the foot, and three for the horse–is derived from Firth's* Cromwell's Army *pp. 95-6, 131-3.*

Map 5   An Army in Battle Array: Great Civil War

body of horse that none of the Parliament side as yet could resist.

Rupert, in one of the first of his many quarrels with his brother generals, insisted that the Royalist cavalry should fight at Edgehill [OCT. 1642.] in line three deep, after the Swedish fashion, and charge home with the steel, instead of lumbering slowly up in column six deep after the old Dutch fashion and halting to fire off their pistols. The more spirited modern tactics of the Swedes were soon adopted in both armies, notably by Cromwell's Ironsides.

The infantry, however, continued to fight in masses six deep, occasionally reduced to three for the purpose of attacking a position. The pikes were in the centre, the musketeers on the two flanks. When 'the shot' had delivered their fire, they clubbed their muskets and closed in, 'the strongest soldiers and officers clubbing down' the enemy. But the struggle at close quarters was mainly decided 'at push of pike.' In rough or enclosed ground, indeed, well-led musketeers were more valuable than pikemen, and infantry than cavalry. But in the open, since bayonets had not yet been

Map 6   England and Wales in the Winter of 1643–44

invented, an attack on the flank by cavalry was fatal to the
musketeers, and often to the whole regiment if it was engaged on its front against other infantry and had no leisure
to re-form and shelter its 'shot' under the protection of the
long extended pikes. On some battlefields, like Lansdowne
or Newbury, and in the later wars Preston or Worcester,
hedges or woodland gave protection and scope to the activities of the foot, but much of the landscape of the
North-East and Midlands of that day was open heath or
unenclosed field. On Marston Moor and the gently undulat-

ing lands of Naseby, the infantry were exposed to cavalry attack as they would not have been in the woodlands that encumbered those sites in primæval times, or amid the hedges that line and traverse them to-day.

For these reasons the decisive battles of the war were won by cavalry. The man who led the best cavalry, like Rupert in 1642–43, and Cromwell in 1644–45—at least if, like Cromwell, he had also a general's eye for the course of the battle as a whole—that man would make his side master of England.[1]

In 1643 the Royalists had not only the best cavalry upon the average, but the best single body of infantry in Hopton's astonishing Cornishmen. With these advantages they overran the whole South-Western quarter of England, destroying one after another the small, ill-disciplined armies, privately or locally raised, which then represented the Roundhead cause.[2]

The Parliamentary generals wandered aimlessly about with no objective, and were cut up in detail. The Cavalier chiefs began to conceive a large strategic plan to end the war by a triple advance on London from Yorkshire, the Thames Valley, and the South-West at once. Hopton's advance on London from the South-West was to unmuzzle the suppressed Royalists of Kent upon its way. It was a hopeful plan. But it foundered on the irregular and local character of the Royal armies: the men of Cornwall and Devon were not well-paid, long-service regulars, but volun-

[1] Cannon were used in the field, but decided no important battle except the peculiar battle of Langport in 1645. But once the King's armies were broken in the field, the siege train of the New Model, a fruit of Parliamentary taxation, made short work of his garrisoned towns, castles and manors, and speedily finished the war.

[2] The various bodies composing the Cavalier armies were of a no less private character than the Roundhead regiments, though at first combined under better generalship. 'The honest country gentleman,' says a Royalist playwright, 'raises the troop at his own charge, then he gets a Low-Country lieutenant to fight his troop for him, and then sends his son from school to be cornet.'

teers who were unwilling to remain indefinitely away from
their work and homes, the more so as Plymouth was still
held from the sea by Parliament, threatening their own
county in their rear. Bristol indeed had been taken, but
Gloucester and Taunton, centres of the Puritan clothing
industry, still held out. It became apparent that before
London could be attacked, these places must first be reduced. Close siege was laid to Gloucester, but the London
'prentice trainbands marched across England and relieved
it, their masters being willing that work should go slow
for two months while the stronghold of the 'good old cause'
in the West was being saved. [AUG.–SEPT. 1643.]

Clearly a war waged on these terms could be won by
the side that should at first create a long-service army with
regular pay and discipline. The King had not the money
to do this. Parliament had the money if it had the wit.

Meanwhile in the North the advance from Yorkshire on
London was stopped, partly by the resistance of the seaport of Hull, corresponding to Plymouth in the South-West,
partly by the greater solidity of Roundhead civil and military organization in the counties of the Eastern Association,
where Puritanism was strongest and had found its ideal
leader.

Oliver Cromwell was the Puritan type of squire, farming
his land himself, closely connected with the middle and
lower classes of town and country in business transactions
and in local politics. As champion of the common rights of
small peasants and fishermen in the matter of fen-draining,
he had won the first place in the affections of his own countryside before ever the Long Parliament met. He had
fought at Edgehill, and had there noted, as he told his
cousin Hampden, the superiority of the high-spirited Cavalier horse over the 'old decayed serving men and tap-
sters' opposed to them. Returning to East Anglia he set
himself to raise, among the yeomen and small freeholding
classes whom he knew and by whom he was known, well-
mounted regiments of cuirassiers whom he taught to combine a strict military discipline with their religious zeal.
They were 'of greater understanding than common soldiers,
making not money but that which they took for public fe-

licity to be their end.' From the first they were marked by a democratic tone on social and political questions and unorthodoxy in the forms of their Puritan faith. At this period Cromwell wrote:

I had rather have a plain russet-coated captain that knows what he fights for and loves what he knows, than what you call 'a gentleman' and is nothing else. I honour a gentleman that is so indeed. It may be it provokes some spirits to see such plain men made captains of horse. But seeing it was necessary the work should go on, better plain men than none.

These East Anglian regiments, who began a new era in English war and politics, became best known to the world by the nickname of 'Ironsides,' which had first been applied to their leader in person. They were the real origin of the New Model and of all the later Cromwellian armies. Their first important service was to check the half-hearted advance of the northern Cavaliers through Lincolnshire, at Gainsborough and Winceby fights, and in doing so to get into touch with Sir Thomas Fairfax, who was still upholding the Roundhead cause north of Humber from the sea-base of Hull. [1643.]

But it was not enough that the Cavalier advance on London had been checked. The country was weary of the war, and a strong party even in the Capital was clamouring for peace by 'an accommodation with His Majesty,' not very different from surrender. In these straits Pym's last act of statesmanship was to negotiate an alliance with the Scots. [AUG.–SEPT. 1643.] After the satisfaction of their national demands, they had withdrawn their army to their own side of the Tweed in August 1641. They now undertook to send it back into England as the ally of Parliament. In return they demanded the reformation of the English Church upon the Scottish model.

The Parliament men could not accede to the demand in its entirety, for although they desired to abolish Bishops and the Prayer Book, and to introduce some lay element into the ecclesiastical organization, they were, like all Englishmen, jealous guardians of the supremacy of the State over the Church. There was the further difficulty that the

Scots and their English partisans demanded the persecution of all unorthodox Puritan sects, even while the war against the Prelatists was still unwon. Only so, it was held by many, could they look for God's blessing on their arms.

Now popular Puritanism in England, during this period of its most rapid expansion, was markedly unorthodox, full of fresh individual vigour and variety, and breeding a hundred different forms of doctrine and practice. The great religious ferment of English humble folk which laid its strong hold on young George Fox and John Bunyan, taught men to think that—

New Presbyter is but Old Priest writ large.

Honourable members at Westminster would not indeed have thought twice about clapping into gaol all tinkers and shoemakers who took to prophesying, whether or not they were afterwards going to produce *Pilgrim's Progress* and the Society of Friends; but it was a more serious matter that the best English soldiers of all ranks from Cromwell downwards were the most rebellious against orthodoxy. 'Steeple Houses' and 'hireling ministers' were coming in for hard words from the hardest fighters. In half the regiments and on half the local committees that upheld the authority of Parliament, Independents were bearding Presbyterians, and Presbyterians were demanding the dismissal of Independents. For the Independents wanted a Church made up of free, self-governing congregations, not under the scrutiny of any general organization bound to enforce orthodox opinion and practice.

This quarrel in face of the enemy almost ensured the triumph of the King's armies. However, in the autumn of 1643 the Scots were for the moment satisfied by Parliament itself taking the Covenant, and by vague promises of 'a thorough reformation' of the English Church 'according to the example of the best reformed Churches,' but also, as was inserted by way of safeguard, 'according to the word of God.' On these somewhat equivocal terms Pym purchased the aid of the Scottish arms, and died in December.

Next year the policy of the dead statesman bore fruit in the victory on Marston Moor. [JULY 2, 1644.] The three

united armies of Cromwell's East Anglians, Fairfax's Yorkshire Puritans, and the Scots under Alexander and David
Leslie, twenty-seven thousand in all, destroyed the forces
of the northern Cavaliers joined to those of Rupert, num-
bering together eighteen thousand. It was by far the largest
battle in the war. Rupert in person and his best troops of
horse, hitherto unmatched, yielded before the impact of
the Ironsides. At a blow the whole of Northern England
was subjected to the Roundhead power.

Marston Moor was set off by the capitulation of Essex
and all his infantry at Lostwithiel in Cornwall, whither he
had rashly and aimlessly penetrated. [SEPT. 2, 1644.] Instead of trying to destroy the royal forces, he had sought
prematurely to overrun the royal territories, with fatal results. This disaster cleared the way for the rise of Cromwell.
The older type of general, high in social rank, moderate
in politics, and orthodox in religion, which had served Parliament well to begin the war, suffered at Lostwithiel an
irremediable loss of prestige. The sectaries and 'russet-
coated captains' who had reaped the bloody harvest on
Marston Moor stood proportionately higher in the minds
of the Parliament men. If it was a question of God's blessing, the sectaries seemed to have had the larger share of it
that year.

The war was decided by the statesmanlike decisions of
the House of Commons in the winter of 1644–45. The development of the Roundhead armies into the most perfect
military weapon of the age was curiously involved in the
quarrel of Presbyterian and Baptist over religious conformity. Parliament had to deal with the two problems together.
Few members sympathized with the sectaries, and many
were bitter against them as turbulent and dangerous fellows; but, on the other hand, the House had no wish to subject the English Parliament to the Scots Kirk, and the
English squires to inquisitorial boards of elders and clergy.
Of the two impending evils they chose, for the time being,
the one that gave promise of immediate success in the field,
although some honourable members intended to cheat the
Independents of 'the liberty they fought for,' after they

had safely won the war for their masters—a game that proved as dangerous as it was dishonest.

For the present, at least, the Houses supported Cromwell against his rival, the Presbyterian Earl of Manchester, because the sectary was the better soldier. By the Self-denying Ordinance they obtained the resignations of all officers who were members of either House, but the right of reappointment was reserved. When the decks had thus been cleared of every encumbrance, they chose Fairfax as their Captain-General; he added to his high military qualifications a politic indifference between Presbyterianism and the Sects. Finally they appointed Cromwell as his lieutenant, with charge of all the horse. His Ironsides constituted half the cavalry of the New Model. The position of Independents and Baptists was now safe, for just so long as the war lasted.

The 'New Model' Army which Fairfax and Cromwell were to command was a regular force, enlisted in the direct service of Parliament, and more regularly fed and rather less irregularly paid than any army on either side had yet been; it was therefore possible to enforce a proportionately stricter discipline. The good conduct which enabled the 'Saints' speedily to finish the war was due to their food and pay as well as to their religion. The Houses had now a better instrument than private regiments and local levies, badly provided for by paymaster and commissariat, and fending for themselves by plunder. For Parliament had the power of the purse and had at last learnt how to use it.[3]

On the other hand, the plundering habits of the royalists were worse in 1645 than in 1642, in proportion as the King was more desperately bankrupt. Discipline had indeed at no time been the strong point of the gallant Cavaliers. Their commanders quarrelled with one another less often on questions of religion and politics than on points of preced-

[3] It is true that in 1646 the pay of the New Model began to fall gravely into arrears, but the pay in 1645 must have been fairly regular; between March 1645 and March 1647 Fairfax's men actually received £1,185,551. See Firth's *Cromwell's Army*, 183–84, 202–3.

ence and personal rivalry. The old spirit of chivalry, the independence of each knight working counter to all regular command, was the bane of the royal armies from first to last. The common Cavalier, brave in battle, but drinking and gambling between whiles, prided himself on his unlikeness to the precisians and psalm-singers of the rebel camp. And as his chiefs for want of money left him more and more to starve, he supported himself more and more by the plunder of the countryside. Finally even the most loyal districts of the South-West were glad to see the back of Goring and his like, and brought in the produce of their farms to the New Model camp for money down.

The King's best servant saw and noted it all:

Those under the King's commanders (wrote Clarendon) grew insensibly into all the licence, disorder and impiety with which they had reproached the rebels; and they again into great discipline, diligence and sobriety; which begat courage and resolution in them, and notable dexterity in achievements and enterprises. Insomuch as one side seemed to fight for monarchy with the weapons of confusion, and the other to destroy the King and government with all the principles and regularity of monarchy.

It was indeed the task of the Long Parliament to prove that 'government' can be even more effectual when it is collective than when it is personal. And in the summer of 1645 that proposition was proved up to the hilt.

Fairfax, unlike Essex before him, had for his military objective the destruction of the King's army in the field. At Naseby he found it and broke it to pieces, thanks to Cromwell and his horse. [JUNE 14, 1645.] After that the morale of the remaining Cavalier armies rapidly degenerated, while the country turned with gratitude or resignation to the side that would give it peace. The well-provided artillery train of the New Model Army, and the zeal and skill of the storming tactics of its infantry, reduced with astonishing speed the numerous garrisons of the King, scattered wide over the West in castle, manor-house and walled town. Twelve months after Naseby, the capitulation of Oxford marked the practical termination of the Great

Civil War. [JUNE 24, 1646.] From Land's End to Berwick the word of Parliament was law.

The progress of these mighty operations had not been effectively disturbed by Montrose's romantic diversion. Riding from the King's camp to Scotland disguised as a groom, [AUG. 1644.] he was a few weeks later sweeping victorious over the Lowlands at the head of a few thousand Highland swordsmen. As a general he was Cromwell's only rival, but it was his destiny to command brave but uncivilized tribes, who slunk back after their victories to store their plunder in their native glens, leaving him with a remnant to be trampled to ruin by the charge of David Leslie's cavalry at Philiphaugh. [SEPT. 13, 1645.] Of Montrose's great enterprise, which was to have broken the secular power of the Kirk in Scotland, nothing remained except the memory, very bitter to Lowland Scots of that day, but very dear to their descendants as a point in the common national pride that has united Highlander and Lowlander ever since the days of Sir Walter Scott.

CHAPTER FOUR

The Failure to Reach a Settlement. Regicide. The Revolutionary Governments. Ireland and Scotland. Blake and the Revival of the Navy. Domestic, Ecclesiastical and Foreign Policy of the Protectorate. The Death of Oliver and the Restoration

The victory of the Roundheads was complete, not in the material and military sphere alone. Moral disintegration had undermined their enemies' resistance. The neutrals had everywhere acclaimed the triumph of the New Model as the only road back to security and peace. Even the Cavalier gentleman who laid down his arms, disbanded his troop and rode off home in a mood between melancholy and relief, felt no such bitter resentment as he and his son were to nurse after a dozen years of military rule, accompanied by heavy fines on their estates, the proscription of their religion, and the execution of their King. When Sir Jacob Astley at his surrender said to the victors—'You have now done your work and may go play, unless you fall out among yourselves,' he was not using the language of irreconcilable hatred.

A great opportunity for settlement was there for the taking. In three years it had been so completely thrown away that the Empire was only saved from disruption and England from anarchy by the employment of despotic military power; and the Restoration settlement of 1660–62, though in itself inferior to what might have been obtained in 1647, was actually the salvation of the country.

The execution of Charles I marks the moment at which the failure to carry on government by consent was admitted and proclaimed, and the 'forcéd power' established, nominally in order to realize Republican ideals, but in fact to prevent utter chaos. How had that situation been reached? Between the end of the First Civil War and the tragedy in front of Whitehall [JUNE 1646–JAN. 1649.] stretch a series of intrigues, proposals, *coups d'état* and military operations, arising out of the character and policy of the four parties actively concerned—the victorious Parliament, the captive King, the Army, and Oliver Cromwell.

Parliament is the party whose conduct in these three critical years it is least easy to praise or even to excuse. It may seem strange that a civilian assembly which had learnt to take the right measures and trust the right men in wartime, should fail only when it came to make political use of its conquests. But history, from the time of the Roman Senate until the Parliaments of our own day, is full of examples of this apparent paradox. Assemblies of men of valiant blood can be made wise by the dangers of war, but the power that armed victory brings, or seems to bring, may deprive them of judgment, and subject them to the mass-emotions of a mob. So in 1647 the House of Commons thought that its hired servant, the New Model Army, had placed in its hands supreme power over the religions and estates of all the subjects of the land, and it proceeded to dispose of all things English according to its own prejudices, with no more respect for the real England than Charles had shown in the day of his supremacy.

The most important cause of the failure of the Long

Parliament to make peace after the Civil War was the same error that had ruined Charles and was to vitiate the Restoration settlement, the inability of any party to admit the need for religious toleration in a divided land. But the Long Parliament had the peculiar audacity to attempt the persecution of the Anglicans and the Sectarians at the same time, on behalf of the narrow Presbyterian orthodoxy which had less hold on the future of English religion than any other movement of the day.

Simultaneously the Long Parliament yielded to the temptation of meeting its great financial difficulties by the too facile expedient of attacks upon the property of its late opponents in the field. If, with reasonable exceptions, security had been given to the lands and fortunes of both sides in the late war, it is not likely that the Cavalier squires would have conceived that intense loathing of Puritanism which governed the conduct of their class during the remainder of the century. They had hitherto felt small affection for Laud and the Laudian clergy. But when the fines on 'malignants,' as the defeated party were called, forced some of them to sell parts of their estates to the victors of the hour, often to war-profiteers of lower social standing than themselves,[1] and when at the same time the Prayer Book service to which they were accustomed was forbidden, the squires began to feel a new affection for the ejected Laudian clergy,—about 2000 in number,—fellow-sufferers at the same rude hands. The breach between clergy and laity, which Laud had made, was healed by Puritan persecution. The political alliance of squire and parson, and the hatred they so long nurtured together

---

[1] Recent research indicates that the amount of land actually sold by Cavaliers to pay fines has been exaggerated. The men, who bought up the land of individual Cavaliers, kept their purchases at the Restoration. Unjustly, but not unnaturally, Charles II was therefore accused of ingratitude towards his own and his father's followers. On the other hand, the more thorough-going Cromwellians, mostly army officers, who invested their pay and gains in buying up Church or Crown land cheap, lost it when it was resumed at the Restoration; everywhere except in Ireland they sank back to the social level whence they had risen.

against the foes of Bishops and Prayer Book, date from feelings engendered at this time.

Not content with rendering the Royalist gentry irreconcilable, the Long Parliament, with almost incredible folly, proceeded to pass measures for the lifelong imprisonment of Baptists, the prohibition of laymen from preaching in public, and the dismissal of all Independent officers from the New Model. [1646–47.] In their harsh ingratitude to the men who had saved them in the field, the Parliamentary majority was egged on by the dominant faction in the City of London. To crown this elaborate edifice of folly, it was proposed to disband the Army without cashing its considerable arrears of pay. This drew together in close alliance officers and privates, enthusiastic sectaries and men who had been attracted into the ranks by the offer of good pay secured upon the taxes. Injustice made the Army a faction in the State, united by its grievances and its anger. All ranks began to listen more eagerly to the propaganda of the radical enthusiasts in their midst, who appealed from the Long Parliament to Republican and democratic ideals based on universal suffrage. These theories proved in that age impracticable, but humanly speaking, the soldiers cannot be blamed for refusing to submit to religious persecution and neglect of their just financial claims, at the hands of the authority whom they themselves had rendered supreme in the State by their magnificent military services.

Yet the coercion of Parliament by the Army [AUG. 1647.], even if justifiable in the first instance, was necessarily fatal to constitutional rule, and led by inevitable steps to the dictatorship of Cromwell. He long strove to keep the soldiers in their duty to the Houses, and said to them with perfect sincerity as late as July 1648: 'What we and they gain in a free way is better than thrice so much in a forced way, and will be more truly ours and our posterity's. That you have by force I look upon as nothing.' This warning, uttered by England's greatest man of action, stands as the tragic comment on all that was yet to come in his own career.

The quarrel of Parliament and Army, which Parliament had provoked, put the balance of State in the hands of the captive King. Both sides made advances to him, and he could perhaps have settled the country by casting in his lot with one or the other. But his virtues and his failings alike made that impossible. His rigid adherence to the principle of monarchical government and its corollary the episcopal regime in the Church, for which he was prepared if necessary to endure in his own person the worst that man can do, made it impossible that he should come to terms either with Army or with Parliament. Furthermore, he was by temperament incapable of coming to an honest agreement and abiding by it. The less admirable side of his character taught him to conceive the plan of winning back power by insincere negotiations with both parties, which should help to set them by the ears together. To play with victorious enemies in the hope of deluding them is always dangerous.

Yet his execution was as much the catastrophe of his enemies' cause as of his own. In the person of his son, his plan was victorious a dozen years later, for his policy had hastened and his death cemented the alliance of Presbyterians with Royalists against the Independents and the Army. The first stage of that alliance led to the Second Civil War [1648.] and the victory of Cromwell at Preston, and so to the execution of Charles. The final result was the Restoration of his son, when the Presbyterians were the catspaw and the dupe of their Episcopalian allies. Crown, Parliament and Episcopacy were restored together, but owing to the action of Cromwell and the Army who had defended and nursed the sects for a dozen years, it was the sects and not the Presbyterian orthodox with whom lay the future of non-conformist Puritanism.

The revulsion of feeling in favour of the King, which began during his trial and execution, and swelled to such vast proportions as years went by, was largely due to the fact that he suffered as the champion of the laws which his enemies were breaking and of the ancient institutions which they were destroying. Apart from the personal aspect of the scene, with its overmastering appeal in favour of 'the royal actor' who played his part with sincere and simple dignity, the conservative instincts of the English nation were rudely outraged. [JAN. 30, 1649.] They felt that they were being carried beyond the historic current of English life into uncharted seas. It was an adventure they had not bargained for. This Republicanism, what was it? The rule of preaching colonels apparently. And yet for many years to come, the men, and in particular the man, who had seized power through means of the Army but in the name of an unconscious and bewildered 'people of England,' had the courage and genius to govern, making out of an utterly impossible situation something not ignoble, and in some important respects very profitable for the future growth of Great Britain and its Empire.

The decisive factor in the triangular contest between King, Parliament and Army had been Oliver Cromwell. As early as 1647, while he was still a back-bench Member of Parliament, and not yet in name the supreme commander of the Army, his force of character made him in effect 'our chief of men.'

King, Parliament and Army each had an *idée fixe* and consequently they could not agree. Cromwell, who was pre-eminently an opportunist,—'none goes so far,' he once said, 'as he who knows not whither he is going,'—could easily have supplied them with a dozen possible solutions if they had been ready to listen to reason. Far the best solution propounded by anyone was the 'Heads of the Proposals,' made by Cromwell and Ireton to Charles, based on wide toleration, the use of the Prayer Book in Church by those who wished, Bishops without coercive power, and a stop to the sequestration of Cavalier estates. [SEPT. 1647.] But the King was only playing at negotiation, and neither Army nor Parliament had any thought of so liberal a treatment of the conquered. Cromwell and Ireton were speaking for themselves and common sense alone. They found that they must either march with the Army or perish. Cromwell underwent one of those sharp revulsions, accompanied by repentance and prayer, so timely that his enemies miscalled them hypocrisy.

The riddle of Oliver must be read not in his mutable opinions but in his constant character. His moderation and his dislike of force were often counteracted by his instinct at every cost to find a practical solution for the problem of

the moment; if agreement failed, as it often does in revolutionary times, then, however reluctantly, he would cut the
Gordian knot, for the nation's government must be carried
on. Moreover, although commonsense was the dominating quality of his intellect, it worked in an atmosphere
of temperamental enthusiasm which left him no doubts
or fears when once he had reached a conclusion after
weeks of brooding hesitation. For his final resolve, when
at last it emerged, always seemed to him the inspiration of
God. God spoke in the victories of each successive war,
pointing—whithersoever Cromwell's latest thoughts were
leading him.[2] When, therefore, he learnt at last that all
his efforts to find an accommodation with the King had
been wasted time, the fanatical mood of the Army about
'the man Charles Stuart' took possession of him. When
he found also that England must be ruled for awhile
through the soldiers or slide into anarchy, he felt the glow
of the Republican faith in which so many of his men returned from the victory at Preston, although it was not
so much his settled conviction as the apparent necessity of
the moment. Ten years later he was veering round again
to constitutional kingship—in his own person this time,—
in order to get rid of military rule and put himself in line
with the strongest current of thought of that day, ebbing
back towards conservative and civil legality. For always
this strong swimmer must ride on the crest of the wave.
How many more successive waves would he have ridden,
if death had not put an end to his titanic strife with circumstance?

Cromwell was not the only able and public-spirited man
who had pushed his way to the front on the Roundhead
side, under the double impulse of the emotional turmoil of
the time and the number of careers opened to talent by

[2] Butler, the author of *Hudibras,* the famous satire on the
Puritans, writes four lines not inapplicable to Cromwell:
'Whate'er men speak by this New Light, / Still they are
sure to be i' th' right. / 'Tis a dark Lanthorn of the Spirit, /
Which none see by but those who bear it.'

civil war and revolution. The era of Vane, Blake, Ireton, Monk, and of Milton as pamphleteer and secretary, was an era of great public servants, worthy to be dignified by the name of 'Commonwealth.' The Regicide government, consisting partly of army officers and partly of members of the 'Rump' or minority which 'Pride's purge' had made supreme in Parliament, were neither poltroons nor blind fanatics. [DEC. 1648.] The position in which they found themselves on the last day of January 1649 was one which must have speedily led to their own ruin and the dissolution of the British Empire, had they not been men above the common in cool-headed courage. The state of public opinion, strongly alienated from them but divided against itself, rendered impossible the appeal to a free election, which their democratic theories demanded but their sense of responsibility and self-preservation forbade. Wherever they looked, the prospect was dark in the extreme. Their authority was denied, not only by Cavaliers and Presbyterians, but by radical democrats like John Lilburne, who at that time had a great popular following. The Navy was paralysed by mutiny; the Royalist privateers under Prince Rupert held the seas; Scotland and Ireland were in arms for the younger Charles; Virginia and Barbados repudiated the authority of the usurpers; Massachusetts, though not unfriendly, had since the beginning of the troubles in England acted as if it were an independent State. Holland, France, Spain and all the continental powers regarded the regicides as pariahs and England as a cypher. Yet in four years the Council of State had overcome these dangers with the help of Cromwell's sword and Blake's broadsides, before resort was had to the final stage of the revolutionary government, the Protectorate of Oliver.

The first step in the reconstitution of the British Empire by the Republican Government was the subjugation of Ireland. It was rendered easier for Cromwell and his army because the Protestants over there, whatever their political allegiance, tended to rally round him as the champion of their race and creed, while the Irish resistance became racial and Catholic instead of Royalist. After the fall of Drogheda, Wexford and Clonmel [1649–1650.] had broken

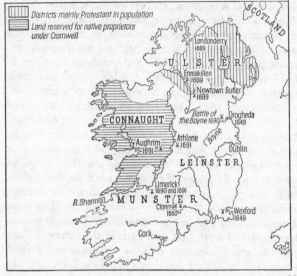

EMERY WALKER LTD. SC.

Map 7   Ireland in the Seventeenth Century

the back of resistance in the East, Cromwell went home, leaving Ireton to carry on the guerrilla war of Celt and Saxon in the West to its bitter end.

The land settlement in Ireland, by far the worst part of Cromwell's constructive work within the British islands, was the part that outlived him substantially in the form he gave it. It completed the transference of the soil from Irish to British proprietors, which had been begun under the Tudors and pushed forward under the Stuart Kings. The object was threefold: to pay off in Irish land the soldiers who had fought and the capitalists who had provided the money for the conquest, in the manner in which the veterans of Cæsar and of William the Conqueror had been rewarded; secondly, to render the English hold upon Ireland secure against another rebellion like that of 1641, even after the army should be disbanded; and lastly, to extirpate Catholicism. The first two objects were attained.

Ireland west of Shannon was reserved for native proprietors. The rest of the island passed to Protestant landlords. The idea of driving the whole Celtic population beyond the Shannon was entertained but not executed. The natives remained for the most part on their farms as hewers of wood and drawers of water to the new alien landowners, who rack-rented them, according to Irish custom, without being obliged to make the improvements and repairs customary in English tenancies.

In Ulster alone had the tenant some protection, and in Ulster alone the population was largely British and Protestant, on account of the immigration of hard-working Scots from the neighbouring coast beginning from the time of James I's plantation. Elsewhere in Ireland, those of Cromwell's private soldiers who were planted out as yeomen failed to preserve their religion and nationality, because they were too widely scattered and were cut off by social barriers from the Protestant gentry. Some of the yeomen threw up their farms, while others intermarried with the natives, with the result that their descendants brought Saxon and Ironside qualities to stiffen the Celtic and Catholic resistance. The landlords were left isolated in their power and privilege, until the end began with Gladstone's Land Bills and Parnell's Land League.

In Ireland as Oliver left it and as it long remained, the persecuted priests were the only leaders of the people because the English had destroyed the class of native gentry. The Cromwellian settlement rendered the Irish for centuries the most priest-led population in Europe.

Cromwell's next task was to reduce Scotland to the obedience of the Commonwealth. North of the Tweed there was no Sectarian or Republican party and, properly speaking, no Parliamentary party. The land was divided between a rigid ecclesiastical Presbyterianism, very different from the political Presbyterianism of England, and the Cavalier interest, which in Scotland was not Laudian but represented the rebellion of the nobility and others against the rule of the State by the Church. Presbyterian and Cavalier hated each other bitterly, for the blood shed in Montrose's wars flowed between them. But they patched up a hollow alliance round the person of Charles II, whom they proposed to restore by force of arms to his throne in England. Their plans were ruined at Dunbar [SEPT. 3, 1650.] and Worcester [SEPT. 3, 1651.], the last and, militarily, the greatest victories of Cromwell's army on British soil.

When up the armed mountains of Dunbar
He marched, and through deep Severn, ending war.[3]

The only sanction of Oliver's rule beyond the Tweed was the presence of the English army and, therefore, the arrangements he made could not be permanent. But the rule of the sword, so long as it lasted, enabled Oliver to carry through without compromise his own enlightened policy for the benefit of Scotland, whose internal feuds had at length subjected her to the great neighbour she had so often defied. He united the whole island in a single Commonwealth, and Scottish members sat in the British Parliaments held under the Protectorate. For the first time Scotland enjoyed the immense advantage of free trade with England and her markets beyond sea. Order was kept and justice administered without favour, as never before in her history. Even the Highlands were garrisoned and the clans kept in awe. The government was good, but as in England, it was costly, and the taxes were burdensome and deeply resented.

The dignity and efficiency of the Scottish Presbyterian Church were preserved, while it was no longer permitted to persecute others or to domineer over the State. 'I verily believe,' a Scottish Presbyterian wrote of the Protectorate, 'there were more souls converted to Christ in that short time, than in any season since the Reformation though of triple its duration.' The English soldiers behaved irreproachably as an army of occupation, save when they endeavoured to found Baptist Churches in an uncongenial soil, or derided the discipline of the Kirk by seating themselves on the 'stools of repentance' during divine worship, to the displeasure of 'grave livers,' and the untimely mirth of the youthful part of the congregation.

[3] During the raid of Scots and Cavaliers into England that ended at Worcester, it is noticeable that so far from Englishmen rising to join them, the militia turned out very readily to put them down. If the regicides were unpopular, so were their enemies, especially the Scots.

But Oliver's direct rule failed to bring the immunity from foreign war which alone could have given his domestic system any chance of financial stability and ultimate popularity. His Protestantism and his desire to help English traders and colonists all the world over, led him into a quarrel with Spain. He revived the claim of Elizabethan Englishmen to trade with the Spanish colonies and to be entirely free from the power of the Inquisition. The Spanish Ambassador replied that this was to ask 'his master's two eyes.' Perpetual hostilities were taking place between the Spanish forces and the English colonists, traders and buccaneers of the West Indian Archipelago, which Spain regarded as her own in spite of the English settlements in so many of the islands. [See Map 8.] Oliver lent to the English of the West Indies the powerful aid of the mother country. He sent out an expedition which, though it failed at Hispaniola, captured Jamaica. [1655.] This proved the most important single step in the enlargement of that West Indian island Empire which, for a century and a half to come, held so prominent a place in British trade, diplomacy and war.

As a factor in European politics Cromwellian England was feared and respected, but achieved nothing great. The protection of the Vaudois was a noble gesture, worthy of the finest sonnet ever written by a political secretary, and was very well managed as a diplomatic feat; but it was not very important. The war with Spain [1655–58.], which was really a trans-Atlantic quarrel, did little good in Europe either to England or to Protestantism. There was glory, no doubt, in Blake's destruction of the Spanish fleet under the forts of Teneriffe, where Nelson afterwards lost an arm, and there was pride in the storming of the slippery sand-dunes near Dunkirk by the red-coated infantry with the army of our French allies looking on in admiration. But the perennial British interest in the Balance of Power in Europe demanded no such vigorous interference, for the balance then stood adjusted without Cromwell's heavy weight in the scale. Spain had already decayed and France had not yet grown to any dangerous height. The Thirty Years' War was finished and, for the time, no opportunities existed for a new Gustavus Adolphus. If Oliver had been on the scene with his army and his fleet in 1618 or in 1630 or again from 1670 onwards, something notable might have been achieved. In 1654 the man was there, but the hour had passed, or not yet come. History is made up of coincidences or their absence.

On the top of the expenses of the Dutch War, the Spanish War increased the burden of taxation on the country and gravely injured its prosperity and trade. Oliver's militarism and imperialism became increasingly unpopular, not only for political reasons, but because they cost too much. That one should be forced to give a large part of one's property yearly to the taxgatherer, though accepted as a normal condition of life to-day, seemed then an intolerable outrage. Yet, in spite of the heavy taxes, the sale of Crown and episcopal lands, the fines on 'malignants,' and the confiscation of half the soil of Ireland, Oliver died in debt. From the point of view of finance alone a change of system was necessary, which would enable the army to be disbanded. But the army could not be disbanded unless some way could be found leading back to government by consent. Oliver spent his last years in the search for that way, but he had lost it, and was doomed to bear his load through the wilderness to the end.

The same arts that did gain
A power must it maintain,

wrote Andrew Marvell, the lesser but not the less shrewd of the Protector's two poet secretaries.

Oliver, unlike Strafford and others who have 'broken Parliaments,' believed to the last in the necessity for Parliamentary rule. And unlike others who have founded Republics, he began and he ended his career as a believer in the uses of constitutional Kingship. Yet it was his fate to ruin the Puritan cause by dissociating it from both Kingship and Parliament, and to clear the way only by his own death for the restoration of the civil legality which he himself desired. It was his fate—was it also his fault? On

that point historians who know the most are the least willing to venture a clear opinion.

His dismissal of the Rump of the Long Parliament when
it endeavoured to perpetuate its power, was perhaps a
necessity. [1653.] It pleased the nation well for a month,
during which the ballad-makers chanted:

Brave Oliver came to the House like a sprite,
   His fiery face struck the Speaker dumb;
'Begone,' said he, 'you have sate long enough,
   Do you think to sit here till Doomsday come?'

But the all too dramatic march of his red-coats up the floor
of the House, and his guard-room jest about the mace, left
in longer retrospect an indelibly bad impression. If the
mace was a bauble and the crown to boot, what counted
but the sword?

After he had become Protector [DEC. 1653.], his later
Parliaments, though elected under such restrictions as
the times demanded, were not able to agree with him.
Whether he should have risked more to bring about an
agreement so indispensable, is a question too detailed for
discussion here, although it is the heart of the problem.
The alternative was government by Major-Generals, the
naked rule of the sword, which outraged the country and
his own instincts. His last two years were spent in the
delicate operation of beginning to free himself from dependence on the army by making terms with the legalists
and constitutionalists. [1657–58.] They demanded of him
that he should revive the Kingship in his own person. He
began to fall in with their view of the matter, but some of
the army chiefs on whom he most depended remained
stubbornly Republican. The desire of many moderate and
practical men, particularly of the lawyers, was that Oliver
should wear the crown,—the same men who two years
later took the lead in recalling Charles for much the same
reasons. Monarchy was seen to be essential to the restoration of Parliament and the rule of law.

It was in an early stage of this new evolution that death
overtook the Protector. [SEPT. 3, 1658.] But already he had
made some headway in weeding the army of its fanatical

and extremist element, and for this reason Monk, the practical man, was able to represent the strongest party among his fellow soldiers, and to possess himself of power at the end of the prolonged crisis of eighteen months that followed Oliver's death. Consequently, the desired disbandment of the army, the Restoration of Monarchy, Parliament and the rule of law took place without bloodshed, in the name of the old dynasty. [1660.] Whether, if Oliver had lived, it could have taken place in his name may be doubted, but it remains an open question.

Oliver would perhaps have regarded the Restoration settlement with more equanimity than we suppose, for he was a good patriot, a great opportunist and at heart an ardent Parliamentarian. His bitterest disappointment would have been the religious side of the new regime. Yet on English religion also he had left an indelible mark. His victory in the First Civil War made Parliament instead of King the ultimate authority on ecclesiastical questions, a decision upon which James II alone attempted to go back and in vain. His victory in the Second Civil War prevented the establishment of persecuting Presbyterian orthodoxy. His long rule had nursed the Sects into such vigorous life that they and not the Presbyterians gave English Puritanism its form and its character in the coming period of non-conformity. The variety of English religious thought and practice, not without its influence inside the borders of the Church itself, and tending always to freedom of opinion, springs no doubt from something fundamental in the English character, but historically it dates from the Cromwellian epoch.

The Protector's policy had combined comprehension within the Church and toleration without it. While he preserved tithe and endowments, he put down persecution. The benefices of the Church were held by Presbyterians, Independents or Baptists indifferently, while free congregations of a more fanciful kind multiplied outside. Oliver thus obtained in the field of religion a reconciliation of all the various Puritan forces which he had signally failed to obtain in politics. He even tolerated the Prayer Book surreptitiously, and would have tolerated it openly but for the political situation which more and more identified Anglicanism with the cause of the exiled Stuarts. The fatal flaw in his ecclesiastical policy was that he had not been able to give to Anglicanism that share in the life of the Church which he had offered to grant it in the Heads of the Proposals.[6] The Roman Catholics were less molested under the Protectorate than under Presbyterian or Anglican Parliaments, and though the Mass was not legally tolerated the Recusancy laws were repealed.

These conditions were much more favourable to the growth of new religious movements than any that recurred until the great age of religion had begun to wane. The Quaker movement was able to come into being, favoured by Oliver himself, though highly offensive to most persons in authority. Under the Protectorate it took such root that the fiercer persecutions of the Restoration period could not destroy it. George Fox made at least the most original contribution to the history of religion of any Englishman. His very spiritual and very unorthodox Christianity had immense success among the Puritan sectaries of the last half of the Seventeenth Century. In this first period of its power Quakerism,—based on the doctrine of the 'inner light,' that is on the direct personal inspiration of each Christian, man or woman,—was revivalist in its spirit and methods among the common people, rather than staid and 'quiet' as it became in later generations.

Both Long Parliament and Protector did their best for education, both by direct grants in aid and by donations of Church lands. The Puritan movement was in earnest about education as the Tudor despoilers of the Church had never been. Largely under Puritan influence the founding of schools went on much more rapidly in the first half of the Seventeenth Century than in the previous hundred years. The motive of educational enthusiasm was largely religious, but the connection of education with religion, and of religion with politics, had the grave disadvantage of continual proscription in the Universities and schools, first of Puritan teachers by Laud, then of Laudian teachers by

[6] See p. 203, above.

the Puritans, and finally of all save Anglican teachers by the Restoration Parliaments. The effect on the two Universities, which otherwise gave signs of vigorous life, was deplorable, and ultimately reduced them to the lethargy of the Eighteenth Century. The enforcement of unquestioning orthodoxy in politics and religion is incompatible with the true life of a University.

The great fault of the Puritans as governors of the land was that they tended to exclude all who were not Puritan from power and influence in the State; by making profession of religious zeal a shibboleth, they bred notorious hypocrites. Their tyrannical and disastrous suppression of the theatre and other clumsy attempts to make people good by force were part of the same general error. When the Restoration occurred, the non-religious part of the community had come to loathe the Puritans as, twenty years before, they had loathed the Laudian clergy. In particular the squires, the strongest class in the social order of that day, had been outraged by the military rule of Major-Generals and by the overturn of the ancient institutions of the country. Whichever side they or their fathers had taken in the Great Civil War, the squires had come to associate the political and social changes which they disapproved with Puritan religion; therefore, by a strange inversion since the days of Eliot and Pym, the anti-Puritan legislation of the Clarendon Code was the work not of the King and the courtiers but of the Parliament and the squires. [1661–65.] Yet under a Parliamentary system the Puritan sects could hope some day to obtain a measure of toleration which they would never have obtained if the Stuart despotism had been prolonged after the pattern of Laud and Strafford.

BOOKS FOR FURTHER READING FOR CHAPTERS TWO, THREE, AND FOUR: Gardiner, *History*, Vols. VIII. to X.; *Civil War* (4 vols.); *Commonwealth and Protectorate* (3 vols.).

Firth, *Cromwell* (Heroes of Nations Series); *Cromwell's Army*; *Last Years of the Protectorate* (2 vols.), completing Gardiner; John Buchan, *Oliver Cromwell*; *Montrose*; C. V. Wedgwood, *Strafford*.

Carlyle, *Cromwell's Letters and Speeches*; Gooch, *Democratic Ideas in the Seventeenth Century*; W. A. Shaw,

History of the English Church, 1640–60; Lady Verney, *Memoirs of the Verney Family*, Vols. I.–III.; Feiling, *History of the Tory Party*, 1649–1714; R. Barclay, *Inner Life of the Religious Societies of the Commonwealth*.

SCOTLAND:—Hume Brown and Andrew Lang's histories; John Buchan, *Montrose*.

NAVY:—Callender, as before; Corbett, *England in the Mediterranean*, 1603–1713 (2 vols.).

This period is rich in particularly delightful and noble contemporary literature: Clarendon's History; George Fox's *Journal*; Milton's *Areopagitica* and *Of Reformation in England*; *Life of Col. Hutchinson* by his widow; *Clarke Papers* (Camden Soc., 1891), being the debates of the army officers and men with Cromwell, etc. (See also books, p. 173 above.)

CHAPTER FIVE

English Village and Town Life and Its Expansion Overseas. Character of Colonization and Colonial Policy in the Seventeenth Century. New England, Virginia, and the Absorption of the Dutch Middle Colonies. England, France and Holland

Everyday life in Stuart times, though full of hardship, ignorance and cruelty as compared with our own, had great compensating advantages. It was neither ugly nor unnatural. It was lived in the country, and whatever man himself added to nature did not detract from the beauty of things. The crafts were conducted by men armed with tools to do their will, not as now by men doing the will of the machines they serve; and it is not man himself but the machine that is the enemy of grace and beauty of line. Before the mechanical age, common craftsmen were in a sense artists, doing nobler and more individual work than the modern employee engaged on mass production. They were therefore more contented with their lot in life, though many of its conditions were such as would not be tolerated in our more humane generation.

These crafts were not carried on in immense urban areas from which nature had been elaborately expelled. London, which numbered half a million inhabitants by the

end of the century, was the only place in England that
could answer to that description. And even there a man
could take his pleasure on the Thames, then the most
glorious of city highways, or, if he could not afford a boat,
could convey himself on foot in half an hour out of roaring
Cheapside to meadows where sportsmen set springes for
snipe and partridge, close under hills haunted by nightin-
gales. Nature could be found and wooed even by the
Londoner without the intervention of mechanical trans-
port.[1]

The other towns of England, all much smaller in proportion to the capital than some are to-day, answered to the
description that Thomas Hardy has given of the Dorches-
ter of his own boyhood:

Casterbridge [Dorchester] lived by argiculture at one re-
move further from the fountain-head than the adjoining
villages—no more. The townsfolk understood every fluctua-
tion in the rustic's condition, for it affected their receipts
as much as the labourer's; they entered into the troubles
and joys which moved the aristocratic families ten miles
round—for the same reason. . . . Casterbridge was the
complement of the rural life around; not its urban opposite.
Bees and butterflies in the cornfields at the top of the
town, who desired to get to the meads at the bottom, took
no circuitous course, but flew straight down High Street
without any apparent consciousness that they were tra-
versing strange latitudes.

Such were the towns of England from Elizabeth to
George III. And, such as they were, they housed only a
small part of the population, for under the Tudors and
Stuarts the crafts and manufactures were increasingly carried on, not in the corporate towns but in the country.

[1] The extraordinary size of London, both absolutely and
relatively to other towns, at the end of the Seventeenth
Century was due to its having become the greatest port in
the world and a vast distributing centre for both wholesale
and retail trade. Its manufactures were carried on not in
factories but on the domestic system as elsewhere; indeed
the domestic system survived longer in London than in
the North and Midlands after the coming of the Industrial
Revolution in the Eighteenth Century, when the *relative*
size of London declined.

Many villages and hamlets manufactured for the national and international market. The mediæval isolation of the peasant was broken down, and he came in contact in his own village with men of various occupations dealing much with distant shires. Community of trade drew the whole nation together, sharpening the wits and broadening the outlook of the villager. When the first Stuart ascended the throne, men were saying to each other:

By the Lord, Horatio, these three years I have taken note of it, . . . the toe of the peasant comes so near the heel of the courtier he galls his kibe.

While the contemporary French and German peasants were still depressed by the survivals of an outworn feudalism, the English villager was ready to play an independent part in any new development, religious or political, industrial or colonial. The Pilgrim Fathers were most of them English villagers in origin. The mediæval serf would never have planted the free and self-sufficient townships of New England. French Canada, founded in this same Seventeenth Century, was the transplantation of the mediæval peasant under the leadership of his feudal noble and his priest; while the English Colonial movement was the migration of a modern society, self-governing, half-industrial, awake to economic and intellectual change.

The new agriculture and the enclosures had upon the whole increased the number and importance of the well-to-do tenant-farmers and freehold yeomen. Thomas Fuller, writing at the outbreak of the Civil War, thus describes the yeomen:

The yeomanry is an estate of people almost peculiar to England. France and Italy are like a die which hath no points between sink and ace, nobility and peasantry. . . . The yeoman wears russet clothes, but makes golden payment, having tin in his buttons and silver in his pockets. . . . In his own country he is a main man in juries. He seldom goes abroad and his credit stretches further than his travel. He goes not to London, but *se-defendendo*, to save himself a fine, being returned of a Jury, where seeing the King once, he prays for him ever afterwards.

The forty-shilling freeholder, who included many of

this sturdy class, enjoyed the parliamentary franchise in
the shire elections. The independent part played by the
yeomen for King Charles' cause in the West, and for the
Parliament in Hampden's Buckinghamshire and Cromwell's East Anglia, showed how far the better class of English peasant had progressed out of the ignorance and
dependence of the serfs over whom the Norman Barons
had ridden roughshod.

The small squires, freehold yeomen, leasehold farmers
and craftsmen formed together a large part of the rural
population. But there existed also an agricultural prole-
tariat. Towards the close of the Stuart period the publi-
cist Gregory King surmised that the 'cottagers and paupers'
considerably outnumbered the yeoman freeholders and
well-to-do tenant farmers, and slightly outnumbered the
'labouring people and out-servants.' All is extremely uncertain, local variations were infinite, and there are no
figures available except such guesswork as Gregory King's.
But it is probable that there was a large class of poor
folk in every village, part of it landless and working for
hire, part of it living from hand to mouth on a few strips
in the common field, or on pasture rights or squattings on
the common waste. Then, too, there was the nomad population of the roads and lanes,—the campers in the dingle,
the tinker and wandering craftsman, the gipsy from far
lands, the highwayman and footpad, the ballad-monger,
the quack and the showman,—a world of infinite variety,
entertainment and romance, which Shakespeare loved in
its prime, and George Borrow portrayed on the eve of its
fading away before the remorseless regimentation of modern 'improvement.'

Every class of the rural community found an additional
means of livelihood and enjoyment in the snaring of hares,
wildfowl and rabbits in places where no one then cared
to preserve them, besides more adventurous poaching in
warrens and parks. During the Civil War, the 'poor foot,'
recruited on both sides from the rural proletariate, had
the gratification of breaking up innumerable deer-parks
of 'rebel' or 'malignant' gentlemen, with the result that
the stock of deer never fully recovered, and fox-hunting

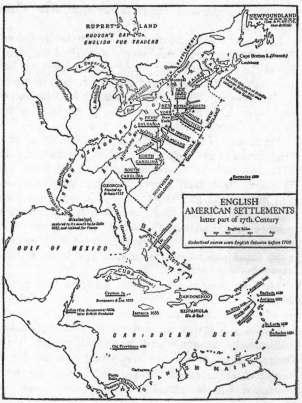

Map 8 English American Settlements, Latter Part of the Seventeenth Century

began after the Restoration to rival stag-hunting as the usual form of the chase. Before that, foxes had been massacred for necessity, not preserved for sport. At the same time the improvement of shot-guns presented an alternative to hawking or snaring as the sportsman's favourite method of taking game. These early gunmen usually stalked the bird for a sitting shot: pheasants were shot roosting, and partridges were shot or netted on the ground. By the end of Charles II's reign, however, many gentlemen practised the most refined form of sport, and actually 'shot flying.'[2]

England under the Stuarts was not sharply divided between an urban and a rural way of life. Since the feudal life of the manor had disappeared and municipal life had become decadent, village and town were both governed by Parliamentary Statutes rather than by local legislation, and were harmoniously related in a single economic system of national dimensions.[3]

Yet in spite of the political and economic unity of England, means of locomotion were still so primitive, and the ill-tended roads so execrable, that provincial differences in speech, custom and character still gave picturesqueness and piquancy to life. The absence of a newspaper press and of a standardized and universal system of education enabled local traditions to survive. Shire differed from shire, town from town and hamlet from hamlet. There was more individuality then than now, at least in the external expression of character.

Men and women were widely scattered through the island, thrown back upon themselves during frequent hours of solitude and isolation; each had space to grow, like the spreading oak tree alone in the field, without troubling too much to conform to any conventional pattern. It was 'every man in his humour.' The typical economic life of the time, as conducted by yeoman, farmer and small craftsman, left the individual more unfettered and self-dependent than he had been in the corporate life of medi-

[2] *The Gentleman's Recreation,* 1686, says: 'It is now the Mode to *Shoot Flying,* as being by experience found the best and surest way; for when the game is on the Wing, if but one Shot hits any part of its Wings so expanded, it will occasion its fall, although not to kill it, so that your Spaniel will soon be its Victor.' Others found the art more difficult, for in *Tom Jones* (Bk. VIII., Chap. XI.) the gentleman supposed to have been born in 1657 says of his brother's expertness with the gun 'though perhaps you may think it incredible, he could not only hit a standing mark with great certainty, but hath *actually shot a crow as it was flying in the air.*'

[3] See pp. 13, 30, above.

æval burgher and serf, or has become in our own day under great capitalist and labour combinations.

But such individualism, greater than is possible in the crowded world of to-day, was qualified by the greater subjection of women to men. It was still the exception for women of the upper and middle class to choose their own husbands, and when the husband had been assigned he was lord and master, so far at least as law and custom could make him. Yet even so, neither Shakespeare's women nor those of authentic Seventeenth Century memoirs, like the Verneys and Hutchinsons, seem wanting in personality and character.

This new English world, so full of vigour, freedom and initiative, laid the foundations of the British Empire and of the United States. The migration of early Stuart times was a world-movement akin in its importance to the Anglo-Saxon and Norse settlement of England a thousand years before. The Elizabethans had prepared the sea-way for the host of emigrants who used it in the following reigns.

The great majority of the first Anglo-Americans came from the south-east of England and represented her most pronounced Nordic stock.[4] They were accustomed not to the hamlets and isolated farms of the West and North, but to the large villages of the South-East and Midlands; it was therefore natural for them, when they reached the other side of the Atlantic, to create the New England township, an institution which spread far, and did much to mould the destiny of all North America. They were indeed the very men to found solid institutions in the wilderness, be-

[4] Of about 25,000 English settled in New England in 1640, it has been calculated by some statisticians and genealogists that fifty per cent. came from Suffolk, Essex and Herts; twenty per cent. from Norfolk, Lincolnshire, Nottingham, Yorkshire, Middlesex, Kent, Surrey and Sussex. The counties on the Welsh and Scottish borders supplied only scattered individuals. These original 25,000, to whom collectively may be extended the term 'Pilgrim Fathers,' were a prolific stock and their descendants were the men who did most to set the political and social tone of the United States in its great developments west of the Appalachian Mountains in later times, until about 1870.

cause in their old homes they had combined self-help and economic individualism with residence in large village groups, where agriculture, crafts and trade had flourished together. The Pilgrim Father did not go out expecting to find a job awaiting him in some specialized employment, but was prepared to turn his hand to anything that circumstances imposed, asking only for land, of which there was abundance.

A great part of the emigration under James and Charles I ran, indeed, not to New England but to the Bermudas, the West India islands, and to Raleigh's Virginia, the first of English Colonies, refounded in 1607. In these latitudes the climate was in some respects alluring; in Virginia tobacco-culture and in the islands sugar offered a way to rapid wealth for a few. The abundant slave-labour of African negroes was only gradually introduced, but from the first there was a tendency to seek 'indentured servants,' whether convict or other, to work the 'plantations' for an aristocracy. Some of the West Indian settlers were Puritan, some Anglicans inclining towards Royalist sympathies, and some were failures of the Old World sent to make a fresh start oversea, not always with happy results for the colony. Local self-government at once became a feature of English settlements in Virginia and the islands, distinguishing them from the colonies of other nations.

But these semi-tropical colonies, important as they became, could not have imposed the English law and language on North America as a whole. The tree whose branches were destined to cover the continent from sea to sea, had its deepest roots in the close-settled, democratic, Puritan land of the New England townships. There the winter was long and hard, the soil thin and stony, the forests came down to the sea coast, covering everything, and the Red Indians prowled around, raiding the lonely farmstead and sometimes the unwary township. Every acre had to be won from nature by axe and plough, and guarded by sword and gun. Yet all the hardships of early settlement in such a land were endured and overcome, on account of the special character of the settlers and the reasons of their coming thither from England. Laud's per-

secution made some of the best types of small gentry, yeomen and craftsmen, desire to emigrate. [1620–40.] Nor
were such men indifferent to the character of their new
home. The English Puritan of that day sought a community large and homogeneous enough to protect him in the
peculiar religious life which he wished to lead and which
he wished to see his neighbours lead. The desire for free
land and economic opportunity was part of the inducement,
but would not by itself have filled the wilderness of New
England with folk. For when in 1640 the persecution
ceased, the immigration thither ceased also. But the prolific stock that had been planted there in the previous
twenty years, held the key to the future of North America.

Immigrants of this type were able to endure and overcome the first winters in that harsh land of snow-bound,
rocky forests. For they were picked men and women,
trusting themselves and one another, with a purpose
strongly held in common. Some of them were well-to-do,
and the colony of Massachusetts was backed by money,
supplies and good organizers in England,—wealthy Puritan Lords, squires and London merchants, who stayed at
home themselves, but supported these ventures, partly
from motives of religion, partly as an investment of their
capital.

Charles I set no bar to these proceedings, for he was
glad to see such dangerous spirits go into voluntary exile.
Indeed their departure goes far to account for the non-
resistance of his English subjects during his dozen years
of autocratic rule. From the time of Elizabeth onwards,
Anglican persecution has always been more than half
political in its motive. The Roman Church persecuted to
save souls, and was therefore less compromising. Rome
could not endure the thought of heresy in any part of
the world; so Louis XIV would allow no Huguenots in
Canada; and Spain would have no Protestants in South
America. But Charles I, and, in later years, Clarendon,
tolerated Puritan and Roman Catholic colonists on the
other side of the ocean, provided Anglican conformity was
observed at home, as the basis of the corresponding system
in the political sphere.

New England was democratic in spirit from first to last. The Saxon township was brought across from East Anglia, but squirearchy was left behind. Abundant land, divided up into freeholds among all who were ready to clear it of trees and till it with their own hands, was the firm basis of the original North American democracy. Squirearchy continued to flourish in an island where land was limited and at a premium, and population at a discount, whereas the opposite conditions prevailed in New England. Feudalism had arisen in the Dark Ages to organize society for self-defence under warrior landlords; but in New England the community acted as a whole, the township and the colony undertaking the organization necessary for fighting the redskins, and the mother country helping to defeat the Dutch and the French.[5]

Above all, the Church was democratic, and religion was the motive of the foundation of the colony; the State in early Massachusetts was ruled by a democratic Church even more than in contemporary Scotland. Full political rights were confined to 'Church members,' who composed a considerable proportion of the whole population. Inside the colony there was no pretence at religious toleration. Dissidents seeking religious freedom from the particular brand of Puritanism represented in Massachusetts, moved away and founded neighbouring Rhode Island, the colony of Puritan toleration, under the leadership of Roger Williams. New England included both kinds of Puritanism, the rigid and the free.

New England was an amphibious community. The seaboard with its fine harbours and inlets, and the neighbouring fishing grounds, held the people to the coast and made them hardy mariners. Their capital was Boston, a merchant city on the sea. The forests on the water's edge of the Atlantic rendered shipbuilding easy for them, until the age of iron ships. Their houses were built of wood as universally as those of the early Saxons in the old English forest.

[5] See Vol. I., p. 123.

The inhabitants of New England and of all the English colonies on the American seaboard, not only found attraction on the coast, but were hindered from penetrating far inland by formidable geographic barriers. The Appalachian and Allegheny mountains and their continuation northwards in wooded wildernesses up to the Gulf of St. Lawrence, effectually cut off the early English colonists from knowledge of the prairies of the interior and the Ohio Valley, where in fact much richer soil awaited them. But no great rivers offered them an easy way into the interior, like the St. Lawrence, the highway of the French colonials. This geographic restriction favoured close settlement and the growth of a number of coastwise colonies, each of great political solidity and numerical strength. When therefore in the Eighteenth Century the English-speaking populations of the seaboard at length burst over the Appalachian barrier into the Ohio Valley and the prairies of the Middle West, they were powerful enough to sweep away their French forerunners in those regions and then to advance across the empty continent with astonishing speed, planting over immense areas the New England idea, modernized and mingled with the spirit of the ever-moving frontier.

The settlement of the shores of the St. Lawrence river by the French, though contemporaneous with the settlement of New England, was its opposite in every respect. The one was the plantation of a seaboard, the other of a great river highway leading far into the interior of the continent. While the early English settlers multiplied their numbers and concentrated their strength in the agricultural townships of a large but limited area, the French went up the St. Lawrence as missionaries and fur traders, discovered the Great Lakes and sailed down the Mississippi. The fur trade was their economic object, and they pursued it by keeping on good terms with the Red Indian trappers from whom they purchased the furs. The New Englanders, on the other hand, wanted the Indian's hunting-grounds to plough, and regarded him as an enemy, only half human. The colour-feeling of the English race is stronger than that of the French.

French Canada was as feudal and Roman Catholic as
New England was democratic and Puritan. The Breton
peasant, the most religious and obedient in old France,
went out under the leadership of his priest and his lord,
and reconstituted on the banks of the St. Lawrence the
clerical and feudal society which alone he understood.
There was no element of democracy or of self-government
in the French North American settlements until those ideas
were intruded late in the Eighteenth Century as a result
of English conquest. The French royal government, which
had organized and subsidized the planting of the colony,
kept it under close control and subjected every male in-
habitant to compulsory military service. No one could enter
the colony without the permission of King Louis, and that
permission was not granted to Huguenots.

The American colonies of England, the offspring of
Dissent by Self-help, were much less submissive to their
home government than the colonies of France, Spain or
even Holland. The English colonies had originated not in
acts of State but in the venture of joint-stock companies
or of individual proprietors. As they were gradually
brought under the control of the Crown, the habit of self-
government within the colony had perpetually to be adjusted, not without friction, to the authority of the Royal
Governor. It was a 'dyarchy' that caused many quarrels,
but was necessitated by the circumstances of the time.

In practice, in spite of the Governor, the colonies were
self-governing as regards their own internal affairs. Laud
had contemplated an attack on the religious autonomy of
New England, and it cannot be doubted that if Charles I's
despotism had become securely established in the old
country a crisis would ere long have arisen out of an attempt to extend the system of arbitrary government across
the ocean. But the civil troubles at home gave the colonies
twenty years in which to nurse their independent spirit:
Massachusetts made war and founded or annexed new
colonies without reference to the home government. It is
true that the victorious Parliament of 1649, in reasserting
the unity of the Empire on a regicide basis, had proclaimed
the novel doctrine that the English Parliament could legis-

late for and govern the colonies; but Oliver as Protector had more carefully respected the sensitive independence of New England, and the Restoration put the colonies back in direct relation with the Crown rather than with Parliament.

Massachusetts had, in fact, early adopted an attitude almost amounting to a claim to independent sovereignty. This led to a long and bitter dispute, occupying the reigns of Charles and James II. It came to a climax in 1683, when the Charter of Massachusetts was cancelled at the height of the Tory reaction in England, when so many English towns were similarly deprived of their ancient liberties. In the case of Massachusetts the provocation had been considerable, but it did not justify the attempt to subject the colony to despotic government. The Revolution of 1689 gave the opportunity to settle this, like so many other outstanding questions. A new Charter was granted and self-government restored on the condition that political rights should be extended not merely to 'Church members' but to the whole colonial community. [1691.] 'Thanks to England,' writes Mr. Truslow Adams, 'the final death-blow had legally been dealt to the theocracy, and the foundation laid for genuine self-government and religious toleration.'

The probability that New England would some day break off from the home government was present from the first. It was made yet more probable when on the Restoration of Charles II the social and religious differences between old and New England were stereotyped. In the homeland puritanism and democracy were once more subjugated by Anglicanism and aristocracy, an arrangement which the Revolution of 1689 modified but did not overset. Cromwell had found it easy to remain on good terms with Massachusetts, though Virginia and Barbados had to be compelled by force of arms to obey the regicide Republic. If a system of religion and society consonant with the ideas of the Protectorate had become permanent in the mother country, the social and intellectual misunderstanding between old and New England would not have become so sharp as it did in the middle of the Eighteenth Century.

Cromwell was the first ruler of England who was consciously an Imperialist. Before him, the attitude of government towards colonization had been permissive only. The Protector annexed Jamaica by force of arms, thereby greatly increasing the importance of the English possessions in the West Indian archipelago.[6] He also annexed Acadia from France, but it was given back after the Restoration.

In spite of their surrender of Acadia, the governments of Charles II's reign, under the influence of Clarendon and of Shaftesbury, were imbued with the spirit of Cromwell's colonial policy. They took intelligent interest in the affairs of America, largely with a view to promoting English trade and finding markets for English goods. Prince Rupert and the Court supported the enterprise of the English fur-traders to Hudson's Bay, turning the northern flank of the French Canadian trappers. Above all, England captured and annexed from the Dutch the group of Middle Colonies between New England and Virginia, turning New Amsterdam into New York, and so forming an unbroken coastline under the British flag from Maine to the new colony of Carolina. [1664.] Behind that line of coast colonies was founded the most strange settlement of all: Charles II's government, at the moment of the strongest Tory reaction in England, permitted William Penn, the Quaker courtier and organizer, to found Pennsylvania [1681.] as a refuge for persecuted Friends in the wilderness, where they practised with success the unwonted principle of just dealing with the redskins.

The annexation and further planting of these Middle Colonies brought to the front two new principles of the utmost importance in the British Empire—the union of a

---

[6] The Civil Wars, from the time of Cromwell till Sedgemoor and after, sent large supplies of unhappy political prisoners and prisoners of war to serve the West Indian planters as 'indentured servants,' practically as slaves, for a term of years. In this miserable way, the English stock was increased.

number of different races with equal rights under the British flag, and religious toleration for all. Those principles had not been the contribution of New England. They were first developed on a large scale in the Middle Colonies seized from Holland, where the Dutch were quickly reconciled by the respect paid to their customs and by the enjoyment of rights of self-government such as they had not known under their own flag. In New York Colony, in Pennsylvania, in Maryland and in New Jersey, there were welded together on equal terms of freedom, English, Dutch, Swedes, Germans, French and Ulster Scots—that is to say, Anglicans and Puritans, Calvinists and Lutherans, Roman Catholics, Quakers and Presbyterians. Thither, as to a most congenial atmosphere, came the Huguenot victims of renewed Roman Catholic persecution in the Europe of Louis XIV, and the Romanist and Puritan sufferers from Anglican intolerance, which operated only in the British Islands.

The North America of the Eighteenth Century that ultimately revolted from Great Britain, was made up of the combination of three types of colony, New England, the Middle Colonies, and the Southern slave-owning aristocrats. The characteristic spirit of modern America, which eventually spread from Atlantic to Pacific, was a blend of the ideas and habits of the democratic township and self-dependent Puritanism of New England with the absence of religious and racial prejudice fostered among the races and religions that were first mingled in the Middle Colonies.

A third element, common to all the colonies from Maine to Carolina, was the frontier spirit. The frontier in American history does not mean, as in Europe, a fixed boundary paraded by sentries, but is the term used for that part of the wilderness into which the white man has most recently penetrated. The frontier was always moving, but the frontiersman was always the same. At whatever distance, small or great, from the Atlantic seaboard, whether in the Seventeenth or the two following Centuries, certain characteristics were always found among the pioneers of the advance into the West. Hardihood, resource and courage;

poverty and the hope of present betterment; democratic equality and dislike of all forms of training and authority, whether political or intellectual; careless generosity and shrewd self-help; lynch-law and good comradeship; complete ignorance of distant Europe—combined to make up a well-known type of character, often in sharp contrast to the settled and conservative habits of the comfortable folk nearer the coast, in districts which had themselves constituted the frontier a generation or two before.

If ever aristocratic Britain were to come into serious conflict with her colonies, she would find some sympathizers at least among the settled and well-to-do folk of the coast towns, who grew richer and somewhat more amenable as the generations went by; but she would find implacable rebels not only in the Puritan farmers of New England, but in the democratic frontiersmen at the back of every colony, an element frequently despised or forgotten by the highly civilized part of society until it was too late.

In the last half of the Seventeenth Century England's statesmen and merchants put a high value on her American colonies. They did not indeed foresee their enormous future expansion; no one dreamed for an instant that the quarter of a million inhabitants of the coast colonies in 1700 would ever be enlarged into a State of a hundred millions. The Appalachian Mountains bounded the vision not only of British statesmen but of the Anglo-Americans themselves. England prized about equally the sugar islands and the colonies of the continental seaboard.

The overseas possessions were valued as fulfilling a twofold purpose. First as supplying an appropriate outlet for the energetic, the dissident, the oppressed, the debtors, the criminals and the failures of old England—a sphere where the energies of men who were too good or too bad not to be troublesome at home, might be turned loose to the general advantage; as yet there was no pressing question of a purely economic excess of population in England. Secondly, the colonies were valued as markets where raw materials could be bought, and manufactured articles sold, to the advantage of England's industry and commerce. 'I

state to you,' said Chatham, 'the importance of America;
it is a double market: a market of consumption and a
market of supply.' Cromwell and Clarendon, Shaftesbury
and Somers, would all have said the same.

The external policy of England was falling more and
more under the influence of mercantile considerations.
Even the restoration of the influence of the old social
order in 1660 did not go far enough to check this movement. The direction of the course of external trade by
government regulation from Whitehall or Westminster, a
scheme of which the Navigation Laws formed part, was
worked in some respects to the advantage of the mainland
colonies; in other respects it sacrificed their interest to that
of the home country or the sugar islands—whereupon the
New Englanders took to smuggling like ducks to water.

At the end of the Stuart period England was the greatest manufacturing and trading country in the world, and
London outstripped Amsterdam as the world's greatest
emporium. There was a thriving trade with the Orient,
the Mediterranean and the American colonies; its basis
was the sale of English textile goods, which could be
carried to the other side of the world in the large ocean-
going ships of the new era. England's commerce, in America and everywhere else, largely consisted of the sale of
English manufactures. In that lay her strength as compared to her forerunners in maritime power. Venice had
been the carrier, at the European terminus, of the trade
between all Europe and the Asiatic markets. Spain had
lived on spoil, tribute and mining for precious metals. Even
Holland had lacked a sufficient hinterland of manufactures
and population in her small territory.

When finally the attacks of Louis XIV drove Holland to
devote her wealth and energy to self-defence on land,
she gradually fell behind England in the race for commercial leadership. [1668–1714.] In spite of maritime
rivalry, it was England's interest to save Dutch independence and to preserve the Spanish Netherlands from falling
into French hands. For if the Delta of the Rhine had become French, the maritime power and the independence
of England could not have long survived. In that respect

English and Dutch interests were identical, as Charles and James II failed to see, but as the English people saw. But it was none the less to the selfish advantage of England that her two chief rivals for naval and commercial supremacy became engaged during this critical period in great military expenditure, France from deliberate choice and ambition, Holland from the necessities of self-defence.

Meanwhile in the England of the Restoration and of the Revolution Settlement, the governing classes were determined to spend as much on the Navy as was necessary, and as little on the Army as they could possibly help.

BOOKS FOR FURTHER READING: Egerton, *British Colonial Policy*; Beer, *Origins of the British Colonial System, 1578–1660*; Osgood, *American Colonies in the Seventeenth Century* (3 vols.); Channing, *History of the United States,* Vols. I.–II.; Truslow Adams, *The Founding of New England* (Atlantic Monthly Press, Boston); Parkman's works, for French Canada.

CHAPTER SIX

The Restoration and the Reign of Charles II. The Formation of the Whig and Tory Parties

The principles of government associated with the names of Cæsar and Napoleon have never been popular in England. Cromwell, like all great English soldiers, disliked the idea of ruling his countrymen by the sword, and they disliked him for doing it. In his last years he was seeking a path back to the rule of law, custom and Parliament. But law, custom and Parliament were in this island so inextricably interwoven with the Kingly office by centuries of continuous growth and by the inherited association of ideas, that a restoration of the monarchy was needed if the nation were to enjoy its ancient rights again.

Had Oliver himself lived, it seems likely that he would have attempted the most difficult task of his life, to restore constitutional rule by reviving the monarchy in his own person. In the person of his feeble son Richard it was frankly impossible. The rule of the sword became more undisguised and more intolerable when there was no strong hand to wield it, when regiment began to fight with regiment, and General to rise up against General as in the worst periods of the Roman Empire. [1659.] To prevent anarchy from becoming chronic at home, and to stay the dissolution of the Empire overseas, there was no way but to recall the Stuart heir. The sooner and the more willingly that was done by Parliament and by the old Roundhead party, the greater would be the freedom of the subject under the restored Kingship.

The lead given by General Monk to the sane and patriotic elements in the army, enabled the Convention Parliament to be freely elected. [1660.] It consisted of moderate Roundheads of the old Presbyterian party, with a strong admixture of Cavaliers. It called back Charles II from his exile in Holland. At this important crisis of the constitution, it was not the King who summoned Parliament, but Parliament that summoned the King. Though the principle of the Divine Right of Kings might be preached as the favourite dogma of the restored Anglican Church, though the lawyers might pretend after their fashion that Charles the Exile had been Charles II from the moment his father's head fell upon the scaffold, the fact was notorious that monarchy had after a long interval been renewed in his person by the vote of the two Houses, as the result of a general election.

The authority of the King and the authority of Parliament were once more regarded as inseparable. Rivals they might long remain, enemies they might on occasion become, but they would never again be two mutually exclusive methods of government as Strafford and the Regicides had made them. Absolutism and Republicanism both were dead; nor except by James II has any serious attempt since been made to revive either the one or the other in England.

So 'the King enjoyed his own again.' The second Charles could indeed be trusted to 'enjoy' whatever came his way, but 'his own' was no longer the full heritage of power which had descended to his ancestors. The crown had been stripped of many of its jewels in the first session of the Long Parliament [1640–41.], and that work was not undone at the Restoration. The great Prerogative Courts, with their rival system of jurisprudence based on the laws of ancient Rome, were not revived as an eyesore to the Common Lawyers and a weapon of the Prince against the Subject: Star Chamber and High Commission remained abolished and illegal. Taxation could no longer be imposed save by vote of Parliament. Strafford's old enemies, 'Sir Edward Coke and his Year-Books,' Hampden and his scruples on Ship-money, triumphed at the Restoration no less than Laud and his surplices.

Of all that generation of the illustrious dead one survivor remained to become the architect of the Restoration settlement,—Edward Hyde, now Earl of Clarendon and Lord Chancellor, the faithful servant of the royal family in its long exile. To him the Stuarts owed it that they ever returned from foreign lands, because even there he had kept young Charles in some degree of connection with the Anglican Church and the constitutional royalists, in spite of the Queen Mother and the swordsmen. And now, in the critical first months of the reign, Clarendon's wisdom and moderation, in harmony with the King's shrewdness and loose good-nature, gave peace to the land, stayed the furies of revenge, and made it to the interest of all parties to live as loyal subjects of the restored monarchy.

Clarendon, who had been the bosom friend of Falkland and the ally of Hampden against Strafford, was still the man of 1640. To that year he undertook to bring back the body politic, as though the two most crowded decades in English History had not intervened. Nor was he wholly unsuccessful. The balance of power between King and Commons was fixed in 1660 at the point where it had been set in the first session of the Long Parliament. The restored equilibrium of the Constitution served as nothing else could have done to give a breathing space for recovery and regrowth after the storms of the revolutionary era. But mere equilibrium would not provide a permanent form of government for a vigorous and growing State, as Strafford and Pym had both foreseen. State action, especially overseas, was paralysed by the division of executive and legislative into two rival bodies, neither the acknowledged master of the other in case of dispute. Until Parliament controlled foreign policy as well as finance, until the King's Ministers were also the servants of the House of Commons, the King's government would remain suspected, impoverished and hampered; and the struggle between Crown and Houses would proceed once more, whether the Parliament were called 'Cavalier' or 'Whig.'

Clarendon indeed had little joy of his chosen part as mediator between King and Commons, for both fretted against the limits he set. His other sorrow was that he could nowhere find the integrity and public spirit of the men he had known in his youth. The character of English politicians, and, to a less extent, the character of the class of landed gentry as a whole had degenerated under the corroding influence of war, confiscation and revolution. Politicians and poets, with one or two grand exceptions, had learnt to change their principles and their allegiance like summer and winter clothes. And the young royalist squires who now rode roughshod over the land had been ill schooled for the parts they were to play. Some had spent what should have been their schooldays in garrets over the Arno and the Seine, amid the riffraff of foreign cities; while those who had stayed in England had grown up among grooms in a corner of the dismantled manor-house when the estate had gone to the hammer. Mean shifts to gain their daily bread had been their education and discipline, and hatred of the Puritan spoiler had been instilled in the place of religion.

An upper class so brought up was not likely to resist the incitement to cynicism and profligate life afforded by the spectacle of the supremacy and downfall of the Puritans. The distinction between virtue and hypocrisy was dim to the first generation that laughed over *Hudibras*. Charles II, himself a product of these conditions, made broad the primrose path for the world of fashion in his charming and heartless Court. Clarendon's antiquated virtue di-

vided him from his master and from the new generation
of Parliament men. His grave integrity might indeed, like
Pitt's or Peel's, have won the confidence of the uncorrupted
middle classes, where family prayers were said daily and
virtue was not mocked. But political and religious affinities
disabled him from becoming their leader; he was the last
man in the kingdom to court the popular suffrage, and he
left to libertines like the young Buckingham and to sceptics
like Shaftesbury the task of leading resurgent non-conformity and organizing the political aspirations of the mercantile world.

The greatest work of Clarendon and Charles, for which
both deserve high credit, was their steady refusal to permit a general revenge upon the Roundhead party. Only
so could the King fulfil the promises made in Holland that
had brought him home in peace, only so could the throne
be re-established as a national institution accepted by all
parties. The Act of Indemnity and Oblivion was stigma-
tized by the Cavaliers as 'Indemnity for the King's enemies
and Oblivion for the King's friends.' [1660.] The royalists
had looked to glut their revenge in the blood and the
estates of the rival faction; but in the main they were
disappointed, and they never forgave Clarendon.

A dozen regicides, and Vane the noblest survivor of
the Commonwealth statesmen, were offered up as scape-
goats, and their deaths appeased the cry for blood, never
prolonged in England. But the cry for land was louder and
more lasting. Land was still the chief goal of ambition,
the chief source of wealth, power and social consequence.
On the land-question a compromise was effected by
Clarendon which secured the acceptance of the new
regime by the great body of former Roundheads. Church
and Crown lands, and private estates of Cavalier magnates
that had been confiscated and sold by the rebel governments were resumed, without compensation to those who
had purchased them. But the lands which Cavaliers had
themselves sold to pay the fines imposed on them as
'malignants' were left in the hands of the purchasers. A
large body of new men thereby made good their footing
in the English squirearchy, at the easy price of attending

the restored Anglican worship. Many of these prosperous
ex-Roundheads became local leaders of the Whig party
in the coming era.[1]

Under this arrangement many Cavaliers failed to recover
lands which they had been forced to sell as a price of their
loyalty in evil days; they were bitterly aggrieved against
the government, and continued to hate the former Roundheads of every shade with a personal as well as a political
hatred. This temper dictated the policy of the Cavalier
Parliament that was elected at the height of the reaction
in 1661. The majority of the new members formed a
party—afterwards known as 'Tory'—that was more Anglican and squirearchical than royalist: it kept the Crown on
a short allowance of taxes, scouted the advice of Charles
and Clarendon, remodelled the Corporations in the interest of their own Church and party rather than of the
Court, and set on foot by Parliamentary statute a persecution of Puritan non-conformists more cruel than any desired by the King or even by that stout Anglican the Lord
Chancellor.

Indeed the so-called 'Clarendon Code' of laws [1661–
65.] against Dissenters was not the work of Clarendon,
still less of Charles, but of Parliament and the squires.
By insisting on a fiercer religious persecution than ever,
at the beginning of a new age that needed above all else
religious toleration, Parliament sowed dragon's teeth, destined to spring up in the plots, factions and violences that
convulsed the latter years of the reign. The 'Clarendon
Code' was the Cavaliers' revenge for their long sufferings
and their lost lands. Balked by the Act of Indemnity, they
found this other outlet for their feelings. They were
prompted less by religious bigotry than by political passion and the memory of personal wrongs and losses, many
of them still unredressed.

The root of what the Dissenters were now to suffer may
be traced to the Parliamentary fines on 'malignants' and to
the executions of Laud and Charles I. It was not merely
vengeance: the 'Clarendon Code' was also a measure of

[1] See p. 200, above, and note.

police against the revival of the Roundhead party. The Act of Uniformity of 1662 restored the Prayer Book and turned adrift without compensation 2000 clergy who could not assert their 'unfeigned consent and assent' to everything the book contained. The Conventicle Act of two years later made prison and transportation the lot of those caught in acts of dissenting worship. These Statutes were the policy of Parliament, not of the King. Laud's religion triumphed, but not through the royal power nor through the clerical jurisdiction and authority which he had striven to restore, but through the action of the Parliament of squires whose right to pronounce upon religion he and Charles I had died rather than acknowledge.

The religious settlement of the Restoration was not conceived in the spirit of compromise which marked the political and social settlement. Yet it may at least be questioned whether it has not led to more religious, intellectual and political liberty than would have resulted from a wider extension of the boundaries of the Established Church. If the plan to 'comprehend' Baxter and the moderate Puritans had succeeded at the abortive Savoy Conference of 1661, the Quakers, Baptists, and more advanced sects, who must still have been left outside, might have been too isolated and inconsiderable ever to enforce the claim of toleration for themselves. The arrangement actually made, under which the Church of England and the various Puritan Churches followed each its own lines of development, rendered toleration inevitable ere long, and led to the variety and competition of religious bodies characteristic of modern England, utterly at variance with mediæval, Tudor or Stuart notions of Church and State.

It is true that the Puritan sects lost greatly by exclusion from the culture of the Universities and from their natural share in social influence and political power, but their very disabilities and grievances forced them to remain for two hundred years vigilant champions of liberty and critics of government. Our two-party system in politics flourished so long and so vigorously because religion also was based upon the two great parties of privileged and unprivileged.

But in the interim between the Restoration and the

Revolution, the nation was torn and tortured by the active persecution of so large a body as the Protestant Dissenters. The squires indeed, Whig as well as Tory, conformed to the Anglican worship, although the two parties were diametrically opposed to each other in their attitude towards the Church. But many of the middle and lower classes, in the days of Baxter, Bunyan and George Fox, suffered ruin and imprisonment rather than give over the attendance at services which Parliament had made illegal. The merchant class suffered so severely from the penalties enforced on Dissenters, that statesmen were at length alarmed by the havoc wrought by persecution in English manufacture and commerce. They felt less concern for the grave injury done to education by the Five Mile Act [1665.], which forbade any clergyman or schoolmaster from coming within five miles of a city or corporate town unless he swore that he would 'not at any time endeavour any alteration in Government either in Church or State.' Puritanism was strongest in the towns, and the loss thus inflicted on its culture was never completely made good.

The number of Dissenters was kept down by twenty-five years of severe though intermittent persecution. But even in their worst sufferings the faithful looked forward to the next general election to bring them relief through Parliament. For this reason there was no general exodus to America as in the days of Laud and Strafford. The Puritans continued to have faith in the House of Commons, although so long as the Cavalier Parliament sat,—and it sat for seventeen years,—it was the prime source of their troubles.

In Charles II's Court at Whitehall, where Roman Catholicism and scepticism were both more influential than among the Parliament men at Westminster, a larger measure of toleration found advocates. The King, a Romanist at heart, desired to tolerate and promote Catholics, and he knew that it was not safe to do so unless the Puritans were relieved at the same time. Moreover, this expert hedonist took less pleasure than the virtuous in punishing other people for their opinions. The persecuting statutes were on more than one occasion suspended by a royal Declaration of Indulgence. [1662, 1672.] This wholesale tampering with the execution of laws was declared illegal by Parliament, and the Puritans who gained occasional respite by these Declarations, were embarrassed by the knowledge that they were acts of arbitrary power and that their benefits were shared by the Roman Catholics. Parliament was determined that both Puritans and Romanists should remain under the full weight of the penal laws. It was a curious 'triangular duel' between Rome, Canterbury and Geneva, between King, Parliament and the distressed subject. It passed through a variety of phases until the decisive crisis of 1688–89.

In the second decade of the Restoration regime the Protestant Dissenters began to spy a hope of relief in a quarter that suited them much better than the royal prerogative. A minority in the two Houses of Parliament, that was steadily increased by the process of by-elections as the old members died off, held out the hope of statutory relief to 'tender consciences,' and opposed both the Cavaliers and the Court.

This 'Whig' party, as it was eventually called, had religious affinities in its rank and file with Puritanism, and in its higher grades with the latitudinarianism and rationalism of the new age. Puritan and Rationalist were drawn together into common opposition to the dominant High Churchmen. The Baptist preacher, dogged by spies from conventicle to conventicle and haled from prison to prison by infuriated Justices of the Peace, when he heard that the Whig chiefs had taken up the cause of Parliamentary toleration for all Protestants, was too greatly rejoiced to enquire whether Algernon Sidney was in a state of grace, or what Shaftesbury meant by 'the religion of all wise men.'

The Royal Society and the great scientific movement that reached its full intellectual splendour in Sir Isaac Newton [b. 1642, d. 1727.] at Trinity College, Cambridge, was nursed in its infancy by the patronage of Charles II and the sceptical courtiers, who had at least the virtue of curiosity. The scientific and latitudinarian movement slowly created an atmosphere favourable to the doctrine of religious toleration as propounded by the Whig philosopher,

John Locke, while outside the realm of politics it is noticeable that the hunt after witches, that had raged horridly in the first half of the Stuart era, began to abate, as first the Judges and then the juries began to feel the prickings of philosophic doubt.

Within the national Church, latitudinarianism had a party, respectable for its learning and eloquence rather than for its numbers, and more powerful in London than in the countryside. This was the 'Low Church' party, a name that then denoted not evangelicalism but what we should now call 'broad' or 'liberal' views. Politically the Low Churchmen, like Stillingfleet, Tillotson and Burnet, were the advocates of Toleration and the friends of the Protestant Dissenters. Similarly the name 'High Church,' given to the great majority of the clergy and their more ardent lay supporters, did not then mean ritualist; it betokened strong antipathy to Dissenters as well as to Romanists, belief in the doctrine of non-resistance to Kings and their divine hereditary right, a great reverence for King Charles the Martyr and—at least among the clergy—a high view of the authority of the Church in politics and society. Dr. Johnson, though he lived a hundred years later, is an excellent example of the 'High Church' mentality any time between the Restoration and the French Revolution.

It is, indeed, remarkable how much of Puritan, or at least of strongly Protestant thought and practice survived the political and ecclesiastical fall of the Puritan sects. Family prayer and Bible reading had become national custom among the great majority of religious laymen, whether they were Churchmen or Dissenters. The English character had received an impression from Puritanism which it bore for the next two centuries, though it had rejected Puritan coercion and had driven Dissenters out of polite society. Even the Puritan Sunday survived. The anxiety of James I and Laud that the English people should continue as of old to play games on Sunday afternoon, was, one would have supposed, calculated to meet with the approval of the most athletic and 'sporting' of all nations. Yet even at the Restoration, when the very name of Puritan was a hissing and a reproach, when the gaols were crowded with harmless Quakers and Baptists, the Puritan idea of Sunday, as a day strictly set aside for rest and religious meditation, continued to hold the allegiance of the English people. The good and evil effects of this self-imposed discipline of a whole nation, in abstaining from organized amusement as well as from work on every seventh day, still awaits the dispassionate study of the social historian.

A reduction in public expenditure was one of the most popular consequences of the fall of the Cromwellian system. The King was indeed put by the Cavalier Parliament on an absurdly short allowance, which hampered all branches of the administration and ere long tempted him to sell the control of his foreign policy to Louis XIV of France. But the shortage was a natural result of the return to 'the just balance of the constitution,' which Clarendon believed to be the last word of political wisdom. Till Parliament could control policy and expenditure, it would not consent to open wide the public purse. When the Commons insisted on searching the royal account books to trace the actual use made of money voted for the maritime war with Holland, Clarendon and the courtiers were scandalized at such an invasion of the province of the executive by the legislative. [1666.] Yet this was a first step on the road to that Parliamentary control of expenditure, which alone could secure for the King's government the liberal and continuous supplies from the taxpayers essential to a great nation in modern times.

It was the military and not the naval establishment that bore the brunt of the reductions from Cromwell's lavish standards. By a single great financial effort, the New Model Army was paid off and disbanded at the Restoration, as might have been done thirteen years before if the Long Parliament had been well-advised. It was replaced by no other considerable force. Besides the King's splendid royalist 'Life Guards' designed to ride by his coach and protect him from fanatics and Fifth Monarchy Men, only a few regiments were kept on foot, and those chiefly in foreign possessions like Tangier.[2] The oldest regimental traditions of the British Army derive either from the few Cromwellian units whose life was continued like the Coldstream Guards, or else from the famous regiments in Dutch service like the Buffs.

The Cavalier Parliament, reflecting the passionate feeling of the English country gentlemen, hated and feared the very name of 'standing army.' They were well aware that lawful Kings could play them tricks with such a force, as easily as usurping Protectors. The King alone, as all good Cavaliers believed, had the right to nominate to military commands and give orders to the armed forces. To claim any such powers for Parliament was to be a rebel and a Roundhead, for the Great Civil War had broken out on that issue. But it followed from these loyal premises that the Army must be kept very small, lest His Gracious Majesty should be tempted to arbitrary conduct.

How well grounded was this caution appeared too late when James II was permitted to keep on foot 30,000 men. Only as a consequence of the Revolution that he then provoked, did Parliament gain practical security that the Army would not be used against the liberties of the land. Only then, in the reigns of William III and Anne, did fear of a standing army begin to subside, first among Whig statesmen whose hearts were in the land war against Louis XIV. The mind of the Tory squire moved more slowly; for a hundred years after Naseby the sight of a company of regulars on the march recalled to him the red-coats who had blown in the door of his grandfather's hall, ruined his estate, proscribed his religion and beheaded his King. The only force he trusted was the ill-trained militia of the county, officered by rustic squires like himself.

No such fears and memories affected the upkeep of the Navy. The Court and Parliament of the Restoration both

[2] Tangier and Bombay came as the dowry of Charles II's wife, the Portuguese Princess, Catherine of Braganza. In return England helped to maintain the recovered independence of Portugal from decadent Spain, and the commercial and political relations of England and Portugal began which have lasted over two centuries and a half.

accepted the traditions of the Commonwealth's fighting fleet, which the dying Blake had bequeathed to posterity. Charles II and his brother James took a personal and well-informed interest in naval matters, and the Admiralty was well served by men like Pepys and his patrons. The Cavalier Parliament and the Tory party regarded the Navy with special favour.

[1665–67.] Another maritime war with Holland soon broke out, a resumption of the quarrel of the two mercantile communities begun under the Commonwealth. It was conducted on both sides with the same splendid qualities of fighting seamanship and on the same colossal scale as before. Again the larger country had rather the better of the war, and, at the Treaty of Breda, New York was ceded by Holland to England.[3] [1667.]

But while the treaty was still being negotiated, the Dutch fleet under de Ruyter, piloted by English seamen, sailed up the Thames and the Medway, and burnt and captured our finest warships as they lay at anchor off Chatham. [June 1667.] The disgrace made no marked difference to the terms of the treaty, but following as it did close on the Plague [1665.] and the Fire of London [1666.], it deeply affected the imagination and the politics of the English people. The sound of the enemy's guns in the Thames was new to Londoners. Men began to 'reflect upon Oliver,' whose corpse they had so recently gibbeted, 'what brave things he did and made all the neighbour Princes fear him.' 'The King,' the world said, 'minds nothing but his lust and hath taken ten times more care and pains in making friends between Lady Castlemaine and Mrs. Stewart, when they have fallen out, than ever he did to save his Kingdom.' Already there were rumours that we were 'governed by Papists' at Whitehall. With less reason it was believed that the 'Papists' had burnt down London; a few years earlier the Fire would have been ascribed to the Puritans. In this changed atmosphere, more formidable opposition parties and policies

[3] See pp. 211 and 232, above.

were engendered than any that had hitherto been known in the Cavalier Parliament.

And yet the principal cause of the Medway disaster had been the unwillingness of the House of Commons to vote money liberally to a government it could not control and was beginning to suspect. The ships had been laid up and the crews disbanded as a forced economy. Indeed the British sailors had gone unpaid for so many years that large numbers had deserted to the Dutch, who rewarded their seamen with dollars instead of unmarketable 'Treasury tickets.'

The Plague, the Fire, the Medway, the persecution of Dissenters, and the 'flaunting of Papists at Court' caused a temper to rise in the nation that foreboded storm. Yet in face of these signs Charles decided to 'drop the pilot.' [Nov. 1667.] It was indeed tempting to make a scapegoat of Clarendon, for he was regarded by the nation as responsible for all that had gone wrong; he was hated by the unpaid seamen, by the persecuted Dissenters, by the royal mistresses to whom he would pay no court, by the Parliament men whom he would fain keep within their appointed sphere, and by the whole world of young ambition whose path he obstructed. Indeed with his old-fashioned views he was no longer in a position to render great services to England. But the men whom Charles chose in his place led King and country into dangers which he would have avoided, for they betrayed the interests of the nation to France, and some of them plotted with their master to betray the Protestant Establishment as well.

[1667–73.] The 'Cabal' contained not one sound Anglican and scarcely one true patriot. Clifford was an ardent Romanist and Arlington more of a Romanist than anything else; Lauderdale and Buckingham were unprincipled adventurers, and Anthony Ashley Cooper, Earl of Shaftesbury, was the man destined first to found the Whig party and then to ruin it by furious driving. Released by these mercurial companions from Clarendon's control, Charles, his own master at last, entered upon strange courses.

The great fact of the new age in Europe was the advance of French arms and influence across the continent. The decadence of Spain, and the failure of Germany and Italy to produce one formidable power among the innumerable States into which their vast territories were divided, left the way open for the ambition of France. Her unity and internal organization had been perfected by Cardinals Richelieu and Mazarin, and bequeathed by them to Louis XIV and the brilliant group of soldiers and statesmen who served him in his youth. In the ten years since the death of Cromwell the danger had become apparent to all the world. The States of Europe, Catholic as well as Protestant, were in panic, but their inefficiency, selfishness and mutual jealousy prevented their union for self-defence before William of Orange arose to marshal them. Austria, engaged in defending the approaches of Vienna against the Turk, could only intermittently concern herself with the West. Spain, stricken with the palsy of all her once splendid energies, was fain to leave the defence of her possessions in the Netherlands to her former enemies, the Dutch rebels.

Amid the effete monarchies and princedoms of feudal Europe, morally and materially exhausted by the Thirty Years' War, the only hope of resistance to France lay in the little Republic of merchants, Holland poised between the sand-banks and the sea. Enriched by its Eastern colonies, its world-wide commerce, and its open door for refugees of all races and beliefs, the home of Grotius, Descartes and Spinoza, of Rembrandt and Vermeer, led the world in philosophy, learning, finance, painting, gardening, scientific agriculture, and many other of the arts and crafts that liberate and adorn the life of man. Holland was a rival influence to France in Europe, and stood on this height without the parade of King, noble or prelate. Her first magistrate, the admired De Witt, kept a single servant in his house and walked unattended through the streets.

The destruction of this bourgeois, Calvinist Republic, no less than the extirpation of the Huguenots in France herself, formed an essential part of the schemes of Louis and the French Jesuit body who inspired the ideals and the policy of his reign. In that policy, strongly 'Gallican' and nationalist in spirit, little reference was made to the wishes of the more moderate Italian Papacy, with whom both the French Jesuits and the French King eventually had bitter quarrels.

In 1668 an English diplomat in the Low Countries, Sir William Temple, negotiated with great skill the Triple Alliance of England, Holland and Sweden to check the French advance on the Rhine and in the Spanish Netherlands. The effect was instantaneous. Louis was compelled to accept the terms of the Treaty of Aix-la-Chapelle. If England had steadily adhered to this successful line of policy, she might have saved Europe an epoch of bloodshed. But our subservience to France during the twenty years that intervened between Temple's Treaty and the Revolution of 1688, raised the power of Louis to a point from which it could only be dislodged by the long wars of William and Marlborough.

The English Parliament and nation were at first well pleased with Temple's policy of the Balance of Power and the maintenance of Protestantism in Europe. But it was easy for persons secretly hostile to these interests to appeal in public to the sentiment of commercial rivalry with Holland that had already caused two popular wars. The management of foreign policy was in the King's hands as the constitution then stood. In the middle years of his reign, Charles II's Roman Catholic and despotic proclivities were stimulated by his natural irritation with the Cavalier Parliament, which had thwarted his wishes and starved his exchequer. Could he not enter instead into the pay of Louis, and introduce something of the admired French-Catholic system of government into the confused body-politic of England? Charles himself was half French in blood and breeding, and his family had little reason to love English institutions.

Moreover in 1670 the King of England had a family quarrel with Holland. The oligarchic Republic of the De

Witts was keeping his nephew[4] William of Orange out of the quasi-monarchical office of the Stadtholderate, which William regarded as his birthright and which the Dutch popular party wished to restore in his person. By the Treaty of Dover [1670.] that Charles made with Louis, England and France were to attack and partition the Republic and its possessions. A residue would be left, to be governed by William of Orange as the vassal of France. The idea that a young Prince would object to an arrangement so favourable to his vanity and comfort never occurred to these cynics, any more than the idea that a lad just coming of age would find the means to thwart the combined onslaught of France and England.

Such was the open Treaty of Dover, to which Shaftesbury and the Protestants of the Cabal, to their lasting infamy, consented. But there was also a secret treaty, unknown to them but signed by the Catholic members of the Cabal, by which Louis undertook to supply Charles with French soldiers and money, to enable him to declare himself a Roman Catholic and gradually raise his co-religionists to dominance in England.

The two treaties were a single plan for the subjugation of Europe and England by the French Catholic monarchy. But the finance of this hopeful project had been miscalculated. The war with Holland cost England much more than Louis could supply, and bankruptcy drove Charles to submit again to Parliamentary control. Louis no doubt expected that long before the English squires discovered

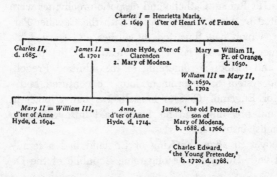

Charles I = Henrietta Maria,
d. 1649 | d'ter of Henri IV. of France.

Charles II,   James II = 1 Anne Hyde, d'ter of   Mary = William II,
d. 1685.   d. 1701   Clarendon   Pr. of Orange,
                            2. Mary of Modena.   d. 1650.

                                        William III = Mary II,
                                              b. 1650,
                                              d. 1702

Mary II = William III,   Anne,   James, 'the old Pretender,'
d'ter of Anne   d'ter of Anne   son of
Hyde, d. 1694.   Hyde, d. 1714.   Mary of Modena,
                                             b. 1688, d. 1766.

                                        Charles Edward,
                                        'the Young Pretender,'
                                        b. 1720, d. 1788.

that they had been duped, his dragoons would be billeted at free quarters on the rich Calvinists of Hague and Rotterdam. And so it would have happened, but for the temper of the Dutch people, the physical conformation of their land, and the qualities that William of Orange now first revealed to the world.

When the great French army entered the almost defenceless territories of Holland, the popular party rose in rage and despair, brutally murdered the De Witts, overthrew their Republic, and re-established the Stadtholderate in William's person,—but not as a preliminary to surrender. [1672.] On the contrary they cut the dykes, letting the water of the canalized rivers flow over the low meadows, and at the sacrifice of their drowned property brought the French armies to a standstill. Meanwhile their seamen at Solebay more than held their own against the united fleets of England and France, and William's genius for diplomacy enabled him to build in haste the first of his many European coalitions against Louis.

These unexpected events gave the squires at Westminster two years in which to take stock of the situation, and to overturn the whole policy of the Cabal and its master. Parliament had the whip hand, for the war had made Charles bankrupt. In 1673 he was forced as the price of supply to assent to the Test Act that excluded Roman Catholics from office under the Crown, thereby bringing to light the alarming fact that James, Duke of York, heir to the throne, was a Romanist. Next year Parliament withdrew England from the war. [1674.]

The Cavalier Parliament had come to realize that this war, properly understood, was not a continuation of the old contest between England and Holland for maritime supremacy, but a design to put an end to Dutch independence as the chief obstacle to the French and Jesuit conquest of Europe. Moreover, the disappearance of Holland as an independent power would be fraught with danger for England's maritime security, because the Delta of the Rhine would then fall into the hands of France.[5] France

[5] By the Treaty of Dover some of the islands of Zealand were to be attached to the British Crown, but they would

too was a maritime rival, potentially more formidable even than Holland, and if established in Amsterdam she would soon make an end of English naval supremacy. It was the issue of 1588, of 1793, of 1914: England could not suffer Holland and Belgium to pass under the domination of the greatest military power in Europe.

Holland was saved for the time, but the issue was not yet decided. It governed English and European politics for forty years to come. After 1674 Louis could no longer hope for the assistance of British arms in subjugating Europe, but thanks to the 'just balance of our constitution,' he secured our neutrality until the Revolution of 1688, by playing off King and Parliament one against the other, bribing the Parliamentary leaders and subsidizing the King. The active agents of this policy over here were his ambassador Barillon and Charles' French mistress, Louise de Querouaille, Duchess of Portsmouth, whom our ancestors spoke of as 'Madam Carwell.'

England had been saved by the narrowest of chances from laying Europe at the feet of France by the destruction of Holland. This policy, insane from the point of view of English interests, was explicable as part of the dynastic and religious designs of the House of Stuart. When this was perceived, a reaction took place against the King and his brother and their 'Popish counsels,' which gave four years of power to the Cavalier Parliament, on the basis of Anglican, national and constitutional principles. Charles, thoroughly alarmed at the storm he had raised and determined not 'to go on his travels again,' threw over his Roman Catholic schemes and sought safety in alliance with Anglican and Tory sentiment. Such was the policy which, during the remainder of his life, he played with consummate nerve and skill.

Charles' change of front involved the abandonment of the discredited Cabal Ministers and submission to the leader of the Cavalier Parliament, Thomas Osborne, Earl

not long have been tenable against French power stretching from Brest to the Zuyder Zee.

of Danby. A Yorkshire squire in origin, Danby sincerely
held the political and religious tenets of his class. [1674–
78.] Though greedy of wealth, titles and power, and ambitious to found a great family, he was, like Clarendon, a
man of principle, though with more brilliancy and versa-
tility in his statecraft. He depended more completely on
Parliament than Clarendon had done, and was indeed the
first royal Minister who owed his position by the throne
to the goodwill of the House of Commons. He further secured his majority in the House by systematizing the brib-
ery of individual members which began at the Restoration
and continued in the eras of Walpole and George III. The
expense, corruption, and elaboration of election contests
were also on the increase; in proportion as the power of
Parliament rose in the State, a seat and a vote were worth
more in the world's market. The patriots of an earlier age
had not had their purity thus tempted.

Danby may be called the founder of the Tory party.
Yet this theoretic champion of non-resistance did more
than any Whig to prepare the way for the Revolution and
the reign of William III. During his four years of power he
befriended Holland and opposed France. And he arranged
a splendid though distant future for this system of alliance
by effecting the marriage of William of Orange with Mary
[1677.], daughter of James and heir after her father to the
thrones of England and Scotland. James disliked the match,
but Charles, convinced of the necessity of conciliating the
nation, supported Danby's scheme and the marriage took
place. [See note, p. 252, above.] The Tory Minister saw a
thing which his party afterwards forgot for awhile, the
necessity of a Protestant succession if a Parliamentary monarchy and an Anglican Church were to be maintained.

During the period of Danby's Ministry, the Tory party
was more devoted to the House of Orange and more hostile
to France than were the leaders of opposition. The Whigs
feared the high monarchical principles of the young Stadtholder, and, when Danby tried to force on a war against
France, they dreaded to see an army in the hands of their
political enemies. These considerations were reinforced by
the bribes which some of the Whig members took from

the hands of Louis' ambassador. Charles and the Whigs, otherwise poles asunder, were both secretly against war, and between them they managed to prevent it.

The Cavalier Parliament had sat for over fifteen years. A general election would certainly produce a new House of Commons more favourable to Protestant Dissent, but even less favourable to the Court and the Roman Catholics. Therefore Danby and Charles had each his reason for dreading a dissolution. If Danby had already been as wise as he became in later years, he would have considered how ill the country was represented by his party and by the existing Parliament, and would have relaxed the persecuting laws. He preferred to join with Charles in evading a dissolution as long as possible, and used the precious interval to crush out the political and religious enemies of Toryism by the strong hand. The Clarendon Code was re-enforced with fresh vigour, and only an accident prevented him from passing his 'non-resisting Bill,' which proposed to exclude from Parliament all who would not utter the Tory shibboleth, of non-resistance to the Crown under every provocation. [1675.] A dozen years later Danby set his party the example of repudiating this doctrine by leading the rebellion of Yorkshire against King James.

The chaos and violence of British politics in the ten years before the Revolution were due to the fact that the two separate quarrels were being pressed by unscrupulous antagonists, that of Parliament against Crown involving the question of Protestant against Catholic, and that of Tory against Whig involving the question of Church against Dissent. The cross-currents and changes of issue were consequently bewildering. Danby still calculated in the spring of 1678, that by applying the rigour of the law he could crush the Dissenting and Whig interest before the long overdue dissolution came, while keeping Court and Roman Catholics subject to Parliament. It was a dangerous and unjust policy, and it provoked Shaftesbury, now the leader of the Whig opposition, to desperate courses.

[1678.] In such a world Titus Oates' 'Popish plot' acted like a match applied to powder. His elaborate lies for a time gained credit with almost everyone, and turned the Cavalier Parliament in its last months virtually into a 'Whig' assembly. For the belief in Oates' falsehoods was confirmed by the publication of a truth sufficiently astounding. The correspondence of Coleman, who acted as the Duke of York's confidential secretary, was seized and published. It contained letters to the French King's confessor discussing plans for the forcible reconversion of Great Britain.

We have a mighty work upon our hands [Coleman had written], no less than the conversion of three kingdoms, and by that the subduing of a pestilent heresy, which has dominated over a great part of this northern world for a long time. There was never such hope of success since the death of Queen Mary as now in our days when God has given us a Prince who is become zealous of being the author and instrument of so glorious a work. . . . That which we rely upon most, next to Almighty God's providence and the favour of my master the Duke, is the mighty mind of his Most Christian Majesty (Louis XIV).

What measures should the country take to prevent the overthrow of their religion by the accession of Coleman's master to the throne? The Whigs proposed to exclude James from being King even in name. The Tories proposed to limit his powers. In the prevailing temper of party violence and religious intolerance the attempt to carry out either 'exclusion' or 'limitations' would very probably have led to civil war. Nothing could have saved the country in 1679 but a union of Whig and Tory statesmen, laying aside their mutual animosities and compromising their rival claims, as they did ten years later after a cruel schooling in adversity.[6]

The Whigs, with whom the game first lay, behaved disgracefully. Instead of seeking to fuse the favourable heat of the hour into a national settlement, they tried only to kindle the furnace sevenfold and to fashion out of it their party advantage. They pursued innocent Catholics to death, exploiting Oates' plot even after the credibility of the evidence had begun to wear thin. The violence of

[6] Swift long afterwards wrote of the Tory scheme of 'limitations': 'It was wisest, because it would be less opposed, and the King would consent to it; otherwise an exclusion would have done better.'

the three successive Whig Parliaments [1679–81.] against
their Tory rivals no less than against the Court; the system-
atic intimidation of moderate men by the London mob and
by Shaftesbury's 'brisk boys'; the refusal to consider for
the sake of peace any compromise short of complete Exclusion; and finally the coquetting of the party with the
bastard Monmouth as the candidate for the throne, in disregard of the rights of William and Mary who did not
promise to be Whig puppets,—all these phenomena, and a
belief that '1641 was come again,' drove a large body of
moderate opinion, led by the subtle and eloquent Halifax,
to rally to the Tory and Royalist side. Moreover the Tories
and the Court, rivals since 1661, were consolidated into
a single party by the dread of a Roundhead revival.

Whig violence was soon countered by Tory violence no
less pernicious. The party that Danby had founded might
perhaps have been led by him along wiser courses, but
Whig malevolence kept him in prison awaiting impeachment. And although sage 'trimmers' like Halifax were the
most formidable advocates of the Tory cause in Parliament,
the party owed them no allegiance and hated their moderation. The rank and file of squires and High Church clergy
became ultra-royalists, prostrating themselves at the feet of
Charles, who had become in effect the able leader of their
party, and prostrating themselves yet more abjectly before James, who enjoyed for awhile a ludicrous popularity
with the Church that he was longing for the opportunity
to overthrow.

After the dissolution of the Third Whig Parliament at
Oxford in 1681, Tory reaction had full licence. The persecution of Protestant Dissenters, in abeyance during the
Whig fury, was renewed with a redoubled zeal. Some of
the Whig leaders finding themselves beaten constitution-
ally, plotted an insurrection, while old Roundhead soldiers
planned to waylay and murder the Royal brothers at the
Rye House, as they came back from the Newmarket races.
[1683.] When these villainies were discovered, the rage
and power of the Tories reached their full height. The
Whigs were scattered like chaff. Shaftesbury died in exile
in Holland. Russell, Sidney and others perished on the

scaffold. The cynicism of the age was shown in the employment against Whig prisoners of false witnesses who were known by the Court and the Tories to have sworn away the lives of Catholics.

During the last four years of the reign, Parliament did not meet. [1681–85.] It temporarily dropped out of the constitution where for some years it had held the leading position. And whenever the House of Commons met again it would not be representative of the old constituencies, or of any free electoral body. The town corporations, including London itself, had been 'remodelled' to the exclusion of the Whigs. No Tudor had ever interfered in this manner with the local franchises of the English boroughs, and nothing but the assistance of the Tory party could have enabled the monarchy to strike so deadly a blow at the local liberties of England as the 'surrender of the Charters' implied.

No more was heard of the scheme of 'limitations.' The Tories in their zeal for the Anglican Church against the Dissenters had abandoned all her defences against Rome. They were prepared to hail with enthusiasm the accession of a Roman Catholic zealot to powers greater in many respects than those of Queen Elizabeth. In their zeal against Whig disloyalty, they proclaimed the most slavish doctrines of non-resistance to the King, even if he should behave like Nero, doctrines new in the history of England and not really believed by the foolish men who proclaimed them with a violence that coming events would render absurd in the retrospect. The University of Oxford made itself conspicuous in these protestations of unconditional submission to the royal will, and James knew so little of human nature that he afterwards took the dons at their word.

The Court, completely victorious and no longer troubled by a House of Commons, was swayed in its policy by Palace intrigues alone, as in days before the Long Parliament. There were two parties at Court in Charles II's last years. Halifax and the moderates were opposed to 'French counsels' and wished England to maintain the Balance of Power in Europe. But the heir to the throne, and the courtiers who had attached themselves to his rising star, were all for France. And Charles, being without Parliamentary supply, depended on French gold. The influence of Halifax declined. It was in these years that Louis, ever advancing into new territories on the Rhine and in the Spanish Netherlands, acquired that ascendancy on the continent which England had afterwards to wrench from him by twenty years of war.

The violence of rival factions in England had prepared slavery for Great Britain and for Europe. But these misdirected energies of the nation in the latter years of Charles II had given birth to the two great parties whose internal cohesion and mutual rivalry made Parliamentary government a success in the coming centuries, as a method of ruling the British State and Empire. From the Exclusion Bill struggle date not only the names of Whig and Tory,[7] but a new perfection of party organization and propaganda, and the peculiarly English art of 'electioneering.' A country that had once excited itself so profoundly in electoral and Parliamentary strife was not likely to be long quiet under a despotism. Shaftesbury and his enemies had introduced the astonishing customs of the Eatanswill election, with all its noise, expense, anger and fun—a peculiar and valuable national heritage, because it fostered that interest in the conduct and result of elections for want of which the Parliamentary system has withered and wilted in more than one continental country in our own day.

In this same period of the Exclusion Bill struggle, the idea of 'party loyalty' grew up among leaders and underlings; it was indeed the only loyalty that was practised by some very important statesmen in the reigns of James, William and Anne. Party loyalty has great attendant evils, but it renders strong Parliamentary government possible. In the end Louis XIV was defeated and the Union with Scotland carried by the mutual confidence of the Whig Junta and its supporters, and the Peace of Utrecht was obtained under no less difficult circumstances by Tory cohesion.

The bond that held together the Whig and the Tory

[7] In their application to English parties they were both originally hostile nicknames, 'Tory' meaning an Irish Catholic bandit, and 'Whig' a Scottish Covenanting zealot.

organizations respectively, so that each had a continuous life of nearly two centuries, was not altogether theory or principle,—for theories and even principles change with changing circumstances,—but permanent religious and social cleavages to which the two parties gave political expression. The Whig party founded by Shaftesbury remained, till long after the Reform Bill of 1832, the party of the unprivileged Dissenters, and of the mercantile and middle classes arrayed under a section of the higher aristocracy. The Tory party, alike in the days of Danby, Pitt and Peel, was in its heart of hearts the party of the landowners and of the Anglican clergy and their adherents, though often with strong allies in other classes. Only in the latter part of the Nineteenth Century the removal of the disabilities of Dissenters and the complete transmutation of social grades by the Industrial Revolution, led towards a gradual shifting of the party system onto new social bases, and the disappearance of religious difference as a leading motive in English politics.

Few political philosophers would have prophesied well of the party system or of Parliamentary government in the year 1685. The two parties, in their first wild boyhood, had set fire to their own house. But the severity of the immediate chastisement that fell first on the Whigs and in the new reign upon the Tories, taught them lessons of wisdom that enabled them in a few years to save Britain and to save Europe.

CHAPTER SEVEN

James II and the English Revolution, 1685–88. The Revolution Settlement, 1689

Government in the last years of Charles II had been based upon a close understanding between the Court on the one hand and the High Church and Tory Party on the other. [1681–85.] What the Privy Council decided at Whitehall was promptly and joyfully executed by the rustic magistrate in the shire, and was praised from the pulpit in the parish church. To crush and silence their common adversaries the Whigs and Dissenters, to set the whole machinery of the law and its officers, the Justices of the Peace, the partisan Judges and packed juries to invigilate against every smallest movement of opposition or free speech, appealed alike to the Court and to the High Tories. The latter found in the Church doctrine of non-resistance to the Crown a religious sanction for these violent proceedings against all critics of the royal policy. Forgetting much and foreseeing little, they held it to be in the eternal nature of things that royal policy should be identified with their own wishes and interests. But this eternity was limited to the life of Charles. So long as he lived there was no revival of the Roman Catholic designs he had abandoned in 1674. He still, indeed, drew his pay from Louis, but it was to enable him to dispense with Parliament and to keep the peace with France, not to attempt anything active for the Roman Catholic cause at home or abroad. Only on his deathbed was he formally reconciled to the Church to which he at heart belonged. [Feb. 1685.]

James II inaugurated the new reign by summoning Parliament. It was a packed assembly, in which many members owed their seats to the remodelled corporations from which every Whig had been excluded. So long as the Tories and the Court held together, they would never again have cause to dread a general election. Never again could there be a Whig Parliament. And it was only a question of years before the 'Dissenting interest' would be crushed out by the Clarendon Code, steadily applied without any more of those unsettling intervals of 'indulgence,' which the misunderstandings between King and Commons had so often caused in the past.

The Parliament of 1685 was more royalist in sentiment than the Cavalier Parliament, but there was one thing which it would never help James to do,—to subject Church and country to Roman Catholicism. The quarrel on this issue between James and the Tory House of Commons was hastened by an event which for the moment made them faster friends than ever before,—the rebellion of Monmouth in the West. [June–July 1685.]

Monmouth's insurrection made no appeal to the Whig

gentry or to the moderate elements that were the strength of the Revolution three years later. It was a rising of Puritans against the persecution they suffered, not in the spirit of the modern Whig but of the old Roundhead party. But whereas in Cromwell's day the Roundheads had had very effective upper-class leadership, Puritanism was now a plebeian religion, confined even in Somerset to the shopkeepers of Taunton and the yeomen and labourers of the countryside. In the campaign that ended at Sedgemoor, they gave their lives with admirable devotion, not from feudal loyalty to their chiefs such as bound so many Highland tribes to the Jacobite cause, but from the mistaken belief that the worthless Monmouth was the champion of their religion.

The revenge taken upon the rebels, first by Kirke and his barbarized soldiers from Tangier, and then by Judge Jeffreys in his insane lust for cruelty, was stimulated by orders from the King. It was the first thing in the new reign that alarmed and disgusted the Tories. In the general horror felt at the long rows of tarred and gibbeted Dissenters along the roadsides of Wessex, came the first recoil from the mutual rage of parties that had so long devastated English political and religious life, the first instinctive movement towards a new era of national unity and toleration.

But the effect of Monmouth's rising on James was to goad him on to fresh tyranny. Under French and Jesuit advice, he adopted much more rapid methods of Romanizing the country than he seems to have contemplated in the first months of his reign. He had now an excuse to keep on foot an army of 30,000 men, and to make on Hounslow Heath a great camp to overawe the capital. A mistaken reliance on the Army encouraged him to defy the Tory Parliament, the rural magistracy and the Anglican Church. Contrary to the laws of the land, which he claimed the right to suspend at will by his royal prerogative, he officered his regiments with all the Roman Catholic gentlemen whom he could induce to enter upon so dangerous a service. Their numbers were insufficient, and he was even less able to find co-religionists to fill the ranks, till he sent over to Ireland for shiploads of Celtic-speaking peasantry. English soldiers and civilians were agreed in regarding these latest recruits as foreigners and savages, whom it was the task of the Anglo-Saxon to keep docile and unarmed even in their own island. Now they were to be made masters of England herself.

By the time the Revolution broke out, James had already ruined the discipline and loyalty of his fine army, but he had not yet converted it into a force that could be used to uproot the Protestant religion. The Revolution was, indeed, timed by its promoters to forestall the completion of that difficult military evolution. But James had done enough to confirm for another long period the antipathy of the Tory squires against standing armies, which they had twice seen employed, once by Cromwell and once by James II, to subjugate the gentry and subvert the Church.

The failure and execution of Monmouth, while it tempted James along the road to ruin, removed an obstacle from the path of William of Orange. It brought nearer by one stage the union of all English parties under his leadership. He had been on good terms with the Tories ever since Danby's Ministry, but half the Whigs had been misled by the *ignis fatuus* of Monmouth. The removal of that pretender caused all English Whigs and Dissenters to concentrate their hopes upon William and Mary. In 1687 the great majority of Englishmen were united in the hope that James would presently die, and his daughter Mary succeed him before it was too late.

The solid part of the Roman Catholic body in England consisted of country squires, excluded from the magistracy but not from society, and living on very tolerable terms with their Tory neighbours. They had no goodwill for the policy which James was adopting at the suggestion of the French and Jesuit party, and with the applause of unprincipled English sycophants like Jeffreys and Sunderland. The Catholic squires knew their countrymen well enough to be sure that supremacy could never be won for their religion, except by foreign arms and civil war; and a second civil war might end, as likely as not, in completing the ruin of the English Catholics which the first had half

accomplished. In these views they were supported by Pope
Innocent XI, a man of sense and moderation, very different
from the Pontiffs who had excommunicated Elizabeth. Innocent had quarrels of his own with Louis XIV and the
French Jesuits; he dreaded the French power in Italy and
in Europe, and therefore watched with sympathy the sailing and the success of William's Protestant crusade, because it would release England from French vassalage.

What the Pope and the moderate English Catholics
hoped to obtain in England was not political supremacy but
religious toleration. This, William publicly promised to secure for them to the utmost of his power. By temper,
policy and circumstance he stood for religious toleration.
Holland had been successfully united on that basis under
his great ancestors. He was, himself, the head of a league
against Louis that sought to unite Austria, Spain and the
Roman Pontiff with Holland and Protestant Germany.
James himself, with a little patience, could have obtained
from his Parliament legal sanction for Catholic rites, which
were in practice being openly celebrated. But neither the
Tories nor William were prepared to consent to the thrust-
ing in of Roman Catholics to officer the Army, to fill the
magistrates' bench, the Privy Council and finally the benefices of the Church of England herself. Yet that was the
policy pursued by James for three years, with ever-increasing violence and illegality, with no assignable object
but to prepare the way for the forcible reconversion of
England.

During these very years his ally, Louis XIV, was re-
voking the tolerant Edict of Nantes [1685.], persecuting
the Huguenots of France with the utmost cruelty, for-
bidding them even to escape into exile, driving them by
torture to the Mass, separating families as if they had been
negro slaves, sending the men to the galleys and the
women and children to be brought up with stripes and ill-
usage in a faith they abhorred. The sum of human misery
thus wantonly brought about is horrible to contemplate.
In the course of years, some hundreds of thousands succeeded in escaping, mostly into England, Holland or
Prussia. A large proportion were artisans and merchants

of high character, who brought to the lands of their adoption trade secrets and new industrial methods. Religious sympathy prevented their welcome from being marred by trade jealousy. The transference of so many of these men from France to England was not the least of the causes why Britain so far outstripped her great neighbour in commercial and industrial enterprise. Many French industries were ruined and many English industries founded by the greater cruelty of religious persecution in France.

The effect produced on the subjects of James II by these proceedings across the Channel, and by the arrival in their midst of a host of innocent victims of Roman Catholic fanaticism, was comparable to the effect on Elizabethan England of the cruelties of Alva and the Massacre of St. Bartholomew, and to the effect on the contemporaries of Fox and Pitt of the September massacres and the cruelties of Robespierre. The Revocation of the Edict of Nantes prepared the mental and emotional background for the Revolution of 1688 and for the long wars with France that followed. They raised to a height in England the hatred of 'Popery,' though in the great division for and against Louis in which all Europe was now being arrayed, the Pope was on the side of the nation whose delight it was to burn him in effigy.

The English drew their ideas of 'Popery' from their nearer neighbours, the French Jesuits and clergy who were eagerly preaching the extermination of the unhappy Huguenots. The terror lest their system should be extended to England as a result of James's proceedings, gave a fresh actuality to Foxe's *Book of Martyrs* and the tales of the Marian persecution. Protestants of every shade, from Archbishop Sancroft to Baxter and Bunyan, saw the necessity of forgetting old quarrels and standing together against the fanatical policy of the King, and the unlimited power he claimed to dispense with the laws of England. This union of spirit among all Protestants brought into the ascendant the Anglican Low Churchmen and the Whigs with their policy of Toleration, while the Tory doctrine of non-resistance to the Crown left the men who had rashly adopted it with the miserable choice of abandoning their political principles or watching with folded arms the destruction of their religion by the 'Nero' of their abstract arguments suddenly incarnate.

The Tory party, indeed, was rudely thrust out not only from its moral and intellectual position but from its material and political strongholds. In 1685 the Privy Council, the rural and the municipal magistrates, the Lords Lieutenant and the Sheriffs, were almost without exception Tories and High Churchmen. Three years later, on the eve of the Revolution, Tories and High Churchmen had been excluded from positions of central and local authority as thoroughly as if Oliver himself had been at work. James attempted to replace them by Roman Catholics, all laws to the contrary notwithstanding. But there were not enough of his co-religionists ready to serve his rash designs. He therefore appealed also to the Protestant Dissenters, but found very few who were prepared to revenge themselves on the High Churchmen at the expense of the Protestant interest and the laws of the land.

Crown and Church were bidding against each other for Non-conformist support. The Crown offered religious toleration and civic equality by illegal Declarations of Indulgence suspending the obnoxious statutes. The Church promised religious toleration secured by statute, as soon as a free Parliament should meet. The Non-conformists, partly from their traditional preference of Parliamentary to Royal power, and partly from the terror of Roman Catholic despotism on the French model, accepted the less dazzling but far less dangerous offers made by the Church.

The King now openly attacked the possessions and freeholds of the Anglican clergy. The Court of High Commission was revived contrary to law, as the King's instrument for dragooning the Church. Compton, Bishop of London, was suspended for refusing to silence Protestant controversialists. A number of Church benefices were filled with Roman Catholics. The Fellows of Magdalen, Oxford, were illegally disseised of their property, and their great College was turned into a Roman Catholic seminary. [1687.] The effect of this act of tyranny was very great

upon Oxford and on all who looked to Oxford for their
opinions. It transformed the citadel of non-resistance and
divine right into a rebel town, that flew the Orange colours
in the High Street during the most eventful winter in
English history. [1688–89.]

Finally all the clergy were bidden to read from their
parish pulpits the King's Declaration of Indulgence, suspending the laws against Roman Catholics and Dissenters
and admitting them to civil and military posts. Since everyone knew that the clergy held the Declaration to be illegal,
the order to read it was designed to humiliate them; but
unless they all stood together, the High Commission would
deprive those who refused to obey. Seven Bishops, headed
by Sancroft, Archbishop of Canterbury, petitioned the
King against the order. His answer was to put them on
trial for publishing a seditious libel. The trial of the seven
Bishops [JUNE 30, 1688.] and their acquittal by a jury
brought the excitement in the nation to a head, and that
night an invitation signed by seven Whig and Tory chiefs
was sent over to William of Orange, whose agents had been
for some time past in close touch with various leaders of
opinion in England.

The birth of a Prince of Wales [JUNE 10, 1688.], although
the identity of the child was for many years unjustly con-
tested by his enemies, had served as a warning to all that
James's system would not end with his death. Neither
Protestant Mary nor Anne, but their new Catholic brother
would succeed to the throne. It was this consideration
that finally brought round the majority of the Tories to
reconsider their theories of non-resistance. The man who
led the party in this change of ground was its founder,
Danby, ever a man of action and reality. It was he who
had signed the invitation to the Prince, together with the
suspended Bishop Compton, another Tory Peer, and four
Whig Leaders.

The dangers and difficulties of William's enterprise
were enormous; half of them were European and half
were English, and only he understood what they all were
and how they might all be overcome by a rare combination
of policy and luck. Unless they could be overcome, he

knew that he would not much longer make head against Louis in Europe, so he determined to take the risk. He needed England as much as England needed him. Until the day of his death this mutual dependence did duty for mutual affection.

The danger most likely to prevent William's expedition would be a demonstration made by the French armies against Holland. This danger was removed by James himself, who alienated Louis by publicly repudiating his protection at the only moment in his reign when he really stood in need of it. William was therefore able to use the sea and land forces of Holland to bring over to Torbay [NOV. 5, 1688.] an army drawn from all the Protestant races of Europe, large enough to protect him against a fiasco like that of Monmouth. Like Monk, he declared for a free Parliament, to which he referred all matters in dispute. The army of James, divided into factions of Protestant against Catholic, and English against Irish, was deserted at the critical moment by John Churchill, the future Marlborough, and others of its chiefs; it fell into such confusion that James dared not risk a battle. William was for many reasons anxious to avoid fighting. Every day added to his strength. The civil population rallied to his banner and to his programme of a free Parliament. Danby himself led the Northern insurrection; the second greatest Tory chief, Seymour, summoned the men of Wessex to William's camp, while the Whig Devonshire organized the Midlands, and the London mob rose without a leader.

Even then it was probable that James could not have been deposed, so strong was the Tory feeling for the hereditary right of Kings, had he not himself persisted in flying from the country and taking refuge with his wife and baby boy at the court of France. [DEC. 1688.]

For many generations to come the Revolution of 1688–89 was spoken of by our ancestors as 'the glorious revolution.' Its glory did not consist in any deed of arms, in any signal acts of heroism on the part of Englishmen, nor in the fact that a whole nation proved itself stronger than one very foolish King. There was indeed a certain ignominy in the fact that a foreign fleet and army, however friendly and however welcome, had been required to enable Englishmen to recover the liberties they had muddled away in their frantic faction feuds. The true 'glory' of the British Revolution lay in the fact that it was bloodless, that there was no civil war, no massacre, no proscription, and above all that a settlement by consent was reached of the religious and political differences that had so long and so fiercely divided men and parties. The settlement of 1689 stood the test of time. It led not only to a new and wider liberty than had ever before been known in Britain, but to a renewed vigour and efficiency in the body politic and in the government of the Empire. The long and enervating rivalry of Crown and Parliament gave place to cooperation between the two powers, with Parliament as the leading partner. From the external weakness that had characterized England in the Seventeenth Century the country rose through the successive eras of Marlborough, Walpole and Chatham to the acknowledged leadership of the world, in arms, colonies, and commerce, in political and religious freedom and intellectual vigour.

The men of 1689 were not heroes. Few of them were even honest men. But they were very clever men, and, taught by bitter experience, they behaved at this supreme crisis as very clever men do not always behave, with sense and moderation. It was the gravity of the national danger in the first months of 1689, with France in arms against us, Scotland divided and Ireland lost, that induced Whigs and Tories in the Convention Parliament to make that famous compromise between their conflicting principles and factions, which we call the Revolution Settlement. It remained the solid foundation of English institutions in Church and State, almost without change until the era of the Reform Bill.

The Tories, who had already in the previous autumn abandoned non-resistance, found themselves in February compelled to abandon divine hereditary right; they agreed that a slight alteration should be made by Act of Parliament in the order of succession to the throne. Henceforth, unless Parliament were 'divine,' the right of English Kings to reign was of human origin. To avoid this logical defeat, many of the Tories would have preferred a Regency in James's name; and even Danby wished that James's daughter Mary should reign alone, with her husband as Prince Consort only. But when these arrangements were found to be impossible, the sense of the national danger caused the Tories to agree to the change of succession in favour of William and Mary jointly, the executive power being vested in the husband. [FEB. 1689.]

Indeed most Tories, in spite of theory, felt so strongly in practice the necessity of excluding a Roman Catholic from the throne, that they took the initiative in 1701, under Harley's leadership, in passing the Act of Settlement that vested the succession, after William and Anne, in the Protestant House of Hanover. Only the Right Wing of the party remained Jacobite, and a number of High Church Bishops, including Sancroft himself, refused to take the oath to William, becoming 'non-jurors,' and giving up their power and preferment for conscience' sake. The reproaches of these faithful few rendered their more adaptable brethren ill at ease. The Tory party, though upon the whole loyal to the Revolution Settlement, remained so at the expense of its consistency and internal harmony; a subtle transmutation towards modern ideas was going on inside it, more painfully than in the Whig party, leading to the Tory disruption and catastrophe on the death of Queen Anne.

But otherwise the Tory forces in Church and State lost little by the Revolution, except the power of persecuting their rivals. The Church remained Anglican, and the last attempt to extend its boundaries to 'comprehend' moderate Dissenters broke down in 1689. But the Toleration Act of that year granted the right of religious worship to Protestant non-conformists, accompanied by many limitations which read strangely to-day, but which were necessary to secure agreement in an age when Toleration was regarded by many not as a grand principle but as a necessary compromise with error.

The Roman Catholic body, being the backbone of the Jacobite party, obtained no legal relief for its adherents, and from time to time fresh laws were passed against them. But in practice the policy of William and the spirit of the times secured for them a considerable degree of free religious worship in England; the infamous penal laws were usually inoperative, and were only brought into partial vigour in times of Jacobite insurrection. Worship in private houses was hardly ever interfered with, and public chapels were erected and priests often went about openly in spite of the laws. So too the laws against the growing body of Unitarians were silently disused. In the favourable atmosphere of the new age, the spirit of the Toleration Act was practised much more widely than the letter warranted.

Substantially freedom of religious worship had, with certain exceptions, won the day. But religious Tests were fully maintained until the Nineteenth Century. Persons, whether Protestant or Catholic, who would not take the Communion according to the rites of the Church of England, were still debarred from holding office either under the Crown or in the municipalities; the doors of Parliament were still closed to Roman Catholics, and the doors of the Universities to Dissenters of every kind. The Church of England ceased to be a persecuting body, but remained throughout the coming era a body with exclusive political and educational privileges that the Whigs, in the long heyday of their power under the first two Georges, never dared to alter.

Thus the principal institutions of Church and State remained on the foundations of 1660–61, and suffered no Whiggish change. The victory of the Whigs at the Revolution consisted only in the victory of their principles—religious toleration and resistance to the power of the Crown—and in the trend towards modernity, latitudinarianism and Parliamentarism that the whole world was about to take, owing to the fact of the English Revolution and the check which it gave to the power and principles of Louis XIV.

Neither did the Whigs in 1689 gain any such monopoly of office as they gained at the accession of the House of Hanover in 1715. William was by no means their leader, though they were more bound to support him than the Tories, because they would lose more by a Jacobite Restoration. But William only looked to find men who would help him to defeat Louis; he was purely indifferent whether they were Whig or Tory. And when in 1690 the Whigs attempted to go back on the spirit of the Revolution Compromise, and to revenge their ancient party wrongs on the Tories, he dissolved Parliament and successfully appealed to the country against them.

His successor, Anne, greatly preferred Tories to Whigs. Indeed, the only advantage that the Whigs had over their rivals prior to the coming of George I, was the fact that they were more unanimously zealous to conduct the war on land against Louis XIV than were the Tory squires with their traditional dislike of a standing army and a high land-tax.

But the Revolution had done more than arbitrate successfully between the two great parties whose feuds bade fair to destroy the State. It decided the balance between Parliamentary and regal power in favour of Parliament, and thereby gave England an executive in harmony with a sovereign legislative. It was only in the course of years that the details of that new harmony were worked out, through the development of the Cabinet system and the office of Prime Minister. But from 1689 onwards no King, not even George III in his youth, ever attempted to govern without Parliament, or contrary to the votes of the House of Commons. To bribe Parliament was one thing, to defy it quite another.

Nor did any King ever again attempt to override the local liberties of England; indeed the central government in the Eighteenth Century became only too subservient to the Justices of Peace, and only too tolerant of abuse in any chartered corporation or vested interest. The victory of law over arbitrary power was upon the whole an immense gain for humanity; but for the next hundred years and more the victory of law and of vested interests produced an undue admiration of things as they were, in the days of Blackstone, Burke and Eldon, all of whom appealed to the great conservative Revolution as the final standard in human affairs. Because James II had attempted to destroy the institutions of the country, it long remained impossible for anyone else to attempt their reform.

Justice and humanity, divorced from all party considerations, gained greatly from the signal overthrow of James and Jeffreys. The Judges ceased to be removable at the will of the Crown. Trials were conducted with decency and on the whole with fairness. Cruel floggings and exorbitant fines ceased to be a usual weapon of party politics. In 1695 the Censorship of the Press was allowed to lapse, so that Milton's dream of 'liberty of unlicensed printing' was realized in England. The even balance of the powerful Whig and Tory parties protected critics of government who spoke from either camp. The cessation of persecution under the Clarendon Code put an end to a mass of continual suffering, hatred and wrong. After a thousand years, religion was at length released from the obligation to practise cruelty on principle, by the admission that it is the incorrigible nature of man to hold different opinions on speculative subjects. On that stubborn fact the modern State, like the mediæval Church, had broken its teeth in vain. The indirect consequences of this victory of the individual conscience were far-reaching and manifold, not to be revealed in the lifetime of the Whigs and Tories who worked out that curious patchwork of compromise, illogicality and political good sense, the Toleration Act of 1689.[1]

BOOKS FOR FURTHER READING (FOR CHAPS. SIX AND SEVEN):
Besides Ranke and Macaulay, see Feiling, *History of the Tory Party*, 1640–1714; Sir G. Sitwell, *The First Whig*; Osmund Airy, *Charles II*; H. D. Traill, *Shaftesbury*; Mahan, *Influence of Sea Power upon History* (for the Dutch wars); A. Bryant, *Charles II*; D. Ogg, *England in the Reign of Charles II*; G. N. Clark, *The Later Stuarts*.

[1] Further remarks on the Revolution Settlement as it worked itself out in the Eighteenth Century will be found in subsequent chapters, *e.g.* Book Five, Chap. One.

CHAPTER EIGHT

Scotland and Ireland from the Restoration to Queen Anne. The Two Settlements

Cromwell's campaigns had established English rule in both Scotland and Ireland, nor did the return of Charles II put an end to the unity of political control over the British Isles. From 1660 to 1690 Irish and Scottish affairs continued to follow the vicissitudes of revolutionary change in England.

Throughout the reign of Charles II, Scotland was governed from Edinburgh by her own Privy Council, but as that body took its cue from Whitehall, and was under no control either from the Scottish Parliament or the Church Assembly, there was no real restoration of national independence, except in the undesirable form of the loss of free trade with England and her colonies. Parliament was entirely subservient to the Privy Council, and made no attempt to voice the manifold grievances of the nation. [1660–85.]

The Privy Council that governed Scotland in the days of Middleton, Rothes and Lauderdale, relied on the support or acquiescence of the Cavalier interest. The Scottish Cavaliers, with their traditions of Montrose, represented the fusion of aristocratic and royalist sentiment after centuries of mutual opposition; and they represented also the determination of the less fanatical among the laity to prevent the old tyranny of the Kirk, which Cromwell had overthrown, from rising again on the ruins of his power. Many preferred the tyranny of the King's Council to that of clergy and elders. Other choice there seemed none, so long as Parliament had no power or policy of its own. The strength of the Cavalier party lay among the nobles. The alliance of the general body of the nobility with the Presbyterians had always been intermittent and half-hearted, and was already played out as a factor in history, except for the steadfast adherence of the great House of Argyle to the cause that it had chosen. Otherwise it was the smaller lairds who remained a mainstay of the Kirk.

The Privy Council had in fact a strong body of opinion behind it in maintaining the supremacy of the State over the Church. Laud's Prayer Book was not reimposed, but the Covenant was repudiated, Episcopacy was restored, and the clergy were to be appointed by patrons instead of by the democratic choice of the religious community of the parish. This programme, accepted by the greater part of Eastern Scotland, might have received the sullen acquiescence even of the South-West, had the Council proceeded with common caution and humanity. But the drunkards who ruled Scotland in the first years after the Restoration went out of their way to impose tests on the Presbyterian clergy which many of them were bound to refuse. A third of the parish ministers, mainly in the South-West, were deprived of their kirks and manses, and replaced by 'curates,' who maintained themselves, in default of popular influence, by alliance with the dragoons and the strong hand of power. [1662.]

From this state of things arose the practice of 'conventicles,' where the 'outed ministers' preached to the faithful. But whereas the 'conventicles' of the English Non-conformists were held in barns or upper chambers, those of the Scottish Covenanters were held on solitary hillsides, in the scoop of the burn, or the heart of the birch wood, with sentinels set all round to watch for the approach of the red dragoons across the moor. And while in England the Clarendon Code was administered legally, however harshly, by civilian Justices of the Peace, in Scotland the recalcitrant districts were handed over by the Privy Council to the licence of the soldiery or the savage marauding of Highland tribes. Such ill-usage stirred to action the warrior and moss-trooper still alive in the Lowland peasant. The Pentland Rising of 1666 was followed a dozen years later by the more formidable and famous rebellion that began with the murder of Archbishop Sharp, continued with the repulse of Claverhouse by the armed conventicle at Drumclog Moss, and ended at Bothwell Brig. [1679.]

The cruelty with which government provoked and suppressed these fanatical outbursts left a deep impression on the memory and imagination of the Scottish people. In happier days to come the stories of the 'killing times,' and the graves and legends of the martyrs shot down in many a solitary place or 'justified in the Grassmarket,' gave to Presbyterianism all over Scotland a hagiology and a cycle of romance, and secured its moral position as the asserter of national and religious freedom. Yet it was not freedom that the Covenanting martyrs had intended to assert, nor was it to posterity that they had meant to appeal, but to the living God whose sole servants they believed themselves to be in a world gone to perdition.

At the time when the disturbed and bloody reign of Charles II drew to a close, the Scottish people were by no means united in admiration for the zealots of the Covenant. The Privy Council and its torture chamber were indeed abhorrent to all decent folk, but the East mainly supported the government for want of any moderate leadership to follow in opposition, while the West was in a state of suppressed revolt. It was easy for Claverhouse and his dragoons to keep down a country thus divided against itself, so long as there was no revolution in England. It was James Seventh and Second [1685–88.], with his Romanizing policy, who drove his subjects of both Kingdoms into the path of union and self-deliverance.

The Revolution, simultaneous in the two countries, restored Scotland to a state of practical independence of England which she had not enjoyed since Dunbar. English statesmen, Tory as well as Whig, were fain to allow her to settle her ecclesiastical and other affairs to her own liking, provided only she would follow suit by choosing William and Mary as her sovereigns. The dynastic dispute in Britain became a lever in Scotland's hand by which she won her own terms in things both spiritual and material first at the Revolution and later at the Act of Union.

It was the Convention Parliament at Edinburgh that deposed James VII, chose William and Mary as sovereigns of Scotland, and dictated the terms on which they might assume the crown. [1689.] And it was the Parliament that in the following year formally restored Presbyterianism, but without renewing the Covenant. [1690.] The autocratic rule of the Privy Council came to an end, as a necessary consequence of the Revolution. Henceforth the Parliament at Edinburgh was an independent force with which the government had to reckon. It was no longer a mere echo of the Church Assembly as in 1639, or a mere echo of the Privy Council as in 1661. It stood for policies of its own. The feudal method of its election rendered it very indifferently representative of the country, but it represented at least the idea of lay forces, independent alike of Kirk and King, though friendly to both. With that a better age slowly dawned for Scotland.

Yet William's was a troubled reign to the north of the Tweed, where the Jacobite party was much stronger than in England. It contained the majority of the nobles, and the respectable and influential body, specially strong in the East, who clung to the ministrations of the newly ejected Episcopalian clergy. The Episcopalian Church, thrust out of the Establishment and barely tolerated in the new Scotland, could hardly fail to be more Jacobite in sympathy than the English Tories, whose Church was left intact and highly privileged under the Revolution Settlement. Moreover, to the north of the Highland line, the great majority of the kilted tribes were Jacobites, out of jealousy of the dominant tribe of the Campbells and their chief, Argyle, the true head of the Whig and Presbyterian party in all Scotland. The Highland attack upon the South, organized by Claverhouse after the example of Montrose, was checked by his death in the hour of victory at Killiecrankie, and was terminated a few weeks later when the tribesmen were defeated by the Covenanted Cameronians at Dunkeld. [JULY 1689.] But the Highland glens were never systematically conquered and occupied before 1746. The horrible Glencoe massacre [1692.] did much to foster Jacobite feeling and to discredit the government. Amid all these dangers Parliament itself, though of necessity loyal to William as against James in the last resort, was factious with all the inconsequent levity and selfishness of amateur politicians, nurtured under despotism, unaccustomed to the discipline necessary for the management of affairs in a free

community, and untrained in any school of public virtue
or wisdom.

Yet William's government somehow survived in Scotland, because it was at any rate more tolerant than its
predecessors, and because its settlement of Church and
State was in accordance with the new spirit of the times.
Though Presbyterianism was restored as the national religion, the aim of government was the gradual substitution
of the secular for the theological in politics. The Church
Assembly again met freely, to discuss and decide its own
concerns, but no longer to dictate policies to government.
The old-fashioned Cameronians, clearly perceiving that the
Church had not been restored to her ancient power and
glory, refused to acknowledge a King who might be a
Calvinist in Holland but was a Prelatist in England, and
was everywhere a Laodicean and a flat tolerationist. But
the mass of the nation, sick of persecution and bloodshed,
acquiesced in the new regime.[1]

An adequate solution of Scottish ecclesiastical problems
had been found at last. For this reason the Scots, while
continuing for two hundred years to be a profoundly religious people, were able to turn their thoughts to material
problems. In 1689 their poverty was in strong contrast to
their energy of mind and character. Agricultural methods
were mediæval, even in the rich soil of the Lothians. For
want of draining, much of the best land lay water-logged
and unused, while the plough went up the barren hill-
side. The primæval forests had disappeared; and as yet
no modern plantations, hedges or walls broke the monotony
of the windswept landscape, where the miserable sheep
and cattle shivered in the blast. Improvements were impossible because the land was let on very short leases with
no security of tenure. Neither lairds nor tenants had money
to put into the land, and the nobles were interested in
their estates chiefly as hunting grounds. The farms were
cabins of turf or unmortared stone, often without windows

[1] An important concession was made to Presbyterian feeling by the abolition of private patronage as a means of ap-
pointing ministers; in the following century patronage was
revived with various far-reaching consequences.

or chimney, the door serving for light and ventilation. Beer and oatmeal were a monotonous but a wholesome and sufficient diet, save when bad harvests brought starvation, as in the 'dear years,' dreadfully recurrent in King William's reign. Nearly half the acreage of what was nominally the Kingdom of Scotland, remained under the tribal rule of mountain chiefs, dwelling outside the law and civilization of the English-speaking lands.

Trade and industry were still on a very small scale. Glasgow had as yet no shipping of its own. Edinburgh was by far the largest and most wealthy town, but even in the towering High Street glass windows were rare. All told, there were about a million Scots in their native land and only a few thousands oversea, chiefly soldiers of fortune. This poverty-stricken population, with few political rights, and living under social arrangements still largely feudal, was more versed in Biblical knowledge and theological argument, and certainly not less independent in spirit, than the well-to-do farmers and shopkeepers of Parliamentary England. If the Scots should ever apply their well-trained minds and vigorous character to improving their lot in this life, the results might be astonishing.

The great change in the landscape and prosperity of Scotland which the next hundred years were to bring about,—the change from the Scotland of Fletcher of Saltoun to the Scotland of Robert Burns and Walter Scott,—was due to the new direction taken by the energies of every class from landowner to cotter. Two antecedent conditions of this improvement may be noticed. First the introduction of long leases gave reasonable security of tenure, which rendered possible plantation, hedging, walling, housing and new methods of agriculture, grazing and breeding. And secondly the Union of North and South Britain in 1707 opened England's home and colonial markets to Scottish industry and agriculture, and made the Scots participators in England's trade privileges all the world over. In William's reign Scotland had learnt, from the tragic failure of her national settlement at Darien, the bitter lesson that she had not the power and resources needed to open markets and found colonies for herself alone. [1695–1702.]

The Union involved the absorption of Scotland's Parliament and Privy Council in those of England. [1707.] Edinburgh remained the legal and cultural capital, but was no longer the seat of political power. It was a bitter sacrifice of Scotland's pride, but it was the necessary price for her material and economic expansion. The sacrifice was the more tolerable because neither Privy Council nor Parliament was in itself very dear to the people, except as a symbol of national independence. The Church Assembly was more rooted in the affection and the daily life of multitudes, and Scottish religion, like Scottish law, was left intact and separate by the Act of Union.

The inducement that prevailed on Englishmen to invite the Scots into partnership, was not economic but political. Scotland was more Presbyterian but she was none the less more Jacobite than England, and she threatened to bring the exiled Stuarts to reign at Holyrood on Anne's death, while the House of Hanover was being established at St. James's.[2] How far the threat was serious, how far a mere expression of her annoyance with England over Darien and other grievances, it is hard to say. But undoubtedly the British Empire was threatened with the possibility of disruption, in the middle of the Marlborough wars with Louis XIV. To hold together the Empire, the Whig statesmen of Anne's reign, supported by moderate Tories like Harley, offered Scotland the great material advantage of union and free trade, on condition that the Crowns and Parliaments became one. The bargain was reluctantly accepted by Scotland, but she was greatly the gainer by an arrangement which robbed her of nominal but not of real independence, and opened out the paths of her future prosperity. England gained not only the political security which was her immediate and pressing need, but the support of Scottish brains and character in the commercial and political development of the Empire.

[2] Whitehall was burnt to the ground during the reign of King William, who himself inhabited Kensington and Hampton Court. From Anne's reign onwards the British monarchs resided at St. James's Palace, until the move to Buckingham Palace in the Nineteenth Century.

By this great act of modern legislation, England placed upon the world's highway of commerce, colonization and culture, a small nation hitherto poor and isolated, but the best educated and the most active-minded in Europe. The mutual advantage to England and Scotland was immense, and was not confined to the accumulation of wealth. In British literature, science, warfare, politics, administration and colonization, the Scots have played a part out of all proportion to their numbers. The mutual advantage was indeed long unrecognized by the vulgar; it was Sir Walter Scott who first taught the English to admire Scotland, and reconciled the two nations to a joyful pride in their partnership. The statesmen of the Revolution and the reign of Anne had served Britain well. If Scottish talents and energies had for the last two hundred years been turned against England instead of being employed towards common ends, the world would be a very different place to-day. And a little more negligence or folly on either side might easily have brought it about.

On the fall of Cromwell's regime in England, the Celto-Iberian race in Ireland looked to see his work undone over there, and the chieftains of their own blood and tradition restored to the lands they had once owned, among a people who still felt for them much of the ancient tribal loyalty. But with certain exceptions this hope was disappointed. The Protestant landlords remained, as a new race of Anglo-Irish conquerors, nor did they, like the descendants of Strongbow and the Fitzgeralds, become identified with the native peasantry around them.[3] The new barrier of religion perpetuated and emphasized the difference of civilization, and idealized the politics of self-interest and racial pride. Moreover communications with England were much easier, and the arm of England was longer and more powerful than in the Middle Ages. The solid block of English and Scottish Protestants of all classes in Ulster gave a strength to the 'English interest' in Ireland such as it had never had before. The events of 1689 were to demonstrate how much

[3] The Cromwellian yeomen, however, often did so. See p. 207, above.

more effective the Ulster colony was as a 'garrison,' than the Cromwellian landowners thinly scattered over the island among a hostile peasantry.

James II, who tried to make his co-religionists masters of Britain where they were in a tiny minority, attempted the same thing with more likelihood of success in Ireland where they formed the bulk of the population. His Catholic Deputy Tyrconnell and his Catholic Parliament at Dublin decided to undo the Cromwellian settlement and to restore the native landlords. But before the new regime was consolidated, the Revolution in England gave the Protestants of Ireland a rallying-point and a legal position from which to defend their property and power. They were not the men to miss the chance. William was proclaimed King at Enniskillen and Londonderry with more heartfelt loyalty than in Whitehall and Edinburgh. [SEE MAP 7.] The farming gentry and yeomen of the North were frontiersmen accustomed to the life of the saddle and the field, the sword and the plough, and were filled with the businesslike enthusiasm of the Puritan religion. They made Enniskillen the headquarters of a vigorous warfare in the open country. Meanwhile the burghers of Londonderry endured the famous siege [1689.], facing starvation in the spirit that the citizens of Haarlem and Leyden had shown in like case against the Spaniard. These men held England's bridgehead in North Ireland till reinforcements could be shipped over in sufficient strength to enable them, under the leadership of William himself, to advance southward upon Dublin.

In the year 1690 Ireland was the pivot of the European crisis. The fate of Britain depended on William's campaign, and on the fate of Britain depended the success or failure of Europe's resistance to French hegemony. William's throne was tottering in the after-throes of the earthquake of the late Revolution, which had not yet subsided. The English Church and Army were disaffected; the civil, military and naval services were in grave disorder; the Whigs and Tories of Parliament were renewing their old feuds; half the public men of both parties were in secret communication with the Jacobites, not because they desired but because they expected a Restoration. With good hope then, Louis had sent over James as his vassal, with French money, troops and generals, to complete first the conquest of Ireland, where three-fourths of the land already obeyed him. Until Ireland was secured for William, Britain could take no part in the continental war, and might soon herself be in the throes of a counter-revolution.

The battle of the Boyne was fought upon two quarrels. [JULY 1, 1690.] It was the struggle of the Anglo-Scots against the Celto-Iberians for the leadership of Ireland. But it was no less the struggle of Britain and her European allies to prevent a Jacobite restoration in England, and the consequent domination of the world by the French monarchy. The presence, on both sides of the river, of regiments from the continent represented the international issues at stake. The outcome of that day subjected the native Irish to persecution and tyranny for several generations to come, but it saved Protestantism in Europe and enabled the British Empire to launch forth strongly on its career of prosperity, freedom and expansion overseas.

But while Enniskillen, Londonderry and the Boyne were but a stage in the forward march of British and world history, they became the central point of time in the imagination of the ruling race in Ireland. With equal intensity of recollection the oppressed Celt continued to think of the gallant defence of Limerick, and the subsequent breach by the conquerors of the treaty they signed there with the vanquished race. [1690, 1691.] Sarsfield, the hero of the Limerick campaigns, stood to the conquered as the representative man of the new Ireland, the faithful son of the *mater dolorosa*. The place occupied by Sarsfield in Irish history is significant. For he was no scion of an old tribal family, with immemorial claims on the local allegiance of a clan. The English had effectually destroyed the clan society and banished or slain the clan leaders. Sarsfield represented the new nation that was taking the place of the suppressed tribes, as Wallace had represented the new nation that in Scotland gradually took the place of old clan and feudal loyalties.

The restored English rule in Ireland reflected very little of the wise and tolerant spirit of William. In this Catholic island he was powerless to do anything to protect the Catholics, whose lot he mitigated in England. The new regime in Ireland reflected the rash ignorance and prejudice of the Whigs and Tories of the Westminster Parliament, who were the real overlords of the reconquered dependency. While the penal code placed the Catholics in Ireland under every political and social disadvantage that malice could invent, and pursued and persecuted their priests, the only leaders left to them under the Cromwellian land system,—by a masterstroke of folly the sectarian quarrels of English Protestants were transferred to Ulster; Anglican intolerance refused political equality and for some time even religious freedom to Presbyterians who had manned the walls of Londonderry and forded the Boyne water. From the Restoration onwards, English trade jealousy had been permitted to depress the Protestant interest in Ireland by laws against the export of Irish cattle and of Irish cloth. The ruin of the Irish cloth trade, completed at the end of William's reign by the decrees of the English Parliament, effectively stopped the growth of the Anglo-Saxon colony. Many thousands of Ulster Scots who sought refuge beyond the Atlantic in the Appalachian mountains, had more real wrongs to revenge on England in the War of American Independence than had most of those who followed the standard of Washington.

Oliver had at least promoted the Protestant interest everywhere in the British Isles. He saw that if Ireland was to be an English colony it must be colonized by English. But the Protestant interest and the Anglo-Saxon colony were after his death depressed by the commercial and ecclesiastical jealousy of Cavalier, Whig and Tory Parliaments, of narrower vision in these respects than Protector or King. Yet the Catholics were still persecuted with Cromwellian vigour. All that was bad in Oliver's Irish system was preserved, all that was good in it was reversed.[4]

Such were the Scottish and the Irish settlements that resulted from the English Revolution. Very different as they were in their character and ultimate consequences,

[4] See pp. 208–9, above.

they seemed to be equally permanent and equally unchallengeable throughout the greater part of the stable and pacific Eighteenth Century. Indeed in 1715, and again in 1745, the Hanoverian government had much more trouble in Scotland than in Ireland. Yet the Scottish settlement, resting on consent, in the end outlasted the Irish settlement that reposed on force.

It is remarkable that the great events which convulsed England, Scotland and Ireland under the later Stuarts, had no repercussions of a regional character in Celtic Wales. From the Tudor settlement till the Nineteenth Century, Wales had no history except that of slow social and religious growth. The upper class were gradually becoming English in culture and connection, while the small farmers of the hills, the typical Welshmen before the modern industrial era, remained Celtic in character and largely Celtic in speech, but felt no active political hostility to England or to English institutions of which Wales was now an integral part. The level of intellectual activity was low as compared to later times, but native music and poetry persisted among the people; and all through the Seventeenth and Eighteenth Centuries the Welsh common folk were gradually moving from an indifferent acquiescence in Anglican religion towards an enthusiastic evangelicalism of their own, by means of which the national mind and spirit eventually revived.

BOOKS FOR FURTHER READING: Hume Brown, *History of Scotland*; Andrew Lang, *ditto*; W. L. Mathieson, *Politics and Religion in Scotland* and *Scotland and the Union*; Lecky, *History of Ireland in the 18th Century*, Vol. I.; Stephen Gywnn, *History of Ireland*; Bagwell, *Ireland under the Stuarts*, Vol. III.; Dicey and Rait, *Thoughts on the Scottish Union*; G. M. Trevelyan, *Ramillies and the Union with Scotland*, Chapters X.–XIV.

CHAPTER NINE

The Wars of William and Marlborough. The Downfall of Louis XIV and the Rise of Great Britain to Maritime and Commercial Supremacy. The Death of Anne and the Dynastic Crisis

SOVEREIGNS: William and Mary, 1689–94; William III (alone), 1694–1702; Anne, 1702–14

In the winter of 1688–89, foreign and domestic events combined to force England into the leadership of the alliance against France, in accordance with Danby's war plans of a dozen years before which had been thwarted by King Charles and by the Whigs.[1] After the Revolution, resistance to France became the first charge on the energies of the new King and of the reconstituted Whig party, and in a scarcely less degree of the nation as a whole. The continued attempt of Louis to reimpose upon England the rule of James and his son after him, rendered the wars of William and Marlborough unavoidable.

William's war, known as the War of the League of Augsburg, lasted from 1689 to 1697, and was ended by the indecisive Treaty of Ryswick. [SEE MAP 9.] After an uneasy interval of four years, war broke out again on an even larger scale,—the War of the Spanish Succession,—conducted by Marlborough as Europe's general and diplomat in chief, and was ended by the Treaty of Utrecht in 1713. That Treaty, which ushered in the stable and characteristic period of Eighteenth Century civilization, marked the end of danger to Europe from the old French monarchy, and it marked a change of no less significance to the world at large,—the maritime, commercial and financial supremacy of Great Britain.

The prime condition of successful warfare against Louis, whether on sea or land, was the alliance of England and Holland. The understanding was not very cordial in 1689

1 See p. 255, above.

between the two nations, so long accustomed to regard each other as rivals in trade and admiralty; but a united front was demanded by the time, and was ensured by the greatest statesman in Europe who had been placed at the head of the executive in both countries. Under William's tutelage, the English and Dutch Ministers contracted habits of close co-operation for purposes of war, which survived the death of the Stadtholder-King and were continued by Marlborough and Heinsius. Co-operation was the less difficult, because England's commercial jealousy of Holland diminished as the proportion of Dutch ships in the allied fleet dwindled year by year, and as Dutch commerce and finance fell behind the newly mobilized resources of her ally. England throve on the war,[2] while the strain of war taxation and effort slowly undermined the artificial greatness of the little Republic. In the latter part of Queen Anne's reign, the mercantile community in London had so little cause left for jealousy of Dutch commerce, that the Whigs and the 'moneyed interest' proposed concessions to be made to Holland in the terms of peace, which the Tories and the 'landed interest' justly criticized as extravagant.

Throughout this long period of war [1689–1713.], which involved all Western and Central Europe and its American Colonies, the naval operations stood in a close causal connection with the diplomatic triumphs of William, and the diplomatic and martial triumphs of Marlborough. But it is only in quite recent times, under the influence of Admiral Mahan and his school of history, that the maritime aspect of the struggle against Louis has been rated at its true value. For although Sir George Rooke and Sir Clowdisley Shovell were fine seamen, no name like Drake, Blake or Nelson appeared as the rival of Marlborough's fame, and the single naval victory of La Hogue seemed a poor match for Blenheim and Ramillies and the long list of conquered

---

[2] The cost was not out of proportion to Britain's wealth, and the loss of life was trifling as compared to the losses of present-day warfare. At Blenheim the allied army in the field consisted of only 9000 British and 36,000 foreigners. And the British armies only fought one of these great battles on an average every two years.

provinces and towns. Yet all the grand schemes of war and diplomacy depended on the battleships of England, tossing far out at sea; Louis of France, like Philip of Spain before him, and Napoleon and Kaiser William since, was hunted down by the pack he never saw.

La Hogue, the crowning victory at sea, occurred as early as the fourth year in the long contest. [1692.] This is the more remarkable, because the French, as Admiral Mahan tells us, were 'superior to the English and Dutch on the seas in 1689 and 1690.' In the first months of the war Louis had the chance to perpetuate French naval supremacy and to prevent the success of the English Revolution, by the proper use of his then dominant fleet. But the irrecoverable moment went by unseized. He made no naval effort to stop William from shipping his forces to England in 1688, and to Ireland in the two following years. In 1690 the victory of the French over the inferior numbers of the combined English and Dutch fleets off Beachy Head, showed what might have been done to cut the communications between England and Ireland in the year of the Boyne. But the courtiers at inland Versailles lacked the sense of naval opportunity, which was seldom entirely wanting to the statesmen who watched the world's ebb and flow from the tidal shore of the Thames.

In 1692 the tables were turned by the victory in the Channel of the allied over the French fleet, followed by the destruction of fifteen French men-of-war in the harbours of Cherbourg and La Hogue. These losses were not indeed very much greater than the allied losses at Beachy Head two years before.[3] And yet La Hogue proved as decisive as Trafalgar, because Louis, having by his clumsy and arrogant diplomacy defied all Europe to a land war, could not afford to keep the French fleet up to its strength, in addition to the armies and fortresses needed for the defence of all his land frontiers at once. The French fighting

[3] Neither Torrington nor Tourville, the English and French admirals at Beachy Head and La Hogue respectively, was to blame. Both were forced to fight by orders from their governments, against their better judgments, and both made the best of a bad business.

navy in 1690 had owed its temporary superiority to the
war-policy of the Court, and was not, to the same degree
as the navies of England and Holland, founded on proportionately great resources of merchant shipping and commercial wealth. The trade and industry of France were
oozing away through the self-inflicted wound of the Revocation of the Edict of Nantes. When, therefore, the war-
policy of Louis induced him to neglect the navy in favour
of the land forces, French naval decline was rapid and
permanent, and French commerce and colonies suffered
accordingly.

The battle fleets of King Louis retired from serious operations, leaving the passage to the continent open year after
year to the armies of William and Marlborough with all
their supplies and reinforcements, and allowing the pressure of the British fleet to be brought to bear on hesitating
States at moments of diplomatic crisis. In William's reign
the allied fleet saved Barcelona and prolonged the resistance of Spain against Louis. During the Marlborough
wars, our alliance with Portugal and rebellious Catalonia
[1703, 1705.], and our whole war-policy in the Mediterranean and in Spain, depended on our naval supremacy
in those seas, of which Gibraltar and Minorca were pledges
taken and kept. [1704, 1708.]

The seamen of France, when their grand fleet went out
of commission, turned their energies to privateering. Admiral Tourville was eclipsed by Jean Bart. English commerce suffered from him and his like, but throve in their
despite, while French commerce disappeared from the
seas. When the frontiers of France were closed by hostile
armies, she was thrown back to feed upon her own ever
diminishing resources, while England had the world for
market from China to Massachusetts.

In the earlier years of the reign of the Grand Monarch,
his good genius, Colbert, had nourished French industry
and commerce with remarkable success, though often by
State regulations more paternal than would have suited
the individualist spirit of wealth-making in England. But
from the Dutch war of 1672 onwards the malign influence
of Louvois gradually replaced the hold of Colbert on the

mind of the King. Warlike ambitions in Europe and religious persecution at home destroyed the fabric of national prosperity erected in the earlier part of the reign. Louis could indeed tax his miserable peasants at will, but even he could not take from them more than they had, and he had bled them white long before he was rid of Marlborough. Bankruptcy brought his system to the ground, and with it fell the moral prestige of despotism and religious persecution.

Meanwhile the English State, that had been so feeble and distracted in the first two years of William's reign, was gaining internal harmony, financial soundness and warlike vigour all through the long contest, so that the new English principles in Church and State were constantly rising in the world's esteem. England was paymaster to the Grand Alliance, with her subsidies to needy German Princes, and her own well-equipped armies and fleets, that increased in numbers, discipline and efficiency as the years went by.

Parliament, supreme at length in the constitution, was ready to vote supplies to William and Anne such as it had never voted to either Charles. Scarcely less important, from the point of view of the finance of the war, was the alliance between the King's Ministers and the City, leading to a new system of government borrowing on long loans. In the past, royal loans had been made in anticipation of revenue, the capital to be paid back as soon as certain taxes had been levied. Under the new system the patriotic investor, doing well both for himself and for his country, had no wish to have his capital paid back at any near day, preferring to draw a good interest on it for the rest of his life, upon the security of the State. The principal lenders to government were organized in the Bank of England, to which Ministers gave the support of public credit in its banking operations with individual traders. [1694.]

The Bank of England and the permanent National Debt were the outcome of the fertile brains of the Scot, William Paterson, and of the Whig Chancellor of the Exchequer, Charles Montagu; the whole movement was regarded with suspicion by the Tory country gentlemen, jealous of the ris-

ing influence of the 'moneyed interest' over the royal counsels. The City, prevalently Whig in political and religious
sympathy, was bound still more strongly to the Whig party
by this system of long loans to the governments born of
the Revolution. For the Pretender would repudiate his
enemy's debts if he should ever return, and to prevent that
return the Whigs were pledged one degree more deeply
than the Tories.

The movement towards the development of the world's
resources through accumulated and applied capital, was
in this era finding its principal seat of operations in mercantile England. The capitalization of industry was still in the
day of small things, though the domestic cloth-workers
dealt through capitalist middlemen. But the capitalization
of the world's trade was already conducted on a large
scale, and was moving its centre from Amsterdam to London. The London of William and Marlborough was a huge
emporium, less of industry than of commerce and finance.
Its work was done by a turbulent population of cockney
roughs—porters, dockers, day-labourers, watermen and a
fair sprinkling of professional criminals—living uncared-for
and almost unpoliced in labyrinths of tottering, insanitary
houses many of them in the 'liberties' outside the City
walls, especially in the over-populated area of which Fleet
Street was the centre; next, there was a large middle
stratum of respectable shopkeepers and artisans, largely
engaged in high-class finishing trades; and on the top of
all, a body of wealthy merchants and moneyed men to
which no other district in Europe could show the equal,
inhabited 'the City' proper.

London and its leaders were once more hand-in-glove
with government, as in the days of Burleigh and Gresham;
but the methods of State finance and the quantity and
availability of London's wealth had made great strides since
the days of Elizabeth's parsimonious warfare against Philip.
If Drake had had Charles Montagu behind him, he would
have done more than singe the beard of the King of Spain.
The Grand Monarch of this later era was to learn by bitter
experience that the English Parliament and the City of
London between them commanded the deeper purse,

though France had nearly twenty million inhabitants, and England and Scotland about seven.

The East India Company of London had become the rival on equal terms of the once dominant Dutch Company, that had so rudely excluded the English traders from the Spice Islands in early Stuart days. Steady trade with the Mogul Empire on the mainland was carried on from the stations at Madras, Bombay, and latterly from Fort William in the Delta of the Ganges, the nucleus of the future Calcutta. The shareholders in the joint-stock company continued to make fortunes hand over hand during the war with Louis, for although ships were lost to French privateers, the demand for tea, spices, shawls and cotton goods did not diminish, and the demand for saltpetre to make gunpowder greatly increased. The Company, though it was gradually building up a great market for English goods in China and India, was accused of exporting bullion and bringing back mere 'luxuries'; but men and women still clamoured for the 'luxuries,' and for shares in the much-abused Company. In the reigns of William and Anne, the strife in the City between the chartered traders and the interlopers, between the Old Company and the New, convulsed the House of Commons, which had stepped into the place of the Court as the State arbiter of commercial privileges. In the first half-dozen years after the Revolution, Sir Josiah Child, in defence of the monopoly of the Old Company, disbursed some £100,000 to Cabinet Ministers and members of Parliament. In these quarrels, all the furies of party passion and private greed were stimulated by the knowledge that the wealth of the East was no longer an Arabian tale, but a solid fact on which City fortunes were being built and new County families founded every year. The most remarkable and formidable of these self-made magnates was Thomas Pitt, grandfather of the great Chatham, and owner of the Pitt diamond. Having made his fortune in India first as poacher and then as game-keeper, that is to say first as 'interloping' trader and then as Governor of Madras for the Company, he purchased a landed estate at home, together with the Parliamentary borough of Old Sarum.

The coffee drunk in the famous coffee-houses of the period was imported less by the East India Company than by the English merchants trading in the Mediterranean.[4] They had become the chief European influence at Constantinople, and were pushing the sale of English cloth in the ports of Italy, Venice and the Levant. In spite of the Barbary pirates and the privateers who dashed out from Toulon and Brest, our Turkey and Venetian merchants throve during the war. And it greatly added to their security and prestige that after the capture of Gibraltar and Minorca the Western Mediterranean was permanently occupied by the Royal Navy. [1704, 1708.]

On the other side of the Atlantic, the English had the full advantage of naval supremacy. [SEE MAP 8.] There was a rehearsal of the issues brought to a final head by Wolfe and Chatham two generations later. The men of Massachusetts, much the most active of the American Colonies, twice during the wars with Louis XIV captured Acadia from the French; though given back once at the Treaty of Ryswick, it was annexed to Britain by the Treaty of Utrecht and re-christened Nova Scotia. By the same treaty Britain annexed Newfoundland [1713.], subject to certain French fishing rights which remained a constant subject of dispute until their final settlement in the reign of Edward VII. The Hudson Bay territory was also annexed, with its snow-bound forests whence English hunters supplied the fur trade at home. And so—although an attack on Quebec, badly concerted between the Royal and Colonial forces, had failed [1711.]—the end of the war saw the British solidly planted near the mouth of the St. Lawrence and in the arctic rear of the French settlements on the great river.

The war and the peace stimulated another British interest oversea, the endeavour to force our commerce on the great South American market, in spite of the Spanish government's decree excluding all foreign traders. The quarrel with the Spaniards in South and Central America

---

[4] The importation of coffee was criticized in 1680, as being 'most useless since it serves neither for nourishment nor debauchery.'

had been carried on by the English buccaneers ever since James I's peace with the Spanish Monarchy.[5] In the reign of Charles II, the buccaneers of the West Indian islands were in the heyday of their romantic glory, as the unofficial maintainers of England's quarrels along the Spanish Main. In the reigns of William and Anne they were declining into the position and character of black-flag pirates of the type of Teach, their hand against the men of all nations, and every man's hand against them. But the process was gradual; many, like Kidd and Quelch, moved in a doubtful borderland between piracy and privateering, and the attitude of the Colonials and of the British officials differed according to the circumstances and the men.

[1713.] An attempt was made to regularize our relations with Spain in the Treaty of Utrecht, when the Tory government won applause even from their harshest critics by securing the famous *Asiento,* permitting England alone of foreign powers the annual privilege of sending a ship to trade with Spanish America, and of taking thither, besides, 4800 negro slaves. But this limited monopoly was used in the Eighteenth Century as the starting-point for a larger illicit trade, and the quarrel for the open door in South America only came to an end with the termination of Spanish rule in the days of Bolivar and Canning.

With regard to the war in Europe, there is a marked distinction of character between the two parts of the struggle that brought Louis to his knees. In the War of the League of Augsburg [1689–97.], of which William III was the political and military chief, France was engaged on all her land frontiers in operations against Spain, Holland and the German Princes, and even so she held her own; neither side won any sensational victories, though Steinkirk and Landen were successes for the French; neither side anywhere made any measurable progress. [1692, 1693.] The boundary between the Spanish Netherlands and France, where most of the fighting took place, remained practically unaltered. Under William, who was not the man either to

[5] See p. 160, above.

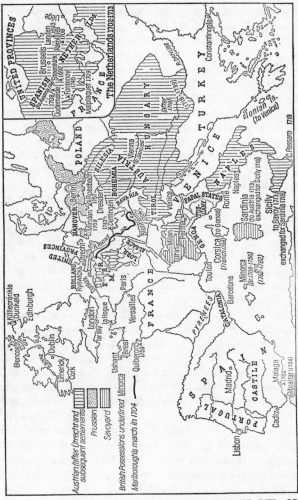

EMERY WALKER LTD. SC.

Map 9   Europe after the Treaty of Utrecht, 1713

win or lose campaigns on the grand scale, the British
troops learnt the art of war, and were bequeathed by him
a fit instrument for a greater captain.

On the other hand, in the ensuing War of the Spanish Succession [1701-13.], France began the contest with every apparent advantage except sea-power. Her armies were in occupation of the whole Spanish inheritance in Europe, in the name of Louis' grandson, Philip V, the new King of Spain. The great Kingdom beyond the Pyrenees, Italian Milan and Naples, and the long-contested Spanish Netherlands with their famous fortresses, were all, for fighting purposes, French territory when the war began. Moreover, Louis had as an active ally the great State of Bavaria, lying in the heart of Germany, on the boundaries of hard-pressed Austria, herself attacked on the other side by the Hungarian insurrection. The situation appeared desperate for the cause of the allies, and for the future safety of Holland and England by land and sea: unless they could turn Louis out of these territories, particularly out of the Netherlands, he would remain what he had indeed become, the master of Europe. But contrary to all expectation, the allies, who in the previous war had seemed no painful inch to gain, chased the French out of every one of these lands with the exception of Spain, where the genius of the Spanish people for guerrilla warfare secured them the King of their choice, the Bourbon Philip.

Austria was saved and Bavaria conquered by Marlborough's march on the Danube and victory at Blenheim in 1704; the Spanish Netherlands were conquered by him at Ramillies in 1706, and that same year Eugene's campaign of Turin secured for Austria Milan, Naples and the hegemony in the Italian Peninsula. Though Spain herself remained to the Bourbon candidate, the Spanish Empire in Europe was conquered and dismembered, chiefly to increase Austria's territories, but also for the permanent security of Holland and Great Britain.

These tremendous victories, as compared to the stalemate of the previous war, can be accounted for in no small degree by the military genius of Marlborough, backed by the fine abilities and faithful co-operation of his friend, Prince Eugene of Savoy, the Austrian General. But the successes must also be ascribed to the ever-increasing maritime, commercial and financial power of Britain and its vigorous application by Marlborough, Godolphin and the Whig Ministers of Anne. Marlborough understood the strategy of world war and the way to combine land and sea power in successful operations, better than any man who has succeeded him in control of England's destiny, with the possible exception of Chatham. Corresponding to England's growth, was the maritime and financial decadence of France, whose efforts at world conquest for fifty years past exhausted and betrayed her just when the prize was in her grasp. The national exhaustion reflected itself in the failing ability of the new generation of Louis' Generals, and the want of self-confidence in his troops after their first defeats at the hand of 'Malbroucke.'

The size and armament of battleships and the tactical methods of warfare at sea underwent no great change between the days of Blake and the days of Nelson. But the methods of warfare on land, when Marlborough took command at the beginning of Anne's reign [1702.], had just undergone a great change from the methods of Gustavus Adolphus and Cromwell.[6] Ever since the Restoration the bayonet had been gradually coming in, and, after the lesson of Killiecrankie, William's reign saw the general adoption of the ring-bayonet that could be left on while the gun was being discharged. Consequently the pikemen, who had composed half the regiment in Cromwell's day, were altogether abolished; henceforth there was but one type of infantry private, with his firelock ending in the dagger-bayonet. In connection with this change of weapon, the six-deep formation of the infantry column, suitable to pikes, was changed to a thin line of three deep, as the method of concentrating the greatest volume of fire upon the enemy. Already we are in the realm of the infantry tactics employed by Frederic the Great and by Wellington, though the drill of the infantry was not yet so perfect or their manœuvring so flexible as in those later times. Cavalry, as at Blenheim and Ramillies, could still decide battles, but their place in war was already smaller than in

[6] See p. 189, above.

Cromwell's day, owing to the increased efficiency of the 'poor foot.'

The warfare of the age of Louis XIV was largely an affair of fortresses. Readers of 'Tristram Shandy' will remember how the two old soldiers of William show even more professional interest in the news of Marlborough's sieges than in his marches and battles. King Louis' military architect, 'the celebrated Monsieur Vauban,' carried the defensive art to a high and complicated perfection, and France and her neighbours watched each other across a network of fortified towns, especially thick in the Netherlands.

The result was a tendency to stagnation in military enterprise and mobility, very marked in the War of the League of Augsburg. [1689–97.] But in the War of the Spanish Succession [1701–13.] the rapid conquest of provinces recalls Gustavus and foreshadows Napoleon. The way for this change had been prepared by the unopposed advance of Louis' armies beyond the frontiers of France into the territories of the Spanish Empire and Bavaria. Marlborough, when he took over the command, found the French far in advance of their usual line of fortresses. He seized the opportunity to restore the war of movement, much to the horror of the more timid and conventional spirits on his own side. When he resolved to carry the Dutch and English armies across Europe to the Danube, to save Austria and win Blenheim, he had to deceive the vigilance of the Dutch authorities and the Tories of the English Parliament, who objected to any such dangerous use of their costly regiments.

Marlborough as a military strategist and a tactician, as a war statesman and war diplomatist, stands second to no Englishman in history. His powers resemble those of Chatham and Clive rolled into one, except that he could not, like Chatham, arouse the spirit of his countrymen at large by magnificent speech and visible ardour of soul. For the purpose of striking down a great military monarchy, he was Wellington and Castlereagh combined, and if the Whigs had left him a free hand he might have made for

Europe in 1709 as good a peace as Castlereagh made in 1815,—or Bolingbroke in 1713.

Cromwell alone seems his match. But Oliver attracts or repels by the peculiarities of his character, and by his political and religious affinities; whereas Marlborough arouses no such prejudices either for or against his claims upon the gratitude of his country and of the world. 'The detested names of Whig and Tory,' as he called them, were less than nothing to him, though fate made him a Tory by birth and upbringing, and a Whig by later connection. Both sides revenged themselves upon him for not being one of themselves, the Tories assiduously blackening his character and the Whigs being lukewarm in its defence. As the contemporary of Louis' English pensioners and of the Whig and Tory correspondents of the exiled James, he was no better, indeed, than the average product of the Restoration Court and the Revolution Parliaments. But if he loved money, he gave England better value for every guinea he received from her than any other of her servants; if he looked to the main chance, his country was the gainer for his shrewdness nine times out of ten; and if he failed to arouse the personal devotion of any class except the soldiers whom he led to certain victory, his featureless calm of Olympian power is perhaps as much above as it is below Cromwell's humorous, passionate humanity, and craving, troubled spirit, never quite at rest either in this world or the other. By the light of his unclouded genius, Marlborough protected the advent of the much needed age of reason, toleration and common sense.

In the successful conduct of a world war there are two distinct operations, both very difficult,—the winning of the victory in arms, and afterwards the making of a stable peace. Unfortunately the temper and qualities required and engendered by war are not always conducive to the proper handling of peace negotiations, and for this reason it was no bad thing that our two-party system enabled the Whigs to win the war and the Tories to make the peace.

Since the Revolution, the Whigs had become the more

inveterate enemies of Louis, as the representative of despotism and the patron of the Pretender. William III, who had less than no predilection in favour of the Whigs, had found in practice that only a Whig Ministry could carry on the War of the League of Augsburg with the necessary vigour and financial ingenuity; but he himself, without help from his English Ministers, concluded peace at Ryswick. In the interval that followed before the renewal of war [1697–1701.], the Tories rose again automatically to the surface, and on the accession of their supporter, Queen Anne, secured almost a monopoly of power. But during these four somewhat confused years of peace, it had been the moderate Tory Harley, a man of Roundhead family and connections, who exerted most influence in the House of Commons. He 'educated his party,' inducing the Tories to pass the Act of Settlement [JUNE 1701.] which fixed the succession on the House of Hanover, in case of Anne's death without children[7]; and to renew the war with France, when Louis, in spite of his acknowledgment of William in the Treaty of Ryswick, insolently declared the Pretender to be James III, King of England. [SEPT. 1701.] The control of the vast resources of the Spanish Empire had been too much for the prudence of the Grand Monarch, who already regarded himself as master of the world.

The War of the Spanish Succession was therefore begun by a combination of moderate Tories and Whigs with Marlborough and Godolphin. [1701–5.] But events led once more to a war-Ministry predominantly Whig, because so many of the Tory party were more interested in passing laws against the Dissenters than in beating Louis. But Harley's heart was in the war, and he remained in the Whig Ministry until Louis had been driven out of the Spanish Netherlands, and the Union with Scotland had been carried. Finally in 1708 Anne was compelled to accept a wholly Whig Ministry without Harley. Marlborough and

---

[7] The Tory party's support of the Act of Settlement in 1701 was probably facilitated by the discredit accruing to Jacobitism from the Assassination plot against William in 1696, curiously similar in its details to the Whig Rye House Plot against Charles II.

Godolphin, altogether detached from the Tory party, remained to act under the orders of the Whig 'Junto.' Mixed
Ministries, though they had often done useful work, were
found increasingly difficult under the Parliamentary system. Ever since the Revolution England had been moving
unconsciously towards the modern system of a responsible
Cabinet all of one political complexion.

The Whigs, who had twice risen and thriven by war,
were slow to make peace. And unfortunately the complete-
ness of their political victory at home coincided exactly
with the period when peace negotiations ought to have
been seriously undertaken and pushed through. [1708.]
Marlborough, having won the Spanish Netherlands for
Austria at Ramillies and Oudenarde, was engaged, during
four more years of unnecessary war, in reducing the fortresses that defended the frontier of France herself. Louis,
in terrible straits, offered in 1709 everything that the allies
could reasonably demand, including the withdrawal of all
assistance from his grandson in Spain. But the Whigs
showed themselves incapable of making peace. They demanded the one thing Louis could not grant—that he
should himself send his armies to expel Philip from the
Spanish throne on which he had placed him eight years before. The cause of this outrageous demand was the difficulty the allies found in expelling Philip themselves, as he
was the favourite of the Spanish people. The Whig for-
mula of 'no peace without Spain' meant in practice no
peace at all. Louis appealed to his subjects, as he had
never deigned to do before; they knew that he had made
great sacrifices of his pride to buy them a peace, but in
vain, so they rallied to him with the well-known valour of
the French people in defence of the soil, and gave Marlborough his first rebuff in his Pyrrhic victory of Malplaquet.
[SEPT. 1709.]

John Bull, also, was hungering for the victorious peace
which the Whig doctors had ordered away from his table.
The cry to stop the war swelled the Tory reaction which
domestic causes were producing. A wave of High Church
feeling passed over the Queen and her subjects, and mobs
who a few years before were chasing Jacobites and sacking

Mass-houses, once more engaged in the alternative employment of burning Dissenters' chapels. Popular emotion was swelled by the folly of the Whig Ministers in impeaching before the House of Lords a certain Dr. Sacheverell, who had preached a sermon against the principles of the Revolution, on the day consecrated to its memory.

The Queen's political and religious sympathies and the influence exercised over her by Mrs. Masham, at length enabled her to throw off the personal domination of Sarah, Duchess of Marlborough. The Whigs fell at once, ere long dragging Marlborough himself after them. [1710.] Anne's initiative in changing her Ministers was confirmed at the General Election. Since the winter of William's coming over, no change in men and measures had been so complete and so instantaneous. Yet this was not a revolution, but a normal process of the new constitution, which was tending more and more towards party Cabinet government by Whigs and Tories in alternation. No change less complete would have secured peace for Europe at that juncture.

The new Tory Ministry took office under the double leadership of the brilliant St. John, prepared to go any lengths to crush the Whigs and extirpate Dissenters in pursuit of his political game, and the slow, moderate Harley, whose chief virtue was a desire, unfortunately rare among contemporary statesmen, to promote unity of spirit in the whole nation. But the government was at least agreed on its first necessary task—the making of peace. Except the betrayal of our Catalan allies to the vengeance of Philip of Spain, it is difficult to find serious fault with the terms of the Treaty of Utrecht. [1713.] The methods by which this excellent peace was obtained are perhaps more open to criticism. The Whigs denounced, and the nation little liked the secret negotiations with France behind the back of the allies—though William had done the same to obtain the Treaty of Ryswick,—the disgrace of Marlborough, and the withdrawal of the British armies from the field in face of the enemy. Yet it was largely the fault of Whig, Dutch and Austrian obstinacy that these methods seemed the only way to settle any terms at all with France and compel the allies to accept them.

British colonial and commercial interests were, as we have seen, amply provided for,[8] and they would have benefited still more if the Tory Ministers' Commercial Treaty with France had not been thrown out by English trade jealousy, organized by the Whig opposition. As regards territorial arrangements in Europe, the terms of Utrecht were based on the formal assignment of the Spanish dominions in Europe to Austria, and the formal assignment of Spain and her American dominions to the Bourbon Philip. [SEE MAP 9.] It was merely a recognition of the state of things established by the events of the war, which the operations of the last five years had failed to shake. England's maritime security was ensured by the transference of the Netherlands to Austria, an inland power of central Europe from whom we had nothing to fear. The French threat to the Rhine Delta had been parried until 1793.

These arrangements proved a stable basis for Eighteenth Century civilization. Europe was never again troubled by danger from the preponderance of France, until the French Revolution had given her a new form of life. If Louis had been treated with the vindictive severity contemplated by the Whigs and Austria, when Marlborough should at length have burst through the network of fortresses and reached Paris, the spirit of revenge might have made a permanent lodging in the soul of the French people, rallied them to the monarchy of the *ancien régime,* and kept Eighteenth Century Europe constantly disturbed with wars more than dynastic.

The Treaty of Utrecht remains the one great act of statesmanship of St. John, Lord Bolingbroke, wherein he showed all his natural brilliancy, together with a moderation in respect to France, that was conspicuously absent from his dealings with those of his own countrymen who were not of his political following.

The Tories, having won the peace, hoped to enjoy the fruits thereof in their domestic programme. They had

[8] See p. 294, above.

passed an Act to prevent anyone from sitting in Parliament, even for a borough, unless he drew at least £300 a year from land. [1711.] But the chief political passion of the fox-hunting Tory squires of the October Club was the desire for a hot run after Dissenters, and Bolingbroke, the free-thinker, was Master of the pack. The first burst had been the passing of the long-disputed Occasional Conformity Bill, which punished with ruinous fines any man who, hav-ing qualified for State or municipal office by taking the Sacrament in an Anglican church, afterwards attended a place of Non-conformist worship. [1711.] But the Schism Act three years later was a much more serious affair. [1714.] It took away from Dissenters the education of their own children, which was to be handed over to persons licensed by Bishops of the Established Church. The many excellent schools that the Non-conformists had established at their own cost were to be suppressed, and their teachers turned adrift. Even teachers licensed by Bishops might teach no catechism save that of the Church. Without di-rectly repealing the Toleration Act, it was intended to cir-cumvent it by extirpating Dissent in the next generation through this peculiarly odious and unnatural form of re-ligious persecution. The Schism Act was the worst blot on the record of the Tory party after the Revolution, and ren-dered its downfall a pre-condition of religious freedom in England. For if the Schism Act had had time to come into force, it must have led to the abolition of varieties of re-ligious belief, or else to a civil war. But the dynastic crisis precipitated by the death of Anne [AUG. 1714.] divided and ruined the Tory party, saved the Dissenters without resort to arms, and established the full Eighteenth Cen-tury era of domestic peace, latitudinarianism and tolera-tion,

When George in pudding times came o'er
And moderate men looked big, Sir.[9]

[9] Both the Schism Act and the Occasional Conformity Act were repealed by the Whigs early in George I's reign, but the Sacramental Test for civil office was retained till Lord John Russell's Bill in 1828. The insistence of the High Church party on using the Sacrament as the key to po-

The reason why the victory of the Whigs on the accession of the House of Hanover meant the victory of 'moderate men' was because the Whigs were the minority party and were in no position to persecute. On the other hand, the Tories in the last years of Queen Anne's reign showed, under Bolingbroke's leadership, a spirit of intolerance natural, perhaps, to a party conscious that it represents the strongest forces in the nation. Prior to the Industrial Revolution the landowners were the most powerful class, and prior to the growth of Wesleyanism the Established Church was by many times stronger than all other religious denominations put together. Against the landed interest and the Church interest the Whigs could put into array only half the peerage, a few of the squires, some of the yeomen, the bulk of the merchants and moneyed men, the Protestant refugees from the continent,[10] and the English Dissenters. This combination, relatively weak in numbers, was powerful in organization and intelligent unity of purpose, because its strength lay in the towns, particularly in London, and because its leaders could pursue the political advantage of their party without its counsels being distracted, as those of the Tory squires often were, by religious and class feeling. For while the ordinary Whig partisan was a middle-class dissenter, the Whig leaders were upper-class churchmen, usually of a latitudinarian or a sceptical turn of mind. Between William Penn and John Bright no Non-conformist was prominent as a leader of political life

litical office was perhaps not very good for religion. 'I was early with the Secretary' (Bolingbroke), writes Swift, 'but he was gone to his devotions . . . to receive the Sacrament. Several rakes did the same. It was not for piety but employment, according to Act of Parliament.' But as long as they were only 'rakes' and not Dissenters, Swift's party saw no profanation.

[10] There were over thirty French Huguenot churches in London when it had about one-tenth of the inhabitants it has to-day. Most of the worshippers in them were skilled men, many of them rising to wealth in the country of their adoption; and almost all were Whigs, on account of the Tory hostility to their forms of religious worship.

in England, though for half that period the Non-conformists were able to keep the Whig party in power.

In time of peace the Tories were normally the stronger by weight of numbers and possession of the land, and would have governed Eighteenth Century England but for the accident of the dynastic question, which proved their division and their undoing. At the end of William's reign Harley had persuaded the party to take the initiative in passing the Act of Settlement, assigning the Crown to the House of Hanover in case of Anne's death without children.[11] This great decision represented the determination of the squires and the Anglican Church never again to trust themselves to a Roman Catholic King. The House of Stuart had only to turn Protestant and the Act of Settlement would have little binding effect on the High Tories, but neither the Old nor the Young Pretender would consent to dissemble his religious beliefs to gain a crown. The fact is greatly to their credit, and their honesty saved Britain a world of trouble and civil war.

Even as it was, the Act of Settlement represented only one-half the feelings of the Tory party on the dynastic question; the other or Jacobite half of their sentiment had a habit of surging up in moments of emotion, and then sinking back checked and uncertain when the practical crisis came. Brought up as boys in the doctrines of Divine Right,

In good King Charles's golden days
   When loyalty no harm meant,

the Tories of the succeeding generation were never quite at ease in opposing the House of Stuart. Old theory and old affection were moreover supported by modern considerations of party advantage and expediency: the House of Hanover was hand-in-glove with the Whigs. The future George I declined to adopt the attitude of indifference between Whig and Tory which William of Orange had shown both before and after he attained the crown. Moreover, the Tory Ministers of the dying Queen could not

[11] For the Hanoverian descent from James I, see tree, p. 163, above; for the descendants of James II, see tree, p. 252, above.

pay court at Hanover without quarrelling with their mistress at home. [1712–14.] For Anne had all Queen Elizabeth's jealousy of a successor; and, like many other Tories, she was a Jacobite in sentiment though not in practice, and detested the German Princes who were to keep her brother out of his inheritance after she herself had ceased to do so.

The Tories therefore clung to the present favour of Anne, at the sacrifice of all chance of future favour with George. The Whigs in opposition adopted precisely the opposite policy. The growing perception that the accession of George I would mean the exclusion of the Tories from power, drove Bolingbroke on his last violent courses, to prepare the way either for a Jacobite restoration on Anne's death, or at least for the complete control of the country by a Jacobitish Cabinet who could dictate terms to either one or other of the claimants. This plan necessitated the extrusion of all Whigs and all moderate Tories from the magistracy, the Army, the Navy, and the government. It necessitated the dismissal of Harley, now Lord Oxford, as a preliminary to consigning the whole machinery of government, central and local, to men of Jacobite sympathy. Oxford was dismissed on July 27, and his rival's hands were free. Five months, five weeks even, might have seen the stage prepared, but the Queen died in five days, and all Bolingbroke's plans fell in ruin around him. [AUG. 1, 1714.] 'Fortune turned rotten at the very moment it grew ripe,' wrote Swift, whom the disaster consigned for life to a Dublin deanery.

The outcome of Bolingbroke's intrigue was that George I came unopposed to the throne, with a rooted distrust of the whole Tory party, which was shared by large numbers of his subjects who were neither Whigs nor Dissenters but who desired undisturbed peace under a Protestant King and Parliament. For forty-seven years to come [1714–61.] the Tory party was out of office, suspected of Jacobitism and painfully divided in its own feelings and allegiance.

Bolingbroke was prevented by the Whigs from taking an active part again in public life. After a period of service abroad as Secretary of State to the Pretender, he left that Court in disillusionment and disgust, and devoted his brilliant powers as a writer to preaching to his countrymen the moderate views of his old rival Harley, the necessity of the Revolution settlement, the evils of party spirit, and the hope of the future in a 'patriot King' who was not to be a Stuart.[12]

The enjoyment by the Whigs of nearly fifty years of uninterrupted power at this stage in our history, though far from an unmixed blessing, secured the political and religious liberties of Englishmen, because the Whigs were the minority party and could not therefore afford to persecute, as the authors of the Schism Act had persecuted. Walpole, who held power from 1721 to 1742, had the sense to see that the Whigs would retain office for themselves and keep the House of Hanover on the throne, only if they left the privileges of the Church untouched, and allowed the government of the countryside to rest very largely in the hands of Tory Justices of the Peace. Under Whig political rule at St. James's and Westminster, the Church and the squirearchy preserved what was nearest and dearest to them in the county, the parish, and the University.

That compromise secured the *Pax Walpoliana*, and saved the House of Hanover from overthrow by the Jacobites. It was a policy very different in spirit from the violence of the original Whig party under Shaftesbury. When Walpole came to power the Whigs had learnt the lesson of 'moderation' very completely, but they had only learnt it step by step. Several times in the reigns of William and Anne they had shown a desire to persecute their political enemies, as for instance in their attempt, thwarted by William, to hold up the Act of Indemnity after the Revolution; in the trials of Fenwick and Sacheverell; finally the impeachment of Oxford in the reign of George I for his share in the Treaty of Utrecht. But a milder and more cautious spirit, which men like Somers, Cowper and Addison usually

[12] Mr. Feiling, in his *History of the Tory Party*, says: 'The man who educated these generations (between Anne and George III) was undoubtedly Bolingbroke, who in the "Letters" and "Dissertations" of his later life Harleyized, that is to say modernized, the whole basis of Tory thought.'

displayed, had been working in the party against the more violent elements represented by Wharton. These pacific and liberal tendencies triumphed in Walpole and his motto —'Let sleeping dogs lie.'

The contests of the two evenly balanced parties in the reigns of William and Anne, the constant appeal made by Whigs and Tories to the intelligence of the public in Parliamentary eloquence, pamphlets, electioneering and the talk of men, had instilled habits of debate and free expression of opinion which continued to mark English political life in the coming era. Though partisan bitterness was guilty of frequent acts of persecution, the shelter generally afforded by the two great parties to their respective advocates enabled freedom of speech and press to grow to its characteristic development in England.

BOOKS FOR FURTHER READING: Lecky, *History of England*, Vol. I.; Feiling, *History of the Tory Party*; C. T. Atkinson, *Marlborough*; Frank Taylor, *Wars of Marlborough*, 2 vols.; Corbett, *England in the Mediterranean*, Vol. II.; Mahan, *Influence of Sea Power*, Chaps. IV. and V.; Coxe, *Memoirs of Marlborough*, 3 vols.; Winston Churchill, *Marlborough*; G. M. Trevelyan, *England under Queen Anne*, 3 vols., *Blenheim, Ramillies, The Peace and the Protestant Succession*.

INDEX

Acadia, 232, 294

Act of Indemnity and Oblivion, 240

Act of Settlement, 307

Act of Six Articles, 65, 70

Act of Supremacy, 57 *n.*, 88

Act of Uniformity, of *1549*, 71; of *1559*, 88; of *1662*, 242

Agriculture, 31–36, 71–72; in Stuart era, 221–22

Alençon, François, Duc d', 134

America, English colonization of, 121, 149–50, 225–34; exploration and settlement, 45–46, 101–4, 229–32; immigration of religious refugees, 169, 170

Anglican Church, establishment of, 56–66; Prayer Book, 68–69; under Elizabeth, 87–90, 129–34; Puritan activity in, 157–58; under Laud, 168–71; as issue of Civil War, 175, 181–84, 193–94; under Commonwealth, 216–17; under Charles II, 237, 242, 259, 261–62; under James II, 263, 266–68; under Restoration Settlement, 271

Anne, Queen, 301–10

Anti-clerical revolution, 38, 41, 48, 49, 50–51, 54–57

Apprenticeship, 137–38

Architecture, Tudor, 140–41

Argyle, Earl of, 177

Aristocracy. *See* Squirearchy

Arlington, Earl of, 249

Armada, Spanish, 104, 118–20

Army, disbandment of, 215–16, 246–47; following Civil War, 199, 201–3; of James II, 263–64; as means of government by Cromwell, 204–9

Astley, Sir Jacob, 198–99

Babington's plot, 117

Bacon, Francis, 155

Balance of Power policy, 16–17, 43–44, 213, 251

Bank of England, 291–92

Baptists, 195–96, 201, 242, 244

Barrow, Henry, 133

Beggars, 32–33, 124 *n.*

Bermuda colony, 226

Best, Captain Thomas, 160

Bible, English translations, 52, 64–65; King James Authorized version, 155

Bible-reading, 38, 64–65, 135–36, 245

Blake, Robert, 205, 210–11

Boleyn, Anne, 53–55

Bombay, 247 *n.*

Bonner, Bishop Edmund, 49, 78, 79

Boyne, battle of, 284

Brooke, Lord, 186

Buckingham, George Villiers, 1st Duke of, 159, 163–65

Buckingham, 2d Duke of, 240, 249

Bunyan, John, 194, 243

Byrd, William, 136

Cabal, 249–54

Cabot, John and Sebastian, 46, 110

Calais captured by France, 81

Calvinistic influence, 73, 132

Cambridge University, 41, 52

Campion, Edmund, 130

Cannon, in Civil War, 191 n., on warships, 47

Cartwright, Thomas, 133

Catherine of Aragon, Queen, 42, 53–55

Catholicism: Reformation under Henry VIII, 49–66; under Edward VI, 69–73; under Mary, 75–76, 78; under Elizabeth, 87–90, 97–98, 117–18, 130–34; under James I, 158–59; under Charles I, 170; in Civil War, 186–87; under Commonwealth, 217; under Charles II, 243–44, 252, 257, 262; under James II 263–68; under Revolution settlement, 271–72

Cavaliers, 154; in Civil War, 185–97; under rule of Long Parliament, 198–99, 200–1; at Restoration, 240–49

Cecil, Robert, 155

Cecil, William, Lord Burleigh, 84, 91, 93, 115–17, 132

Chancellor, Richard, 110

Charles I, 163–204; in Civil War, 184–89, 196; execution of, 202; failure of settlement with, 202, 203; government under, 164–68; Long Parliament, 179–84; religion under, 168–71, 175; Royal Navy under, 162, 168; Scottish revolt, 174–79

Charles II, 148, 205, 237–62; Cabal, 249–50; colonial policy under, 232–35; religion under, 241–46; Treaty of Do-

ver with France, 252–53

Church. See Anglican Church; Religion

Civil War, Great, 174, 185–98; arms and tactics, 188–98; course of, 192–93, 194–95, 196–98; issues of, 183–85; New Model Army, 195–96; resources of, 185–88; Scottish Alliance, 193–94; Second, 202

Clarendon. See Hyde, Edward

Clarendon Code, 218, 241–42

Clement VII, Pope, 53–54

Clergy, under Elizabethan settlement, 88–90; under Long Parliament persecution, 200; marriage of, legitimized, 70; in Reformation, 56–57, 63; in Tudor government, 22, 63

Clifford, Thomas, Baron, 249

Cloth trade, 27–32, 108, 111

Coinage, debasement by Henry VIII, 67, 71; under Elizabeth, 111

Coke, Sir Edward, 154, 166–67

Colet, John, 39–41, 42

Colonial policy under Cromwell and Charles II 232–35

Commerce, cloth trade, 27–31; colonial policy, 234–35; sea, 107–11, 160–62; world patterns before Elizabethan era, 99–101; world-wide, 235, 293–95 235, 293–95

Common Law, 24–25; as Parliamentary cause, 166–68, 182

Commons, House of. See Parliament

Commonwealth, 148, 205–18

Congregationalism. See Independent sects

Constitutional balance, under first session of Long Parliament, 182; at Restoration, 238–39, 246

Constitutional Royal party. See Cavaliers

Conventicle Act, 242

Council of North, 98, 125, 182

Council of Wales and Marches, 126, 182

Counter-Reformation, 98, 130–31

Coverdale, Miles, 52, 64–65

Crafts, Elizabethan, 137–40; in Stuart era, 219–21

Cranmer, Thomas, 52–53, 54, 64, 65, 68–70, 80–81

Cromwell, Oliver, 181, 186 191, 192–95, 199, 203–4; as dictator and Protector, 201, 203, 204–9, 212–17; New Model Army of, 195–97

Cromwell, Richard, 237

Cromwell, Thomas, 54, 58, 65

Crown. See Monarchy

Danby, Earl of, 254–58, 268–69, 271

Davis, John, 110

De Witt, Jan, 250, 253

Declarations of Indulgence, 243–44

Dissenters. See Independent sects

Dissolution of monasteries, 58–63; in Ireland, 128

Divine hereditary right of kings, 153, 237

Downton, Captain Nicholas, 160

Drake, Sir Francis, 48, 59 n., 102, 106–7, 113–19

Dudley, John, Earl of Warwick and Duke of Northumberland, 68, 72–74

Dutch East India Company, 161

Earls, Rising of, against Elizabeth, 97–98

East India Company, 109 n., 110–11, 160–61, 293–94

Economy: cloth trade, 27–31; under Elizabeth, 107–11, 124; industrial practices, 137–39; national control of, 13–14; see also Commerce; Finances

Edict of Nantes, Revocation of, 265–66

Education, 38, 60, 69–70; under Commonwealth, 217–18; among gentry, 142; Grammar Schools, Elizabethan, 131; Renaissance influence, 39–41

Edward VI, 68–74

Eliot, Sir John, 143, 154, 165, 166

Elizabeth, Queen, 81–144; finances of, 111–12, 122–23; gentry under, 140–42; industry under, 137–40; intervention in Scotland, 93–95; Irish policy, 128–29; literature and music under, 134–37; Northern rebellion against, 97–98; Parliament under, 142–44; during reign of Mary, 77; religion under, 129–34; war with Spain, 112–21

Enclosure of open fields, 31–36, 66 n., 71–72

Erasmus, 40, 52

Erastian State, 16

Essex, Robert, 3rd Earl of, 182, 186, 188, 195

Exclusion Bill, 257–60

Exploration, era of, 44–46, 101–11, 116

Fairfax, Sir Thomas, 193, 195, 196–97

Falkland, Lord, 169, 181–84

Finances, of Charles II, 246; of Commonwealth, 214; of Elizabeth, 83, 111–12, 122–23; of Henry VII, 22, 25; of Henry VIII, 67; of William III and Queen Anne, 291–92

Fitch, Ralph, 110

Fitzgeralds of Kildare, 127

Fox, George, 194, 217, 243

Foxe, John, 80

France, 44, 81, 84, 99; American settlements of 102–3, 227, 229–30; control of Scotland by, 92–94; under Louis XIV, 250–54, 260, 265, 269, 287; war of Grand Alliance against, 147; wars of William and Marlborough against, 287–93, 295–98, 299, 301–3

Frobisher, Sir Martin, 110

Gardiner, Bishop Stephen, 49, 77, 78, 79

Gentry. See Squirearchy

Gilbert, Humphrey, 129

Gilpin, Bernard, 87, 95

Gloucester, siege of, 192

Goring, George, Earl of Norwich, 197

Government, under Cabal, 249–53; under Charles

I, 164–68, 175; Commonwealth, 148, 205–18; Elizabethan, 133–34, 142–44; under Long Parliament, 179–205; at Restoration, 237–49; after Revolution, 148–49, 151–52, 273–74; under Tudor kings, 21–26, 48, 56–58; under William III and Queen Anne, 291–92, 300–10

Grand Remonstrance, 183

Great Rebellion, Long Parliament in, 179–85; First Civil War, 185–98; failure to reach settlement and regicide, 198–204; Second Civil War, 202–8

Greenwood, John, 133

Grenville, Sir Richard, 129

Gresham, Sir Thomas, 111

Grey, Lady Jane, 74

Gunpowder Plot, 159

Hakluyt, Richard, 108, 111

Halifax, Marquis of, 258, 259–60

Hampden, John, 143, 154, 168, 181–84, 187–88

Hanover, House of, 307–9

Harley, Robert, Earl of Oxford, 303–9

Hawkins, Sir John, 113–14

Henrietta Maria, Queen, 163, 170

Henry VII, 18–26, 41–42, 46

Henry VIII, 37, 42–43; campaign against Scotland, 92; divorce of, 53–55; Ireland under, 127–28; Reformation under, 49–66; Royal Navy founded by, 46–48; Wales under, 125–27

High Commission, Court of, 132–33, 181–82, 267

Holland, English support of independence, 235–36, 250–51, 254; loss of American colonies to England, 232; maritime achievements, 107–8, 161; Republic of, 113, 120–21; Spanish control of, 79, 84, 99; war with, 211–12, 248, 252–53; wars against France, 147, 250–53, 287–88

Holles, Denzil, 184

Hopton's cavalry, 191

Howard, Catherine, 65

Howard of Effingham, Lord, 118

Hudson's Bay Company, 110, 294

Huguenots, 99, 102, 227, 230, 233, 265–66

Hyde, Edward, Earl of Clarendon, 169, 181–84, 197, 238–41, 249

Independent sects, 188, 192–96, 216–17; under James II, 263–68; persecution of, 200–1, 241–43, 258–59; toleration of, 244–46, 271

India, trade with, 161

Industry, Elizabethan, 137–39; in Stuart era, 219–21

Innocent XI, Pope, 265

Ireland, under Charles I, 172, 178, 183; from Restoration to Queen Anne, 149, 282–86; subjugation and land settlement by Commonwealth, 205–7; under Tudors, 127–29

Ireton, Henry, 203, 205, 206

Ironsides regiments, 192–93, 196

Jamaica, capture of, 213, 232

James I, 152–62; decline of sea power under, 161–62; and Puritan movement, 157–58

James II, 253–57, 259, 262–69

Jesuit missions, in England, 98, 126, 130–31, 158–59; in Ireland, 128

Judicial system, under Charles I, 166–68; Prerogative Courts abolished, 181–82; under Tudors, 23–26, 64 n.

Justices of Peace, 14, 25–26, 151–52; in Wales, 125–26

Kett's Rebellion, 71–72

King-worship of Tudor era, 14, 56–58, 152–53

Knox, John, 91–96

La Hogue, battle of, 288–89

Land system, 33–36; confiscation of Abbey lands, 59–61

Latimer, Hugh, 20 n., 22, 34, 52, 65, 69–70, 72, 80

Latitudinarianism, 244–45

Laud, William, Archbishop of Canterbury, 168–71, 173, 176, 181

Lauderdale, Duke of, 249

Lee, Rowland, Bishop of Lichfield, 125

Leicester, Robert Dudley, Earl of, 86, 115

Leslie, Alexander and David, 178, 195, 198

Levant Company, 109 n., 110

Liberties, personal, under Elizabeth, 133–34; after Revolution, 152

Lilburne, John, 170, 205

Literature, Elizabethan, 135–37

Locke, John, 147, 245

Lollardry, revival of, 38–39

London, 49 n.–50 n., 59; Fire of, 248; Long Parliament supported by, 180–81, 187; in Stuart era, 219–20; under William and Mary, 292–93

Long Parliament, 179–215; first session, 179–83; division into parties, 183–85; conduct of Civil War, 185–98; failure to reach settlement and regicide, 198–204; Republican government under, 204–15

Lords, House of. See Parliament

Louis XIV of France, 147, 235, 250–54, 260, 265, 269, 287–93, 301–3

Lutheranism, 51–52, 73

Lyndsay, Sir David, 91

Manchester, Earl of, 186, 196

Maritime activity. See under Sea

Marlborough, John Churchill, Duke of, 147, 269, 287–91, 297–303

Martyrs. See Persecution

Martyrs, Book of, 80

Marvell, Andrew, 214

Mary I, 74–81

Mary II, 255, 271, 287

Mary of Guise, 92–94

Mary Queen of Scots, 84, 92–99, 117

Massachusetts, self-government dispute, 231

Maurice, Prince, 163

Maurice, Prince of Nassau, 120–21

Mediterranean, English sea-power in, 110, 211, 294

Middle Atlantic colonies, 232–33

Middle classes, 26, 30–31

Military tactics, in Civil War, 189–92; naval, in Elizabethan era, 47; under William and Marlborough, 298–99

Milton, John, 137, 180–81, 205

Monarchy, evolution of Commonwealth to, 215–16, 236–37; under Tudors, 14–15, 56, 133–34

Monasteries, dissolution of, 58–63; in Ireland, 128

Monk, George, Duke of Albemarle, 205, 237

Monmouth's rebellion, 262–64

Montagu, Charles, 291

Montrose, James Graham, 1st, Marquis of, 176–77, 179, 198

More, Sir Thomas, 40, 42, 49, 55

Muscovy Company, 109 n., 110

Music, Elizabethan, 136–37

National Debt, 291–92

Naval activity. See under Sea

Navigation Act of 1651, 211

Netherlands. See Holland

New England, 150–51; character of colonists in, 225–28; geographic factors in growth of, 228–29; independence of, 230–32; policy toward, 232–33

New Learning, 39–42, 51–52

New Model Army, 191 n., 195–97; see also Army

New World, exploration and settlement, 45–46, 101–4; see also America

New York, 212, 232, 248

Newfoundland, 294

Newton, Sir Isaac, 244

Norfolk, Thomas Howard, 4th Duke of, 98

North-East and North-West Passages, 110

Oates, Titus, 256–57
Occasional Conformity Bill, 305
Oxford, capitulation, in Civil War, 197; in Revolution, 267–68
Oxford University, 39 *n.*, 41

Pacific Ocean, Drake's voyage in, 116
Parliament, early Tudor, 14, 16, 23, 48; Reformation, 56–58; under Edward VI, 70–73; under Mary, 76–79; under Elizabeth, 88–90, 133–34, 142–44; in early Stuart era, 153–54, 157, 164–66, 175; Short, 178; Long, 154, 179–215; under Protectorate, 148, 215–16; Convention, 237–41; Cavalier, 148, 241–49, 253–56; Whig and Tory, 257–59; under James II, 262; under William III, 148–49, 151
Parsons, Robert, 130–31
Paterson, William, 291
Pecock, Bishop Reginald, 37
Penn, William, and Pennsylvania, 232
Penry, John, 133
Pentland Rising, 276
Persecution, religious, 41, 65, 76, 79–81, 131, 133, 169–70, 200–1, 241–43, 257–59
Petition of Right, 165
Philip of Spain, ambitions against England, 112–13, 115, 117; friendship with Elizabeth, 84, 97–99; as husband of Mary I, 76–81
Pilgrim Fathers, 225–26
Pilgrimage of Grace, 62, 71
Pitt, Thomas, 293

Pius V, Pope, 98, 130
Poetry, Elizabethan, 136–37
Pole, Reginald, 79
Poor Law, 32–33, 124 *n.*
Portugal, 44–46, 101, 103, 104 *n.*, 108, 160–61, 247 *n*
Prayer Book, Cranmer's translation of, 68–69, 70–71; Protestant emendations to, 73; in reign of Elizabeth, 87, 130
Prerogative courts, under Tudors, 24–25; under Charles I, 166–68; fall of, 181–82
Presbyterian Church of Scotland, 90–96, 173–74; under Stuarts, 156, 174–75; revolt against Charles I, 174–79; under Commonwealth, 208; under Restoration, 275–77; Revolution settlement, 175, 277–79
Presbyterians, 133; in Civil War, 193–94
Pride's Purge of Parliament, 205
Primogeniture, custom of, 35
Privy Council, under Tudors, 14, 21–26
Protectorate of Cromwell, 208–15
Protestantism, 30–31; Lollard revival, 38–39; persecution under Henry VIII, 50, 65; Lutheran influence, 51–52; advancement under Edward VI, 72–73; under Mary, 75–76, 78–81; under Elizabeth, 87–90, 129–34; *see also* Presbyterian Church of Scotland
Prynne, William, 170
Puritans, under Elizabeth, 90, 132–34; under James I and Charles I, 157–58, 169–70; in Civil War

and Commonwealth, *see*
Roundheads; *see also* Independent sects

Pym, John, 154, 178, 181–
84, 186, 188, 193–94

Quakers, 217, 232

Raleigh, Sir Walter, 121,
129, 155, 162, 166
Rationalism, 244–45
Reformation, under Henry
VIII, 49–66; under Ed-
ward VI, 69–73; under
Mary, 75–76, 78–81; un-
der Elizabeth, 87–90,
129–34
Reformation in Scotland,
90–96
Religion, 15–16; anti-clericalism, 38, 41, 48, 49–51;
Lollard revival, 38–39;
Renaissance influence on,
39–41; Protestantism un-
der Henry VIII, 51–52,
65; breach with Pope, 53–
55; Anglican Church es-
tablished, 56–66; Refor-
mation under Edward VI,
69–73; under Mary, 75–
76, 78–81; Elizabethan
settlement, 87–90, 129–
34; Jesuit missions, 98,
126, 130–31, 158; in col-
onies, 150, 169–70, 227–
28, 233; under Charles I,
168–71, 175; division into
political parties and Civil
War, 181–96; Independ-
ent sects, 194, 216–17;
under victorious Long
Parliament, 200–1; under
Commonwealth, 216–17;
under Charles II, 241–
46, 261–62; as issue leading to Revolution, 256–
59, 262–68; under Revo-
lution settlement, 149,
152, 271–72; under

Queen Anne, 304–7
Religion in Ireland, 127–28,
183, 207, 285
Religion in Scotland. *See*
Presbyterian Church of
Scotland
Religion in Wales, 126–27
Renaissance, influence of,
39–41; literature of, 135–
37
Restoration, 216, 236–38;
see also Charles II
Revenge (ship), 121
Revolution of *1688* (Glori-
ous), 148, 151, 264, 269–
74
Roman Catholic Church. *See*
Catholicism
Rome sacked by Charles V,
51
Rooke, Sir George, 288
Root and Branch Bill, 183
Roundheads, 154, 183–84;
in Civil War, 185–98; as
ruling party, 198–205;
treatment of, at Restora-
tion, 240–41; *see also*
Commonwealth
Royal Navy, 46–48; under
Charles I, 162, 168; in
Civil War, 188; decline
under James I, 161–62;
Medway disaster, 248–49;
under Restoration, 247–
48
Rupert, Prince, 163, 188–
89, 191, 195, 205, 209–10,
232

St. Bartholomew, Massacre
of, 99, 102
St. John, Henry, Lord
Bolingbroke, 303–6, 308–
9
Schism Act, 305
Schools. *See* Education; Uni-
versities
Scotland, 44; under Charles
II, 209; under Common-

wealth, 207–9; in Great Civil War, 188, 193–95, 198; under James I, 155–56; Reformation in, 90–96; from Restoration to Queen Anne, 275–82; revolt against Charles I, 174–79; State-Church struggle, 175; union with England, 149, 280–82

Sea exploration and commerce, 46, 107–11; under Commonwealth, 211, 213; under James I, 160–62

Sea-power, 99–104; under Charles I, 162, 168; under Commonwealth, 209–10; decline under James I, 159–60; establishment of Royal Navy, 46–48; under Restoration, 247–48

Sea warfare, 104–6; defeat of Armada, 118–20; against Dutch, 211–12; against France, 289–90, 298; with Spain in West Indies, 213

Sectaries, in Civil War, 188, 192–96; see also Independent sects

Selden, John, 154

Self-denying Ordinance, 196

Shaftesbury, Earl of, 240, 249, 258

Ship Money, 162, 168, 182

Shovell, Sir Clowdisley, 288

Sidney, Algernon, 244

Simnel, Lambert, 20

Slave-trade, 114

Somerset, (Protector) Edward Seymour, Duke of, 58, 68, 70–72, 92

Spain, in balance of power, 44; domination by, under Mary, 75–81; Elizabethan war with, 112–21; exploration and colonization by, 45–46; New World colonies, 101; peace with, 160–62; relations with, in early Elizabethan reign, 84, 97–99; sea-power of, 103–8; war with, under Commonwealth, 213

Spenser, Edmund, 129

Squirearchy, in Commonwealth, 151–52; in confiscation of Abbey lands, 59; in Counter-Reformation, 78; Elizabethan, 140–42; reaction to commonwealth, 218

Star Chamber, 23–24, 170, 181–82

State, sovereign authority of, 11–14, 54–58, 133–34

Statute of Artificers, 137

Statutes of Treason of 1534, 58, 70

Strafford, Thomas Wentworth, Earl of, 171–73, 178, 181–83

Strode, William, 165, 181, 184

Stuart era, political development during, 146–52

Stuart monarchs. See Anne; Charles I; Charles II; James I; James II; Mary II

Stuart Pretenders, 307–8

Stubbs, John, 134

Switzerland, Protestantism in, 73

Tangier, 247

Taxation, for Civil War, 187–88; under Tudors, 25

Temple, Sir William, 251

Test Act, 253

Thirty Years' War, 147, 162–64, 168

Toleration, in colonies, 150, 227, 233; under Cromwell 216–17; under Eliz-

abeth, 87–90, 130, 133–
34; under James I and
Charles I, 157–58, 170;
under Somerset, 70–71;
Whig efforts toward, 244
Toleration Act (1689), 149,
271
Tonnage and Poundage,
165, 182
Tories, 152, 241, 255-64,
266–67, 270–71, 300–10
Town life, Elizabethan, 137–
40; in Stuart era, 219–21
Towns, surrender of Char-
ters, 259
Township, New England,
225–28
Treaty of Aix-la-Chapelle,
251
Treaty of Breda, 248
Treaty of Dover, 252–53
Treaty of Edinburgh, 94
Treaty of Ryswick, 287, 301
Treaty of Utrecht, 287, 295,
303–4
Triple Alliance against Hol-
land, 251
Tudor monarchs. See Ed-
ward VII; Elizabeth;
Henry VII; Henry VIII;
Mary I
Tyndale, William, 52, 64–65

Ulster, English and Scotch
colony in, 172, 178, 183,
207, 282–83, 285
Universities, after dissolution of monasteries, 59–
60; Renaissance influence
on, 39–41

Vane, Sir Harry, 205, 240
Vere, Sir Francis and Sir
Horace, 120–21
Verney, Sir Edmund, 169
Village life, Elizabethan,
137–40; in Stuart era,
219–21

Villeins, emancipation of, 72
Virginia colony, 121, 226,
231

Wales, 286; under Tudors,
124–27
Walsingham, Sir Francis,
115–16, 117
Warbeck, Perkin, 20
Wars, 123; Dutch, 211–12,
248, 252–53; against
France, 147; of League of
Augsburg, 288–90, 295–
96, 299, 301; with Spain
under Commonwealth,
213; with Spain under
Elizabeth, 112–21, 123–
24; of Spanish Succession,
287, 297–98, 299, 301–3;
see also Civil War
Wentworth. See Strafford,
171–73
Wentworth, Paul and Peter,
143
West Indian colonies, 226,
232
Whigs, 151, 241, 244, 255–
61, 266, 272–73, 300–10
Whitgift, John, Archbishop
of Canterbury, 132
William III (of Orange),
147–49, 287–301; Protes-
tant crusade, 264–65,
268–69; as Stadtholder of
Holland, 252, 253; wars
of, 287–91, 295–96, 301
William the Silent of Holland, 113, 115
Williams, Roger, 228
Winchester, Marquis of, 187
Wolsey, Cardinal, 43–44,
48, 53–54, 60
Women, rights of, 225
Worcester, Earl of, 187
Wyatt's Rebellion, 77

Yeomanry, 33–36, 221–22